GREEN EMBER

III: EMBER RISING

Also by S. D. Smith

Reformation Lightning

The Green Ember

Ember Falls

Ember Rising

Ember's End

GREEN EMBER

III: EMBER RISING

S. D. SMITH

ILLUSTRATED BY ZACH FRANZEN

Reformation
Lightning

Reformation Lightning

British Library Cataloging in Publication Data
A record for this book is available from the British Library

First published in the United States of America by Story Warren in 2018

This edition first published in 2023 by Reformation Lightning

Published in cooperation with Story Warren

ISBN: 978-1-916669-07-9

Cover and interior illustrations by Zach Franzen (www.zachfranzen.com)
Maps created by Will Smith and Zach Franzen.
Additional design by Pete Barnsley (CreativeHoot.com)

Printed in UK

Reformation Lightning, an imprint of 10Publishing
Unit C, Tomlinson Road, Leyland, PR25 2DY, England

Email: info@10ofthose.com
Website: www.10ofthose.com

1 3 5 7 10 8 6 4 2

For Dad and Mom

Iustus qui ambulat in simplicitate sua
beatos post se filios derelinquet.

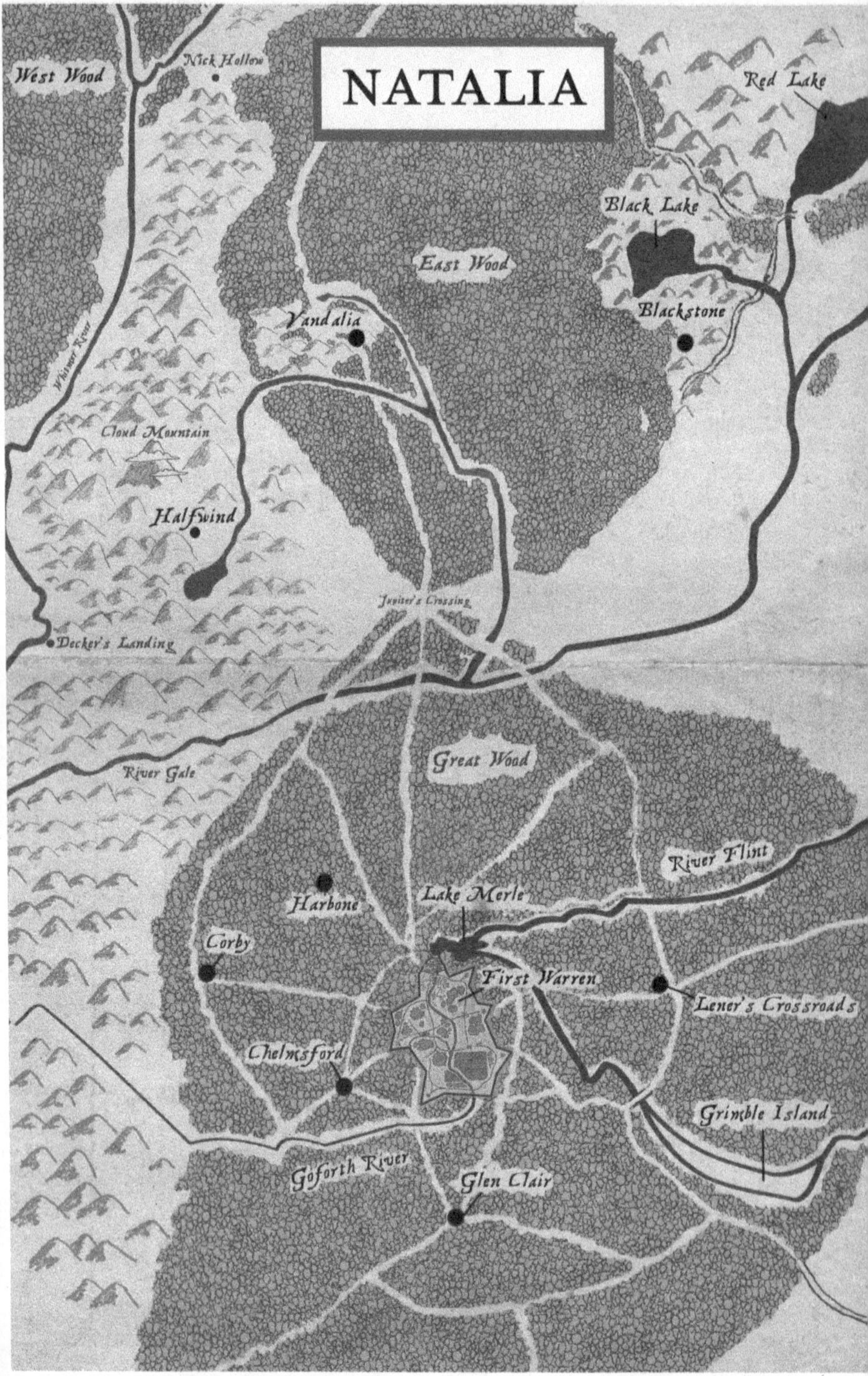
NATALIA
West Wood
Nick Hollow
Red Lake
Black Lake
East Wood
Blackstone
Vandalia
Whitmer River
Cloud Mountain
Halfwind
Jupiter's Crossing
Decker's Landing
Great Wood
River Gale
River Flint
Harbone
Lake Merle
Corby
First Warren
Lener's Crossroads
Chelmsford
Grimble Island
Goforth River
Glen Clair

Red Valley
Deserted Camp
Bog of the Bleaks
High Bleaks
Morbin's Lair
Akolan
The Waste
Grey Grove
Faraway Forest
Low Bleaks
Krebb's Stand
Hammertop
Kingston
Seddleton
River Fay
Massie
Ayman Lake
Halfmoore Hills

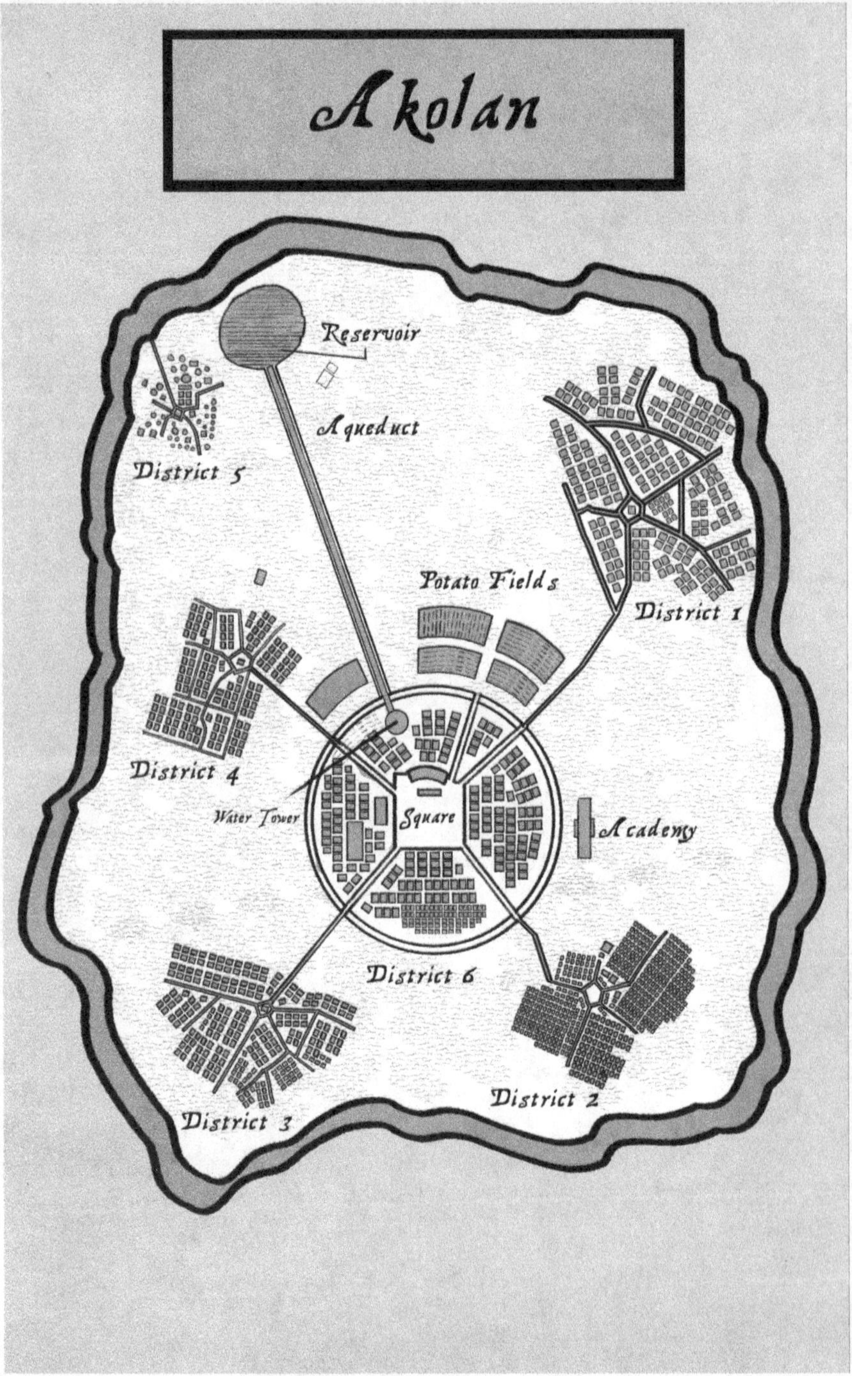
Akolan
Reservoir
Aqueduct
District 5
Potato Fields
District 1
District 4
Water Tower
Square
Academy
District 6
District 3
District 2

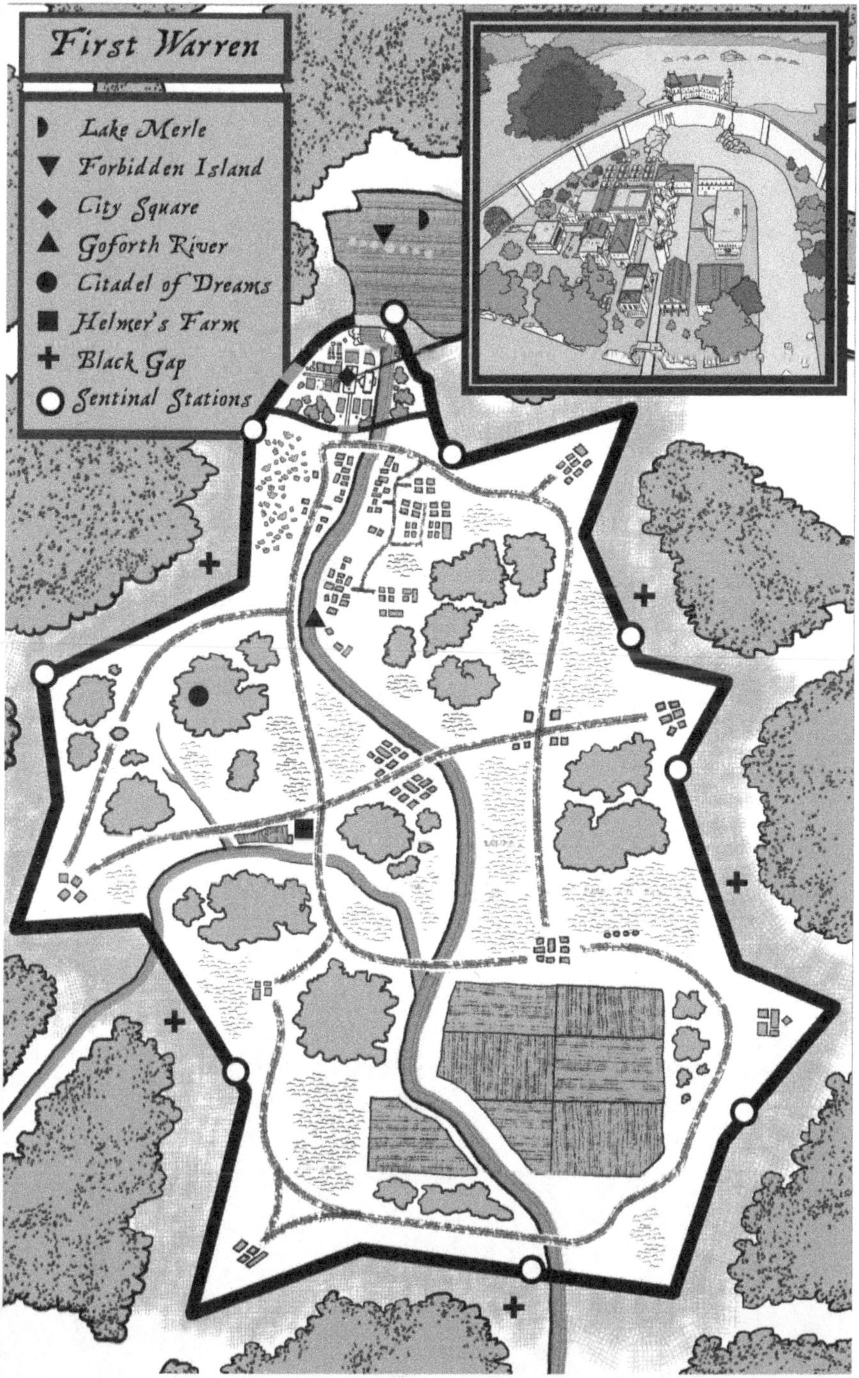
First Warren
Lake Merle
Forbidden Island
City Square
Goforth River
Citadel of Dreams
Helmer's Farm
Black Gap
Sentinal Stations

Prologue

"You've seen the ghost too?" Prince Lander asked, edging near Massie as they slowed to pick their way through a tangled patch of brush.

"The ghost, Your Highness?"

"Something's out there," Lander said, "and it's hard to spot."

"Don't give in to fearful fancy. It's probably nothing."

"I'm not as experienced as you are, Lieutenant Massie," Lander said, "but in my short life I've found it's almost never *nothing*. It's something. Monsters are real; I know that. Ghosts probably are too."

"Just be ready with that sword, sir," Massie said. "I'd wager our steel will find more than mist if this *ghost* attacks."

"I'm ready. Whoever took my mother will answer for it."

Massie nodded. The two emerged through the tangled thicket, and their path was clear for a few minutes. They neither saw nor heard anything unusual. They hurried on.

Massie ducked a dangling limb and emerged into another small clearing, slowing to examine tracks and allow the prince to catch up. He paused over a troubling set of footprints, again trying to determine what might have made such a mark. The prince drew near, breathing hard.

"Are you all right, Your Highness?"

"I'm...completely...fine," Lander managed to say between gasps.

Massie smiled. "What do you make of these tracks? Our ghost?"

Lander, still breathing hard, bent to examine the strange shapes. "It looks like a monster, but not the monsters we've seen."

"Not the monsters we've seen," Massie mused, his brow wrinkled. "If there's anything worse than the monsters you know..." he began.

"It's them you don't," Lander finished.

"Are you scared?" Massie asked.

"Yes," Lander admitted, "but I remember what Captain Blackstar told me. He said we have to keep loving what's on the other side of this fight—the other side of this rescue—and that will have to make us brave."

from *The Wreck and Rise of Whitson Mariner*

Chapter One

The Slave Who Sang

Heather closed her eyes, wincing as she lurched forward. Her uncle shoved her roughly toward the hangar at the far end of Morbin's lair.

"Now you'll join the slaves," Garten Longtreader growled. "You'll see what it means to defy Lord Morbin."

Barbed retorts formed in her mouth, but she swallowed them down. *I need to stay alive now.*

Heather glanced back at the frenzied scene. Chaos reigned in Morbin Blackhawk's lair. A slave had sung a song of defiant beauty in the dark heart of the Preylords' kingdom. Lord Gern was scouring the palace for her. For the slave who dared to defy them.

For the slave who sang.

Gern didn't know who it was. Nor did Morbin know the secret singer's name.

But Heather knew. Heather had heard that voice a thousand times.

The singer was Sween Longtreader, her beloved mother.

"Here!" Garten shouted, signaling for a waiting bird to stoop. Heather followed her uncle onto the raptor's back. At Garten's command, the eagle leapt free of the platform and dropped, descending into the predawn darkness. Heather's heart was in her throat, both because of the sudden drop and because she feared for her mother.

The bird extended his wings, caught a current of wind, and sailed forward through the vast area of uncountable trees. Heather saw, by the light of perched torches, that the trees were honeycombed with elaborate structures of various sizes and shapes. These all clung to the trees, dwellings nestled in the curve of huge limbs. She had never seen structures of this size. Though the sun still slept, there was a buzz of humming industry and innumerable lamps illuminating a busy hive of hurry all around. Silhouetted forms scurried in and out and all along dimly lit paths. Many were rabbit forms. She streaked by in dizzy flight, wondering a thousand things about those lives lived among the enemy's trees. Did these rabbits even see the raptors as enemies?

The bird twisted through the massive heights of the High Bleaks, the historic home of the Lords of Prey. Heather was seeing what no free rabbit had ever seen: the swollen base from which the Preylords hatched their hateful scheme of conquest and enslavement on all of Natalia.

And it had worked. She was, she realized with a pang, joining the slaves. She was no longer free.

But Emma, the princess and heir of King Jupiter, *was* free. And so the cause for which Heather had traded her liberty, and very likely her life, was alive.

That truth was like a flint strike in her heart. A spark of hope.

They broke through the corridor of tall trees, and Heather gasped at the sudden gaping space. In the middle of the high forest lay a barren area, a giant crater in the hard stone of the mountain. A river ran down the mountain and spilled down the high wall in a waterfall. A heap of trash, impossibly wide, rested against the lip of the plunging pit. The vast dump was burning, and scatterings of ash wafted into the acrid air. Ash floated over the pit and drifted, like snow, down and down on a small city at its rocky bottom.

"This is Akolan," Garten called above the howling wind. "It's one of two cities I superintend. The other is First Warren, the former stronghold of the old king. Akolan, here in the High Bleaks, is your home now. If you can stay alive. Your family has a bad habit of trying to get killed."

Did he mean Mother? Did he know she was the slave who sang?

"Of course I know," he said, reading her face. He looked away. "I would know that voice anywhere."

"Is she…?" Heather began.

"She put herself in great danger, of course." There was a look of mixed appreciation and anger on her uncle's face. "But she has a knack for getting away."

"She does?"

"She escaped from my trap all those years ago," he said, eyes staring off into a hazy past. Then he shook his head and went on. "She's no helpless doe. Like you, there's far more to her than what's obvious."

"Is your brother—Is my father here?" she asked, suddenly desperate to know. "And Jacks?"

Uncle Garten's eyes flashed. "We will not speak of him!"

She fell silent.

They were circling the great pit now, avoiding the worst of the falling ash. Heather saw a thousand firelights below and the outlines of neighborhoods sprawled across the bottom of the city cut from stone. She could see a circle in the center, with several distinct groupings of light surrounding this wall in the middle of the city. For that is what it was—a wall. And within that wall blazed the most light.

"For Sween's sake," Uncle Garten went on, calmer, as they began to drop into the massive cavern, "I do not acknowledge any connection. She knows I won't go out of my way to hurt her, but neither will I assure her safety. I am, after all, Morbin's ambassador. That is my first duty."

Heather wanted to say so much, ask so much, yet she knew she must choose her words carefully. But her own anger was beginning to boil.

"To whom are you an ambassador, Uncle?"

"To Bleston—now Kylen, I suppose," he said, "to First Warren, and to everyone here," he pointed at the grim city below, "in Akolan."

"To this prison camp of a city?"

"Yes."

"To these rabbits you helped enslave?"

"Yes," he said, his words growing harder.

"I'm sure Grandfather would be proud," she said.

"You should know, oh great Scribe of the Cause, that we each tell ourselves a story about our place in the world."

"But the story needs to be true," she said.

"Who is to say what's true?" he asked. "All who claim to know it are only seeking power. Which side is right? History will decide in a hundred years."

"If you're on the side that murders, betrays, and enslaves," she said, "that might give a hint."

"To the Lepers' District!" Garten shouted forward, enraged. The bird swooped hard left and dipped down, finally gliding above the far northern edge of the city. They flew past the moonlit waterfall, heard its constant roar and rumble in the otherwise quiet night. There were few lights to be seen here on the edge of the pit, and a foul stench rose from the mangled hovels below. She couldn't make out the ground but could feel that they weren't quite near enough to land. "Here's where you get off," Garten said bitterly. He rammed his elbow into her head, knocking her back to roll off the bird's back.

She fell into the dank, foul darkness below.

Chapter Two

An Emerald Gem Inside

Heather screamed. Panic rose as she fell, limbs flailing, hands grasping for anything in the putrid air. There was nothing to grab, nothing to hold. There was only the air, the night, and a wild, terrific fear.

She struck a canvas sheet, slung taut and pegged in the rock. It gave way against her force, first stretching, then tearing in two in a spray of ash, spilling her into a hard-floored hovel. Heather crunched onto the stone, her shoulder bearing much of the impact. She screamed again, this time from pain. Her eyes bolted wide with fright, and she rolled to an awkward crouch, scanning her surroundings.

Heather was in a dingy tent, further wrecked by her graceless entrance. A foul stench filled her nostrils, and she gagged. A fire blazed in the center of the tent, over which hung a giant pot. Retching repeatedly, she tried to think clearly. Her uncle had called this the "Lepers' District," and she was beginning to understand why.

She heard moaning outside but could only see the jumbled squalor inside the tent, illuminated by the fire and the pale glow of distant stars through the ash falling above the torn canvas.

The moaning grew louder. Muffled whispers and groaning grumbles rose to an angry pitch. She didn't know what to do. Feeling for the satchel that was always strapped over her neck and shoulder, she thought of her duty as a healer. She felt compassion for any rabbit set apart as a leper in this foul, putrid prison. But this bag held far more than medicine. There was an emerald gem inside. Her satchel suddenly felt so heavy that it was hard to hold up.

She needed to eat. She needed to sleep. She needed to get away from whoever was groaning outside this tent.

She had to survive. For Mother. For...did she dare hope? It had been so long since that awful day in Nick Hollow when last she saw her father, a dim grey blur in a haze of smoke, surrounded by countless prowling wolves. To have any hope of seeing him and Jacks again, she had to act now. No matter how tired, wounded, and afraid she was.

Now. *Now!*

Heather crossed the stone floor and grabbed at a half-lit log, catching it up and spinning to face the first of the surging forms breaking through the tent flap opposite her. She didn't hesitate. Heather flung the fiery brand.

The burning log sailed into the corner, striking the rope tied to the peg, splitting the knot and collapsing that side of the tent. Energized to find her feet were still as fleet as

ever, in three strides she bounded through the split canvas and into the night. She sped through a dark street, kicking up a thin chalky residue of ash, while the crowd was left behind, confounded.

Heather had no idea where to go, but she thought anywhere that took her far away from the stench of the Lepers' District was the right direction. She sped on.

The streets were only narrow stone-bottomed paths between tattered tents and ramshackle sheds. She heard the groaning crowd behind as she ran on. After a hard run of several minutes, cutting unpredictable patterns through the shanty-packed blocks of streets, she paused to catch her breath. She looked to the impenetrable sky, obscured by the falling ash, not knowing whether the sunrise was something to hope for or not. *Does the sun even shine in this forsaken crater?*

She heard a muffled curse around the corner, answered by an angry retort. This sent her running again. Glancing back at the pit wall, she shifted her pattern of escape to take her as far from the edge of the high pit as possible. Breaking through the narrow streets, she found she was running free of the hovels and into a rock-strewn waste. In the distance she saw, by moonlight, the vague curve of the high central wall she had spotted from above. She jogged on, forward toward a faint glow in the distance. Soon she saw the outline of more buildings, and, getting closer, she saw by scattered lamplights a neat neighborhood of modest stone houses. Here the ash was mostly cleared away, swept into heaps at the street corners.

She slowed a moment, taking in the stunning contrast between this flickering vision and what she had just escaped. This neighborhood, which seemed to stretch for miles and miles, was only remarkable in contrast to the tract of squalid shacks she had left behind.

She entered a wide street lined on both sides by two-story homes. Stone staircases were cut into the sides of the houses. Hearing footsteps and harsh whispers, she darted up the stairway on the side of the nearest home. Reaching the top, she dropped down, crawled through a film of grey dust to the rooftop edge, and peered over at the moonlit street below.

Three shadowy figures emerged on the far side of the block, walking fast. Then another group rounded the corner, and the two halted some ten steps apart.

"What's o'clock, friends?" an older rabbit asked.

"'Tis seven, I think," a younger replied. "What's the word?" he asked as the groups merged. Heather watched them warily. *It can't be seven o'clock. What can they mean? A code, perhaps?*

"Preylords spotted," the older rabbit replied. "Dropped a package in the L.D."

"They didn't land, did they?"

"No," the older rabbit said, "our scout says it was a drop-off. He was dropped pretty hard."

"Did the Ls get him?"

"No, they did the usual routine. But he bolted before they could close in."

"Great," he said, grumbling. "Stretch."

"Yes, sir?"

"Get your bucks together. We've got to find this interloper, and quick."

"Aye, sir."

"When you find him, bring him to the L.T.'s."

"Aye, sir," Stretch said. "Wisp, Gripple, and Dote, let's go." She heard quick footsteps fading into the night, and the group thinned.

"Speaking of L.T.," the younger rabbit said, "did she make it back?"

"Not yet. That's why he's still at home. Waiting for her."

"I'm headed that way."

"May your feet find the next stone," the older rabbit said, then hurried off.

"Aye," the younger said. He heaved a long sigh and headed back the way he had come.

The group broke up, and Heather remained motionless.

What was she supposed to do? There were bands of rabbits looking for her, and she didn't know who to trust. She was hungry, frightened, and exhausted.

Heather glanced up and down the street, then crouched to creep along the wall. She paused to gaze across the rooftops toward the massive cliff at the pit's edge and the long, thin waterfall that left the crater's lip high above and fell into a reservoir beyond the Lepers' District. She could see movement in the "L.D.", as the rabbits below had called it, torches darting through the streets between ramshackle sheds. Even here, she could still catch the faintest whiff of that horrific smell. She looked around, taking in the spreading rooftops in every direction, separated sometimes by a larger road that gathered the threads of several lanes. The tops were caked with ash. Then she saw the curving wall in the middle distance, higher than her rooftop, so it was impossible to see what was on the other side. She crept down the steps and leaned back into a patch of darkness against the house wall. She felt the need to move, but she didn't know where to go. Surely not to that tall wall that seemed to stretch on and on into the night. But where?

She decided she would head toward the reservoir and try to get some water. That would at least satisfy her thirst, and then she could decide where to turn. Looking carefully back and forth, she stepped into the street and began to jog.

"Hold it!" she heard from behind her. She stopped, glancing around for possible avenues of escape. "Arms where I can see them!" Heather obeyed, her mind screaming at her to run, run, *run*!

"Got something here," she heard. It was a gruff voice, similar to those she had heard earlier.

"Good work." Another voice. Older.

"Who are you, and what are you doing out after curfew?" the older one asked.

"I'm Mags," she said slowly, "and I was with Stretch. We're looking for the package that fell in the L.D."

"A nightpad, huh?"

"Just doing my job," she said. Every escape route was risky. If she ran for the nearest lane, she had no idea if it would even connect to anything. She might be trapped. She assumed they had weapons.

"Your job," the older one said, walking up behind her, "is to do as you're told and follow the law."

"Right," she said. "I'm sorry. I'll just head home." She took a step and heard a click. A bolt flew past her ear and sank, with a thud, into the wall beyond.

They had crossbows.

"Make another move, and you'll never be home again."

"Understood," she answered, nodding as she fought back tears. They had her. She was caught again. Who were they, and what would they do with her?

"Where's your preymark?" the younger rabbit asked, moving into view. He wore a grey uniform with a round red collar. His armor was dark, and one shoulder showed the small, sharp silhouette of wings.

"What?" the older said, grabbing at the white cloth on the neck of her medic's uniform. "No preymark?"

"I left it at home," she said, with no idea what they could mean. "I'm sorry. It won't happen again."

"Let's take her in," the older one said as they grabbed her wrists and bound them tight.

“Where are you taking me?” she asked, a sob starting in her throat as she was spun around to face two large rabbits in grey uniforms.

“Longtreaders, of course,” the shorter one said. “Where else would we take you?”

Chapter Three

The Family Name

They were taking her to "Longtreaders"! Her heart leapt. She wanted to say "That's my family!" and explain all the horrible things that had led her to be here. But something told her to keep silent. Maybe it was the angry caution of the two officers who had caught her. Maybe it was that she had seen so much betrayal she could never trust anyone again.

Kyle—or Prince Kylen as he was known now—had been the first to turn her usually trusting heart wary. He had betrayed her beloved Smalls to the enemy, and it took an incredible rescue from Picket to reverse Kyle's crime. Then there was Perkinson, a close friend to both her and Picket, who had gained their trust and pretended to be their friend while he murdered Lord Ramnor and enabled the great treachery of Prince Bleston. And, of course, her uncle Garten Longtreader, the legendary betrayer of King Jupiter himself. He had brought their family name into dishonor and, much worse, had been the architect of

Morbin's victory, which set in motion the tyranny that had spread to every corner of Natalia.

She walked on, prodded occasionally by the gruff older rabbit. "Get on with ya."

"I'm tired," she said, barely audible.

"You should be in your bed, then, and not out rambling in the night without your preymark like a causer."

A causer? What can that mean? She was too tired to think it through. Her mind was spent. All that remained was a dull, callous caution that urged her into silence. She trudged on, down stone streets, until they crossed a wide space toward that massive wall, which seemed to wrap around the entire center of the city. Guards, with long pikes and crossbows slung at the ready, stood outside a wide gate in the wall. She saw by torchlight the black wings on their left shoulders. When they came near, the guards crouched in a defensive posture. They shouted, "Who goes there?"

"Loyal fellows," her captors replied.

"Then what is the sign?"

"We are here and alive!" they called back together. They walked on, pushing her ahead as the guards called up to others on top of the wall. Then they formed a line, through which she was led, as the gate slowly opened just wide enough for them to enter. She heard the guards shuffling back into place as the gate clanked shut behind her.

She was inside a massive compound encircled by the wall. It was dark, but she saw the outline of many buildings in the moonlight and some activity of uniformed rabbits like the ones at the gate and those who led her on. They turned left and walked alongside the wall until they came to a large stone building with a broad banner above the door. She couldn't make out the symbol, though she strained to see it.

"Go on, outwaller scum," the guard said. She was urged on, and she entered the building.

Inside, she was placed on a bench alongside three other rabbits, two of whom were slouched and unconscious. Both wore red neckerchiefs. The third was huddled on the edge of the bench, head down, with his arms wrapped around his knees. He had a blanket draped around his back. He snuck a glance at her, and she smiled wearily at him. Then his head dropped again, and he rocked back and forth, disappearing into the blanket.

There were guards all over, angry faces showing over stiff red collars as they worked at their various tasks. Several officers scowled at desks, sifting through stacks of paper. Others marked wall charts and sorted forms. She watched them until her vision began to blur.

Heather's tired mind tried to focus, to be present in the moment. She worked to make sense of the anxiety that battled with hope inside her. Would she see Father? Was Mother safe? What about Baby Jacks? Her gaze grew hazy, and her mind dipped in and out of the present until finally sliding over into sleep.

She was in a dark place. The air was thick with fog. A thousand smooth rocks lined the bottom of a damp cave. A slippery voice whispered in her ear. "They will awaken and shake the world. We will have our revenge." Then a scaly hand reached out and grasped her own. She felt her hand shaking, and she screamed.

Then she was awake. She was lying down on the bench, and the shy rabbit was grasping her hand and whispering to her. "It's all right, now. You're okay. Don't scream anymore, please." He patted her hand and made soothing noises. She swallowed hard, her eyes darting around the room. She nodded, coming fully awake and realizing she must have called out, arousing the irritated interest of some of the officers.

But as she calmed and they could see she was no threat, they returned to their tedious work, and she lay still. The shy rabbit had covered her with his blanket, and as the dream dissipated, she found she was almost comfortable. She was still tired, hungry, and very thirsty, but the nap had relieved her very urgent need to rest.

"Thank you," she whispered, reverently touching her ears, her eyes, then her mouth.

The shy young rabbit nodded, smiling as he looked down.

"What is this place?" she asked, as quietly as she could.

The rabbit looked puzzled, peering into her eyes intently, almost, she thought, as if he was trying to figure out if she was being serious or if she had been hit on the head. "You okay, Whitey?" he asked in a mumbled whisper.

"I'm fine," she answered. "I'm just…" She weighed how much to say and decided she could trust this rabbit so far. "I'm not from here."

"I wondered when I didn't see no preymark," he said, grabbing at the red kerchief around his neck. She was beginning to understand what that meant now. "We haven't had any new'ns for quite a while. We'd heard they were finished bringing 'em. Say the Preylords kill all prisoners in the field now. How'd you get here?"

"They dropped me in the Lepers' District."

The rabbit recoiled. "They didn't touch you, did they?"

"No, no. I ran away before I even really saw much of them."

"Powerful contagious, the lepers," he said, wiping his hands on his shirt.

"What's your name?" she asked.

"They call me Hadley," he said, touching his temple.

"Why do they call you that?" she asked.

"Because," he whispered conspiratorially, "it's my name."

"Listen, Hadley," she said, smiling, "what happens here?"

"I'm set to serve a turn in the jake for breaking curfew. As long as I can stay away from Captain Vitton, I'll be okay. But they know who I am. Not sure what they'll do with you. They don't treat outwallers well here," he whispered even quieter, "especially if they're causers."

"So is an outwaller someone who lives outside the big wall?" she asked. Hadley nodded. "What's a causer?"

Hadley glanced back and forth and came close to Heather's ear. "The resistance."

Heather nodded. "They said they were taking me to… to the Longtreaders," she said carefully.

"Of course," he said. "You're here. This is Longtreaders High Command inside the Sixth District."

"Longtreaders High Command? Sixth District?" she asked, a knot forming in her stomach.

"Yeah, Dumbster," he said, pretending to knock on her head playfully, "this is District Six, where all the Longtreaders live, including the head rabbit himself, the main Longtreader."

"Who's the main Longtreader?" she asked, worried.

Hadley leaned in close again. "The Commandant," he whispered. "The most evil rabbit who ever lived. He'd just as soon skin somebody as say good morning. Most folks comes to his attention end up dead, or worse. But don't worry; you'll probably just see one of his lieutenants, and though they're bad enough, they'll just put you in the jake, and you'll spend some time for the crime of being out at dark. Like me. It's none too pleasant, but it's better'n getting mixed up with the Commandant."

She began to weep quietly. All those old fears of her father being a traitor came flooding back. But she knew it couldn't be so. Her father was no traitor. He was loyal to the cause, as everyone said. But so had Uncle Garten been, for a while.

"Buck up, Whitey," Hadley said. "You won't see him. He's above such petty matters. Now Lieutenant Long is no picnic neither. Hope you don't get him. He likes to strike out over nothing. Captain Vitton is worst of all, but he's mainly interested in causers. Only gets at ordinary outwallers when things are slow."

"When you say the Commandant is a Longtreader," she asked, "what do you mean?"

"I mean he's head of the Longtreaders, the peace force here in Akolan. They enforce peace on us. I mean, for us."

"So they're the good ones?"

Hadley's face pinched in a noncommittal twist, and his head bobbed back and forth. Heather nodded. She relaxed a little. It was clear they were just using the name *Longtreader*, probably based on the fact that Garten Longtreader was the highest ranking rabbit in Morbin's order. "So, this Commandant is just a Longtreader in office alone, right? What's his real name?"

"Welp, that's the funny thing," Hadley said, bending closer. "He's a real Longtreader all right." Heather gasped. There was motion near the door. Hadley continued. "They say he's Ambassador Garten Longtreader's own brother."

"All right, girl," an angry guard called. She turned to see an open door. "The Commandant will see you now."

Chapter Four

Escape from Cloud Mountain

Picket ran. He never expected to be back at Rockback Valley so soon, but here he was, rushing through the moonlit night across the pocked and ruined field at the base of Cloud Mountain. He and Helmer were leading a band of rabbits, mostly soldiers, who were evacuating the mountain hideaway, home of the heralds of the Mended Wood. They were one of ten divisions, all fleeing in different directions at the same time. The plan had been ordered by Emma, after quickly consulting with her council. It had been Mrs. Weaver's idea to split into so many parties, some intended to regroup miles away and others to continue on to safer havens. The wounded, old, and infirm were headed for Halfwind Citadel, away from danger.

Picket and Helmer had a different destination.

"This way," Helmer called, his tone urgent. The company formed up behind him and sped toward the woods that lined the valley. Picket dodged craters and quickly picked his way through in the moonlight.

"Watch your step, bucks!" Picket said, pointing to a charred ruin of a catapult tilting on the edge of a bombed-out crater. It hadn't been long since a catapult like this, perhaps this very one, had sent him sailing into the sky to glide and fight at impossible heights. He shook his head and ran on, resuming his keen attention to their surroundings. "When should we split?" he asked, jogging up beside Captain Helmer.

"When we get to Jupiter's Crossing, I think," Helmer replied. "I want to see these bucks to some degree of safety. I think we have a little while yet before word of Heather's trick gets back to Morbin's army."

Picket's uncle, Garten Longtreader, had said there would be no attack on Cloud Mountain by the massive second force waiting not far off. That is, if Princess Emma, King Jupiter's heir, was turned over to Morbin Blackhawk. Emma had made the deal, but Heather intervened, bravely taking Emma's place and buying the rabbits time to escape from the waiting army of wolves and raptors, commanded by Morbin's Preylord lieutenants.

"I hope you're right about Morbin's forces," Picket said.

"I know what you're thinking, lad. I'm less settled about the Terralains."

Picket *was* worried about them. The Terralain army had seemed to be allies at first, but later Lord Bleston, their leader and the brother of King Jupiter, had betrayed them to Morbin and tried to turn over Princess Emma. Picket had intervened, and now Bleston was dead. His son and heir, Prince Kylen, was weak from wounds but alive.

"Me too," Picket said. "Who knows what Kylen's army will do after they find out what I did to their king?"

"You ended him," Helmer said with a growl, "as any noble buck must have done in your place. Though few could have done what you did."

"I let him fall," Picket said, his eyes wide with the memory.

"You did right, and you rescued the princess. You saved the cause, son."

"But if we have to fight Morbin *and* Kylen, well…" His voice trailed off.

"Don't worry," Helmer said, "things will get worse."

"Very comforting, Master," Picket answered. "But fighting both armies would be unimaginable."

"We can't really hope to beat either," Helmer said, "which is why we're retreating."

"I prefer to think of it as regrouping."

"If only nicer words could make an awful thing less so," Helmer said, limping as he ran, "we'd be having a *good* time."

Picket smiled and moved apart from Helmer, slowing to be sure the rear of the group wasn't lagging. After an eerily quiet run, they reached the edge of Jupiter's Crossing, and Helmer called a halt. There were nearly fifty rabbits in this company, and they had been sent this way to draw any enemies away from the more vulnerable units.

"This is where we leave you," Helmer said, motioning for a tall rabbit to step forward and stand beside him and

Picket. "Lieutenant Drand will lead you to the rendezvous. Be bold, move quickly, and stay sharp. This war is far from over. I hope Captain Picket and I will see you again soon." He motioned to Picket.

"Only do your duty," Picket began, "and remember that our side fights because of love and loyalty. We fight for freedom and for the vulnerable—"

"So says the murderer!" A shrill call rang out in the forest, stopping Picket with his mouth still open. The company turned to see Tameth Seer, the old guide to Prince Bleston, emerge from the woods. Behind him stepped a band of tall, strong Terralain rabbits. "So says the assassin. So says the killer of kings."

Even at this distance, Picket could see the anger seething on the faces of the old rabbit and the strong-armed soldiers with him. They looked furious, their muscles tense, eager to act on their rage.

Helmer stepped toward them. "Listen, wise one. I'm not sure who told you what happened, but Bleston betrayed us. He tried to take Princess Emma and made a deal with Morbin. Picket only defended himself, and the prince was killed."

"*King* Bleston never betrayed anyone!" Tameth Seer screeched. "*King* Bleston was the noblest of rabbits. When Prince Kylen, the heir of all Natalia, is well again, he will set things right with all parties. But for now, the assassin Picket Longtreader must be handed over."

Picket stepped forward and began to speak.

"Stay back, Picket," Helmer ordered. "You're wrong, Tameth Seer." He looked past the old rabbit to the soldiers virtually snarling behind him. "I speak as a soldier to soldiers. We have been led into many battles by the delusions of corrupt leaders who lie for their own ends. Please don't let this withered old fool warp your minds with his poison."

A tall Terralain officer stepped forward and drew his sword beside the grizzled old rabbit. He looked into the seer's eyes, then back up at Helmer. "Tameth Seer is a holy rabbit. You profane the land of Terralain and all her own when you speak thus of him. Turn the murderer Picket Longtreader over to us. He will kneel to justice," he said, raising his sword, "or justice will make him kneel."

The rabbits on either side of the wood had stepped forward so that the Terralains were lined up with the tall captain, and Helmer's company was lined up with him. Picket's fellows did not like the way the Terralains spoke of one they considered a hero.

"The Silver Prince tried to kill Emma, his own niece, then tried to kill me," Picket said, stepping ahead of his band. "I didn't want to do what I did. I had no choice!"

"We have no choice but to condemn you for murder!" Tameth Seer growled in his brittle, breaking screech. The Terralains began walking forward. Picket noticed that there were fewer of them across the way, but they were, unlike his own company, well-rested and much stronger.

"Please!" Picket said, drawing his sword. He raised it and then dropped it to the ground. "We're all rabbits. Morbin is out there. We should be allies!"

But they kept coming, moving in with malicious looks.

"This is your last chance," Helmer called, bending to pick up Picket's sword and handing it to him as he drew his own. When there was no reply and they kept coming, he spun to his band.

"What do we do, sir?" Lieutenant Drand asked.

Helmer's face bent into a sour frown. "Knock 'em stiff, bucks!"

Chapter Five

A Poised Sword

The two sides clashed in the moonlit wood, sparks leaping off crossed blades. The quiet of a few moments before vanished in the harsh noise of close battle. Picket leapt in, heartsick grief giving way to anger. True, these rabbits had once saved them from certain death at Halfwind against an army of wolves, but their leader had also betrayed them. And the rescue at Halfwind was probably only part of the plan with Morbin. Picket seethed at the injustice of his accusers. He was no murderer, but neither was he afraid to raise his sword.

He did so now, grappling with a Terralain soldier nearly twice his size. He blocked an overhead slice, deflecting it deftly as he spun and drove his own blade toward the soldier's middle. It glanced off the black breastplate, but Picket saw the shocked look on the soldier's face. He had underestimated the smaller rabbit. Picket followed the jab with a leaping spin and kick that sent the soldier stumbling back. The tall rabbit tripped on a root and pitched backward. Picket loomed over him with his sword poised, his heart pulsing with rage. Just then, Picket saw the woods swell with more rabbits, and his heart sank. Another band was charging in.

Then, from the shadows, out stepped Jo and Cole.

Jo raised his bow, as did the next thirty archers with him. "Terralains, drop your weapons!" Cole shouted. Picket glanced from Jo to the soldier lying beneath him. It was all he could do to stop his sword from doing its awful work. His hand was shaking. He looked across at Tameth Seer. The old rabbit seethed as he was covered by several rabbits with swords.

The sword trembled in Picket's grip as all the injustices he and Heather had experienced flashed through his raging mind. Heather, who was in the clutches of Morbin himself because of their betrayal. His face was contorted with anger as he raised his sword overhead, glaring at the silver stars on the soldier's breastplate. The Terralain arms. The symbol of the Silver Prince.

"Pick?" Jo whispered, putting his hand on his friend's shoulder. "We have them, Picket."

Picket glanced back at Jo. The archer's face was firm, an eyebrow arched with a question.

Picket looked from Tameth Seer to the soldier, then back at Tameth Seer. "I am no murderer," he whispered fiercely, sheathing his sword.

Helmer emerged from the woods nearest the crossing and nodded to Jo and Cole and the archers. "Well done, lads. Any more where they came from?"

"There's a large camp withdrawn from the ridge," Cole said, "but our units seem to have skirted them. This is the only band we know of to be out."

Helmer nodded. "So now, Tameth Seer," he said, walking up to the old rabbit. "My princess, the queen-to-be and true heir of Natalia, has put life and death in my hands. I am charged with protecting her community and furthering the cause. You are an obstacle to all our aims. You did not have to be. You do not have to be in the future. But here you are, mere yards from Jupiter's Crossing, taking up Morbin's part in the story." Some of the Terralain soldiers looked down. "We have no wish to fight with you, as rabbits should not shed one another's blood, but we cannot be allies with Morbin Blackhawk."

"Prince Kylen will arise and sweep all before him!' Tameth Seer said, his high, shrill voice a seesaw of wild glee and gravity.

"Who is the senior military officer present?" Helmer asked, turning from Tameth in disgust. "Who can speak for the army?"

"I can," said a brawny rabbit, the same who had come to the seer's side before the fight began.

"So, Captain?"

"Captain Vulm," he answered.

"I am Captain Helmer," Helmer said, crossing to stand before him. "I do not ask you to chart a course for your entire land. I only ask you for these terms. Do not raise arms against us this day, or the next. Let us go our way and you go yours, in peace. Shed no rabbit's blood."

"Our arms?"

"Keep your weapons, all of you. You go your way in peace, and we go ours. This is no surrender," he said quietly, "only a cessation of hostilities. So we can regroup and think about whether or not we should be fighting one another at all. But that is a matter for our principals. We are only soldiers, and we see what soldiers see." This last he said while glancing at Picket.

Captain Vulm frowned, looked down, glanced at his soldiers, then back at Helmer. "I cannot speak for all the army, Captain. I do not have such authority. But for the soldiers here, I give you my word as a warrior. We will not fight with you or yours for three days."

"Then it is agreed," Helmer said, extending his hand. They caught one another by the wrist and, nodding solemnly, broke apart.

Wordlessly, Captain Vulm motioned for the Terralain band to turn back. They moved with him, sheathing their weapons and stalking off.

"The flood is coming," Tameth Seer cried as he was led away, "and Prince Kylen will turn the tide and win the day! I have seen it!"

"Should we have shown such mercy, sir?" Cole asked, frowning at the retreating soldiers as he walked up.

"I don't want to fight them again," Lieutenant Drand said, feeling at his torn coat for the wound he'd just received.

"I wanted to kill him." Picket's heart was still racing.

"No one could have blamed you if you had," Jo said. "But I'm glad you didn't."

"Who knows?" Helmer said. "Picket refusing the battle may one day win the war."

Chapter Six

A Token of the Broken World

"Listen, now," Jo said as he put his arm around Picket and took him aside. Cole followed. "After you and Captain Helmer left with your company, some more of the band that had gone with Prince Smalls and Captain Wilfred came in."

"My father among them," Cole added.

"Is Lord Blackstar okay?" Picket asked, a stab of guilt driving into his heart. He had begged the prince to attempt a rescue and later learned that it had gone horribly wrong, resulting in Uncle Wilfred being badly wounded—and worse news still. The worst news he had ever received.

"Father is hurt," Cole answered, "but he'll recover. He's well enough to travel with Emma, and she is seeing to his wounds."

"Did he confirm..." Picket began, but he couldn't go on. He dared not hope.

"Yes," Jo said, "Lord Blackstar saw what Captain Wilfred saw. He was run through and carried off, limp as a rag. The prince is dead."

Picket nodded, looking down, tears starting in his eyes.

"But Father brought back a few of the prince's things, which he gave to Princess Emma. And she wanted you to have this," Cole said, drawing out of his pack a long black scarf.

Picket took it and collapsed to his knees, a crippling grief overwhelming him. "It was my fault, my fault!" he sobbed.

They bent to lay gentle hands on his shoulders as he felt the crushing weight of it. After a little while, Cole spoke up. "Princess Emma said this would happen, but she wanted you to carry this token with you, because despite the one mistake you made, you were her brother's true friend—you and Heather and Wilfred, his truest friends—and because you saved his life and have saved the cause again and again, the prince's scarf belongs with you. She said, 'Give it to him, with all my love.'"

"So take it, brother," Jo said, lifting Picket

to his feet again, "and carry on. Bear this token, and bear the flame."

Picket nodded, wiped his eyes, and breathed in deeply. He closed his eyes, took another long breath, then opened them and looked at Helmer. Helmer nodded to the moon. Picket said, "Right."

"Time to go," Cole said.

"Yes. This is goodbye." Picket hugged Jo and Cole in turn.

"For now," Cole answered.

"Watch out for her," Picket said, looking Jo in the eye. Both rabbits' eyes were wet with tears. "Keep that bow ready. And Cole, please keep her safe. I hate to leave like this."

"We'll do our best, Pick," Cole said. "Anyway, your task is far more dangerous than ours."

"I don't envy you, my friend," Jo added. "But we'll take care of the princess...till the Green Ember rises..."

"...or the end of the world," they said together.

They embraced again, then parted. Picket crossed to Helmer. Helmer nodded to Cole and Jo and said, "We'll send word via Harbone Citadel. Wait for the signal, and then don't hesitate. She must be decisive."

"Yes, sir," Cole said, saluting. Jo touched his forehead and bowed. Helmer stared a moment at them, then turned, and he and Picket walked briskly out into Jupiter's Crossing.

Without a word, they began to run. Because of his leg injury, Helmer's gait was ungainly, but it didn't seem to slow him down. Picket carried wounds of his own, in every sense, and he carried them into that sacred crossroads.

Jupiter's Crossing was a complicated place, and it always had been. An unsafe rabbit crossing between two forests for centuries, it became a symbol of King Jupiter's reign when it got to be as safe as any forest road. King Jupiter had won such victories over the birds of prey that they were pressed back into their home in the High Bleaks. This crossing, and many other such places, had become secure for rabbitkind. But that was before. Nowhere felt safe now.

When they came to a tree on the edge of the crossing, Helmer slowed, then bent to kneel, and lowered his head. Lost in his own sober reflections, Picket knelt as well.

As every rabbit knew, it was now very near the anniversary of the day when King Jupiter had died here. The great king was killed by Morbin Blackhawk after being betrayed by Heather and Picket's uncle, Garten Longtreader. When the king died, so died the golden age of rabbits, and the Great Wood became a broken, scorched remnant of its former glories. Ever since, Jupiter's Crossing had been a sad place, hallowed but unhappy for rabbits. But then Picket had rescued Prince Jupiter Smalls here, on this very soil. It was a feat that reverberated throughout Natalia and hummed with hope in the heart of every rabbit who heard of it. Most learned of it through Heather's own startling account, copied and passed from hand to hand. She had become "the Scribe of the Cause" as a result, telling how Picket had soared above and struck down Redeye Garlackson, rescuing the prince, fueling the fire of the cause, and vindicating the Longtreader name.

But the prince he had saved was now gone, and he wept to think of his part in it. Picket had never meant to endanger the prince; he was only desperate to see his lost family saved. He was wrong, he knew, to plead with Smalls to attempt the rescue. And he felt the loss keenly, both for the cause and because Smalls was his friend. His best friend, really. Heather had hopes as well with Smalls that went beyond him being her king one day, and Picket felt the weight of the world that now could never be. He buried his face in the black scarf.

As they slowly got to their feet and walked on in silence, Picket wrapped the scarf around his neck. It felt good to have it close, like the stitching that hurts on a wound, even as it slowly helps it heal.

* * *

Picket and Helmer traveled until they could go no farther. They rested in the well-hidden hollow of a thorny thicket, each sleeping deeply from total exhaustion. When they awoke, they ate and drank from their hefty travel packs, then resumed their march without much talk. Picket had never come this way, heading toward the heart of the Great Wood. Helmer was determined, even though Picket could see his master's leg was aching, and the older rabbit pressed on through the pain.

"Will they know us at Harbone Citadel?" Picket asked.

"They'll know me," Helmer replied. "And they'll know of you. Don't forget that you're a war hero."

"You were a war hero before I was breeched," Picket said.

"That's true, Ladybug," he said, smiling, "but I never did the things you did, nor anything like."

"You like to make war the old-fashioned way."

"It suits me better, yes. On the ground, as rabbits always have, just going straight at the enemy."

"Very noble."

"I think so."

They fell silent again for a while, moving quickly, Picket matching Helmer's efficient hustling gait. He never stopped to check his bearings but plunged ahead, as if he traveled this path every day of his life.

"You know the way, I presume?" Picket asked.

"I could find it on a moonless night while blindfolded."

"I have studied the maps, as you so vigorously commanded, and I wonder if we haven't taken a few paths out of the way."

Helmer smirked. "You are gifted, *young* Picket, it is to be admitted, at routes and calculation. But what you don't know is the most likely spots for scouts or the places that can and can't be seen from great distances. So all your theoretical knowledge of maps is well enough, but I'd rather take my way and keep us alive."

"That's so unreasonable," Picket said, laughing.

"I've been accused of worse."

"You've been guilty of worse."

"That is also true," Helmer agreed. He laughed through his nose in a short, gruff snort.

"You've been this way many times?"

"Yes," Helmer said, but his smile faded. Picket thought his master was remembering days gone by, and he let him remember. He would not break in on his thoughts. Finally, Helmer spoke again. "My sister and I...we walked these paths a thousand times together."

A sister? They walked on, and Picket replied, "I didn't know you had a sister, Master Helmer."

"I do. And she is ten times as bad tempered as I. Her name is Airen, and she's my twin."

"I had no idea..." Picket began. He left a lengthy pause before finishing, "that it was possible for anyone to be even half as ornery as you, Master."

"She is full of fire," Helmer said, now grinning. Actually grinning! Picket was astonished, so he felt freer to speak than he usually would have.

"Where is Airen?" Picket asked.

Helmer's face bent in a frown again. He said, "Airen's in First Warren. She's lived in the grip of Morbin's claw for so many years. And I haven't seen her for ages." He swiped at his eyes. "The truth is, son, I don't know if she's alive or dead."

"I have only just lost my sister. Dead or alive, I don't know. And it is unbearable. I feel as though a part of me is gone. The best part of me. It's awful that you've been separated from Airen so long."

"A good sister is a gift," Helmer said. "I only wish I would have appreciated her more when we were young and together. And I wish I had never left her."

"I'm very sorry, Master."

"We all carry our burdens, Picket," Helmer said, his head hung low and his limp more obvious than earlier. "Wounds unhealed and griefs..." But he could say no more.

"It will not be so," Picket said after a decent pause, feeling for the scarf at his neck, "in the Mended Wood."

Chapter Seven

Family History

After hours of hurry through wide woods, they slowed to cross a particularly tricky thicket, swiping at vines and shrugging off grabby patches of thorns. The sun fell in dappled splashes as evening set in, and Picket followed Helmer into the tangle of trees. Winter was less dominant the farther south they went, and here and there green gathered around the pervasive brown of the forest. Picket had to trust that his master knew what he was doing, for he could not help but calculate a host of faster paths to their destination.

Their destination.

Will we even be welcomed? Picket had felt the chilling dismissal of hard-set opponents before, and he hoped that their reception would at least be a little warm. "Will they welcome us at Harbone Citadel, Master?"

"They have no reason not to," Helmer answered, swiping at a knotted vine, which split and lay limp on either side of their path.

"Except that I'm a Longtreader."

"I think," Helmer said, pausing to draw breath and wipe his brow with a handkerchief, "that the days of your family name being used for ill purposes are over. Thanks to your particular heroics and your sister's gifted pen, the name Longtreader is inspiring the free rabbits of Natalia. I even expect your harshest critics, like Lord Ronan at Blackstone Citadel, to come around."

"I hope so."

"Those at Harbone have no reason to be against us. And besides, anyone who has a problem with you has a problem with me."

"Thank you, Master."

"I accept you," Helmer said, putting his hand over his heart.

"I am accepted," Picket replied, hand over his own heart, completing once again the conclusion to the vows of an apprentice. They had been through much since his unexpected and informal calling ceremony on the village green at Cloud Mountain, but Picket saw that his master still believed that the ritual mattered and that Picket was under his solemn protection.

"With Airen and her family…well, who knows where," Helmer said, drawing his sword again and forging ahead, "you're the only family I've got."

Picket blinked, eyes widening. He stopped. Then he smiled and followed Helmer deeper into the forest.

After hacking through the disused path for an hour, Picket spoke up again. "Have you known Harbone Citadel's lord long?"

"Lord Hewson? You could say that. We hated one another as young bucks, fought like ancient enemies. He from a highborn family and I low, we clashed often. But we came together as soldiers. Battle, as I should guess you've noticed, has a way of forging some durable bonds."

"Yes, sir," Picket answered, looking away. He thought of Jo and Cole.

"Anyway, Lord Hewson is a good friend. I once saved his life from a particularly heinous wolf. Not so fierce and famous as your Redeye Garlackson, no, but no toothless pup either."

At the mention of their enemies, an enormous cloud passed between them and the sun, and the thicket grew darker still. A chill wind picked up, and they felt a sudden shiver. Picket glanced around, uneasy. "It's only the wind," he said, barely aloud. "It's nothing."

"Or it could be that the old forest is trying to tell us to be wary," Helmer said, eyes keen and voice a soft rasp.

Picket lowered his own voice as well. "Isn't that—I don't know—childish?"

"Maybe. Children can, I think, feel things that grownups can't. They are awake to the warnings in the wind. Or so my wise old nurse believed."

"There can never be a wise young nurse, can there?" Picket said, still looking carefully around.

"There can never be a wise young *anything*," Helmer answered, smirking as he took in their surroundings.

"What was that?" Picket whispered, crouching at the sound of a snapping twig in the distance. He gripped his sword hilt tightly.

"Possibly that 'nothing' you spoke of earlier," Helmer whispered back, but he motioned for Picket to stay low and follow. Picket moved close behind his master as they stalked to the edge of the thicket and lay down, well-hidden, to peer out into the small glade before them and the dense forest beyond.

After staring silently for a while—Picket could see nothing—Helmer whispered, "If we get separated, take the most direct route to Harbone, and don't stop for anything."

"Yes, sir. How close are we?"

"For you? A twenty-minute dead run."

Picket nodded.

"Something's out there," Helmer said, and Picket saw the creases deepen at the edge of his eyes. "Friend or foe? I don't know."

"I'm ready," Picket said, adjusting his pack and preparing to move.

"I'll cross the glade," Helmer said, "and you follow after I signal you."

"Yes, sir."

Helmer breathed deeply, then stood and stepped carefully into the glade. An arrow sped toward him. Picket heard the bowstring's *thwick*, saw the blurry arrow collide with Helmer and his master spin and fall.

"No!"

Chapter Eight

The Commandant's Gifts

Heather held her breath and slowly walked down the long dark hallway toward the Commandant's office. She felt she might faint with fatigue, hunger, and fear. The door at the end of the passage bore an emblem of a hawk in silhouette, his sickle in hand and a black crown on his head. At his feet lay skulls. Rabbit skulls. A single word stood out beneath the grizzly emblem.

Longtreader.

Hadley had said the Commandant was Garten Longtreader's brother. Heather knew her father was here in Akolan. *But how? Have I* ever *been told the truth by anyone?* Her knees felt weak. She wanted to run away, to never see what she had to see. But the door opened, and she was shoved inside. She fell to her knees, afraid to look up.

"Well, my dear. What brings you here?"

She looked up, brows knit. A tall rabbit stood before a wide window. The full day's brightness shone behind him, and she could see only an outline in black, much like the symbol on his door.

"Who are you?" she asked, for he was *not* her father. She knew it, and her heart beat faster at the certain knowledge. The world, so wrong, was righting itself at least this much. She could tell it was not Father from his voice and frame. But who was he?

"I ask the questions here!" he barked. "Have you not heard that you must not ask questions of your masters?"

"Who told you this rule?" she mumbled, tired eyes defiant.

He smiled, took two long strides, and struck her in the face. She toppled back, rolling over with the heavy blow. "On your feet!" he screamed. It took her a moment to comply. When she had only gotten to her hands and knees, he crossed and kicked her in the stomach so that she rolled again. Wincing in pain, she got to her feet and, eyes blurry, glanced around the room. Ten rabbits in uniform surrounded her, officers all, she thought, by the gold bands on the sleeves of their black uniforms. Gold bands on their arms. Red collars. Wings on their left shoulders. These rabbits were, she now knew, what Akolan called "Longtreaders." Followers of her uncle Ambassador Garten Longtreader. They obviously ran this slave city, and this violent rabbit before her was their leader.

"I am the Commandant," he said, pacing around the room. The full light fell on his face, and she barely withheld a gasp. One side of his face was ordinary, but the other side was cruelly scarred. Crossed with many wounds, his eye gone and a patch to hide it, his face was a catalog of pain. "I believe you were dropped in the Lepers' District last night, is that correct?"

"It is, sir," she answered, head down.

"Good. Good," he said, brushing at a sleeve that bore five golden bands around it. "It has been some time since Lord Morbin has authorized a new drop. If you live to see the outwallers, they may be glad to have some of the horrible news you can bring and so wallow more deeply in the putrid pool of their sorrows." He spat. "Bring her!" he called, exiting the office through a side door.

Two of the officers grabbed her and shoved her through the door and up several flights of stairs. They pushed her through a stout door, and she stumbled out onto a balcony. No, not a balcony. She could see, as her eyes adjusted to the bright morning light, that it was not a balcony. It was the roof of the building they had been in. They moved her to the edge where she could see, glancing around wearily, almost the full city around and below her.

It was amazing. The vast wall stretched around the center of the massive pit, and inside it were homes and other buildings. The ash fell lighter now but still spread across the sky in wispy flight, piling on the building tops and the streets below. Beyond the wall, several different neighborhoods, almost like little towns, held clusters of stone homes. She saw the Lepers' District, a blight on the otherwise orderly condition of the city. She saw that, despite the ash, Akolan was an orderly place. The Lepers' District was the gross exception. It was especially tidy inside the thick wall, where buildings were cut straight and the lanes and streets were neat. Sweepers worked to move the ash out of sight, especially inside the wall. Just below, there was a large open space surrounded by buildings like the one she was on. Outside the wall and past the L.D., the waterfall ended in a wide reservoir, where high-propped aqueducts carried great quantities of the water into the walled-off district. There she saw it spill into another reservoir, where it was then channeled into several places, including just outside the wall, where rabbits hoed and dug in large fields. The workers pulled up potatoes in great quantities, then loaded them into wheelbarrows and carts. It was a large-scale operation, and, even in her deep fatigue and pain, she marveled at it all.

A blow to the back of her head brought her attention back to the Commandant, who stood sneering with his half-ruined face. She spun to face him, her back now to the low-lipped edge of the roof. "You see what I have to administer here?" he asked coldly.

"I do, sir," she answered. "It is amazing."

"It has been thus since the Longtreaders have come," he said, spinning to survey the pit, extending his hand to reveal it all. "It was not always so for rabbits in Akolan. But now, thanks to Ambassador Garten's vision, we are largely left to our own measures and have no sentinels here." Heather had heard rumors of the sentinels in faraway First Warren, the birds of prey on watch from the wall around that distant city, quick to swoop in and take horrific action at any sign of trouble. She shuddered as he went on. "We rule ourselves in most ways, and Lord

Morbin leaves us to it. We provide skilled labor for his kingdom, and we live our lives. We have a kind of peace. Do you see it?"

"Yes, sir."

"I will not have any disruptions to my peace. Do you understand?"

She nodded. He touched his ear, and she said, "Yes, sir," again, louder this time. He nodded. Then he closed his eye and recited,

"We are here and alive,
Let us make a life for ourselves,
Among our own kind,
And end our rebellion,
Against destiny.
Peace and prosperity forever!"

"Peace and prosperity forever!" repeated the gathered officers in unison.

The Commandant smiled, contempt and total confidence unified in his hard grin. "This is our creed in Akolan. You will have it by heart by Victory Day, which is very close at hand."

"Yes, sir."

"We celebrate Victory Day here, and we fill the square and say our oaths. We keep allegiance to Lord Morbin because he is the ruler of all Natalia and that is the way of peace. But there are those in Akolan who have not yet surrendered to the inevitable. I advise you—no, command you—to avoid and, if information becomes available, inform on these traitors. You will be placed in a home, assigned a job, and given rations."

"Yes, sir."

"Your rations are a gift. Your water is a gift. Your job is a gift. Your quarters are a gift. *Everything* is a gift of the administration."

"Yes, sir."

"You are a nurse, yes?" he asked, looking at her uniform, now badly torn and filthy, and the battered satchel still swinging at her side.

"Yes, sir."

"Then you will report to..." he glanced at a lieutenant, who consulted a sheaf of paper.

"District Four, Commandant," he said.

"You will report to the clinic in District Four for assignment in, let me see," he said, looking her over, taking note of her injuries, "no more than four days. And you will be wearing your preymark. At all times. At no time are you ever to be seen without clear red at your neck. All times! It is the law."

"Yes, sir." Heather was barely able to stand. She sagged and was held up by the officers on either side of her. She blew away some drifting ash that threatened to land on her face.

The Commandant came close, looking intently into her eyes. Heather thought, for just a moment, that there was a hint of kindness in his eye. He took her face in his hands and whispered softly, "We are here and alive. Let us make a life for ourselves, among our own kind. And let us end our rebellion against destiny."

He released her face, gave her one last smile, then struck her so hard that she toppled over the edge of the wall and fell.

She screamed, panicked in mid-air, then struck the first of several slung canvas awnings. She fell from one to another, unable to stop, until she finally spilled onto a high mound of cut stones. The jarring impact made her gasp and lose her breath.

Pain. Intense, pulsing pain.

She wanted to cry out, but her air was gone. She knew it would come back, but that didn't stop the panic. She tried to stand but toppled hard down the steep slope of the rock pile. Coming to the bottom, she gulped in air as the spasm stopped, and she tried to stay upright. But it was too much. Too much pain. Too much exhaustion. Hunger. Thirst. She fell to her knees as a small band of soldiers walked up to her, the first kicking dirt in her face.

"The Commandant is done with you," he said, stepping forward, "for now." She felt sharp pain travel up her back and shoot down her right arm. Possibly rebroken, she realized with a wince. Her vision blurred. Blackness.

Heather blinked, awake again, and realized she was moving. But she wasn't walking. She saw that the surly Longtreaders had her feet. They were dragging her toward the massive wall. She felt the hard stone tear at her back, the wrenching twist in her legs. Her right arm ached. She drifted out again.

When she awoke once more, she looked up to see… no one. Not a single soul. Only the hard stone wall some yards away and an abandoned ash pile. Not even the gate. They must have dragged her down the street along the wall to get her away from their comings and goings at the entrance. She rolled off her right shoulder and onto her left. Still no one. Only rows of homes in the distance.

Her body was in agony, but the fatigue was more insistent. She felt concern, but like a distant call, however urgent, that she could only barely hear. Her mind just had room to inventory her various pains. She knew she was dehydrated, exhausted, and famished. She knew of several sprains, innumerable bruises, and a few likely breaks. Distantly, she remembered the cause and the reasons she had exchanged her life for Emma's. Through her anguish, she weighed the cost and settled in her heart that it was worth it.

Why should I despair here at the end, when death is just what I expected?

Chapter Nine

A Good Dream

For Heather, there were songs and there were dreams, and they seemed to be at war.

The dreams came often. A cycle of dreams. Repeating themes, fading in and out over what felt like months. A damp cave, dark but for a pinprick of light high above. The ground packed with slick moss-covered stones. Slime and mire, slippery mud. A voice in the darkness, echoing the brittle shriek of Tameth Seer, cried out. "Sleep, or death?" Laughter. Darkness. Darkness. Down, down, *down*. A flood, an inescapable flood, and the end of all Natalia at hand. Kylen, terrible in his anger, surrounded by an army and marching on her friends. Darkness, and restful interludes. The songs came and went in doubtful snatches. Then more dreams, more falling. Once she dreamed she was awake and back in Nick Hollow. She drank something cool; then there were more and more troubling scenes. The songs were still there, poking at the edges of her meager store of hope. Then she was lost again. Lost in sleep.

She woke on the third day.

But she didn't know she was awake. Or couldn't be sure. She felt herself in a bed but dared not open her eyes for fear of seeing all that had so terrified her in an endless sequence of unsettling scenes.

Heather yawned. She heard a gasp. Then, a soft singing began.

"Are you come home, my baby girl?
Were you alone, my baby girl?
Fear not, Love, you are safe in my arms,
Home and home and home, again.
Home and home and home, again.
Fear not, my love, where'er you've been,
You're home and home and home, again.
Home and home and home, again!"

Heather smiled and opened her eyes. *Mother!* Mother was there, rising from her chair across the room. Sween Longtreader wept and smiled and ran to Heather, wrapping her in those warm, familiar arms. Heather's pains were gone for the moment as wild joy and gratitude swelled inside her. She clung to her mother tightly with her good left arm and felt she must never let her go.

They stayed like that, clasped together, for a long, long time.

Finally, Heather tired, and Mother helped her lie back down on the bed. They looked at one another, tears flowing freely, grins impossible to displace. It was Mother who finally spoke. "Welcome home, dear Heather."

For a moment Heather wondered if everything had been a dream and she was back in Nick Hollow again, safe and away from whatever troubles the wider world might hold. But she felt her right arm bound close to her body and remembered it was likely broken. Then, like the flood she'd dreamed of so vividly, the world and its woes came rushing over her again. "We're in Akolan," she said.

"We are," Mother replied, nodding. "But this is truly our home for now. Jacks is at school, or what passes for a school here, and Father is working. He should be home soon. He will be so happy to see you awake. We were very worried."

"Father is alive!" Heather said, a sob choking her. "And our Jacks?"

"They're both alive, my sweet girl."

"You're all alive! Say it again, Mother. Please, tell me it's really true."

"It's true, Heather, my love," Mother said, wrapping Heather once again in a long embrace.

"You sang!" Heather said, suddenly panicked. "At Morbin's lair, you sang. Didn't they find you?"

"Hush, dear," Mother said, patting her head. "I escaped through a trash chute and made my way back. I arrived not long after you were brought here."

"Someone found me at the wall?"

"Father did. Word got to him quickly."

"Hadley? The timid buck at the…at the *Longtreaders*?" she asked, saying the name painfully.

"I know, dear," Mother said, and she made the nonsense noises she had always used to calm Jacks when he was a baby. "It's a troubling thing to see our name so ill used."

Heather nodded. "I'm sort of used to it."

Mother frowned. "I want you to rest again. I know we have so much to discuss. I want to hear everything about your life and any news you might have of the world, how you came here and everything. But you must sleep. You must recover. Drink this," she said, bringing a bowl of broth to Heather's mouth. Heather drank it greedily, then followed it with water. "Not too much, my baby. More later. Rest now, my love." She backed up and crossed to the door, smiling at Heather through tears.

Heather started to object to more rest but felt a weight of exhaustion descend on her even as she began to voice her protest. "Thank you, Mother."

"I love you so much, Heather."

"We missed you," Heather said, wiping at her eyes. "We were so scared."

"I know, I know," Mother said, crossing back to sit beside her, taking her hand. "We tried to get away, to find you. Father fought them—he fought so hard and so bravely—but there were too many." She bowed her head. "I am afraid to ask, but I must." She took a deep breath and, almost flinching as if she expected to be struck, she said, "Picket?"

Heather frowned and Mother staggered back, an expression of deep sorrow on her face. "No, Mother! I'm sorry; come back," Heather said, extending her left hand. "I was only thinking how I miss him. Picket is well." Heather smiled wide and squeezed Mother's hand. "More than well, he is a lovely buck, full of courage, strength, and goodness. He's a hero, Mother. He killed Redeye Garlackson. He saved the cause. Mother," she said, wide-eyed, "he flew!"

Mother smiled uncertainly and patted Heather's head. "There, there," she said. "Is he really alive, Heather?"

"Yes, Mother. Alive and well," Heather answered, yawning. "I will tell more later. And you will believe me. I am something of a storyteller myself, now. Father will be very proud..." she trailed off and, eyes heavy and ears full of gentle singing, she fell fast asleep again.

And she did not dream.

[illegible] I was only thinking how I miss [illegible] [illegible] [illegible] [illegible] and [illegible] Mother's hand. [illegible] [illegible] [illegible] [illegible] [illegible] full of courage, strength and goodness. He was a hero, Mother. He [illegible] [illegible] [illegible] [illegible] [illegible] [illegible] [illegible] [illegible] [illegible] [illegible].

Mother [illegible] and patted father's head. "That [illegible] [illegible] [illegible] [illegible]."

"Yes [illegible]

[illegible] and he did not dream.

Chapter Ten

To Make Us Brave

Heather woke before anyone else got home. She dressed in new clothes made for her by Mother, sipped some soup, and drank more water. Then she walked slowly around their small home. She ran her hand over the elegant brickwork of their simple fireplace. Father's work, she had no doubt. Over the fireplace, mounted on the wall, were imperfectly painted pictures of Heather and Picket. Mother plainly didn't have access to the ingredients for the paints she once made in Nick Hollow, but the likenesses were striking, even with only a few drab colors.

She looked at the painting of Picket and tried to imagine where he was, what he might be doing. *I cannot wish you here, brother, but I do wish we were all together.*

"They are poor work," Mother said, stepping in from the small kitchen to check on Heather again. "But we wanted you both to have a place with us. We never forgot about you, and you were always in our hearts. But we wanted your faces in our home, so I made these."

"We never forgot you either, Mother," Heather replied. "And the paintings are good, though Picket looks older now. We saw many lovely paintings at Cloud Mountain, from masters like Finbar Smalls and Jim Toiner, but the painting we always longed to see was the one you painted of our home in the Great Wood."

"Ah, that one is lost in the ashes of our old home," Mother said.

"But the dream of home cannot be so easily destroyed," Heather said, accepting help to get into the comfortable chair set out for her in front of the fire. "It is there, in the Mended Wood."

"That old home was in First Warren," Mother said, sighing. "And we are far from there. Even if we could get there, it's now enemy territory as well."

"But it will not be so…" Heather began.

"In the Mended Wood," Mother answered.

Heather accepted a warm mug of what passed for tea in Akolan and smiled gratefully at her mother. "When will he be home?" she asked for the tenth time.

"Soon," Mother answered.

"Soon," Heather repeated, nodding. Mother had explained that Jacks was at school, and this meant staying there for around ten days, day and night, before coming home on leave for three days and two nights. He would be home in a few days, though they couldn't say for sure, exactly. Heather was impatient to see them all. She closed her eyes and felt herself rise on a wave of gratitude. That Mother and Father and Jacks were alive at all and that she would see them again—it seemed beyond belief. She smiled.

* * *

Heather must have slept again, for when she stirred and opened her eyes, she saw Father, standing by the fire, gazing at her with such deep affection that Heather came fully awake and sprang from her chair. She was in his arms in a moment, never worrying about how weak she was or if he could hold her. He could. And he did, spinning around slowly as he cried and squeezed her and said, "My Heather, my girl! My only daughter, dear. My lovely Heather," and on and on with endless expressions of how tenderly he loved her and happy he was to hold her in his arms again.

"Oh, Father!" was all she could say. And she said it again and again, spinning there before the fire as night fell on Akolan.

When he set her down at last and she sat back in her chair, she smiled and wept some more, sobbing into a handkerchief her father produced. Mother brought her more to drink and fussed over her losing all she drank through crying, though Mother's eyes were wet as well.

"The poet Herbare Fond mused that 'We cry more intensely in our joys than ever we do in our sorrows,'" Father said, wiping at his own eyes.

"That doesn't even rhyme," Heather said, laughing and wiping her eyes.

"Well, it's not all he mused," Father wheezed. "Herbare had a way with words, to be sure. He could muse like lit blastpowder."

"No doubt he was an excellent scribe," she said, "but I'm certain he couldn't keep up with the wordsmith behind such epics as 'Goofhack the Blabber' and 'The Brittle Wits of Sharpe Dulls.'"

"Certainly not," Father replied. He doubled over and gasped in his mirth. "Oh, Heather. I am so happy to see you. You're grown! I am amazed."

Heather smiled. Father had changed too. She noticed he had lost all the weight that had made him a little pudgy in the past. He was lean, too lean, and his face was creased with care. But otherwise he appeared the same. Mother was mostly unchanged, though she too was a little leaner and careworn. But their faces shone now. Mother retreated back to the small kitchen area, and Heather heard familiar noises.

"What are you doing over there, Mother?" Heather asked.

"I'm making a cake, for when you're recovered."

"I'm recovered enough for cake," Heather replied.

"Perhaps she hasn't changed much after all," said Father, winking.

"No cake until you're eating properly again," Mother said in mock severity. "The doctor came a few times while you slept, and he'll be back again tomorrow morning."

"I am training to be a doctor myself."

"We saw your poor ruined uniform and satchel, and we guessed as much," Father said. "We are so—"

Heather cut him off. "My satchel!" she said. "Where is it?"

"It's here, dear," Father said, getting up and crossing back toward the room she had been sleeping in. "Sit down and settle your heart. It's here, and we haven't touched it."

"The doctor wanted to see if there were any important medicines you might have," Mother said, "but we insisted that it be left alone, as long as he had what he needed to treat you."

"And he did," Father added, reappearing with the satchel in hand.

"Thank you, Father," Heather said, receiving it. She unfastened the straps and opened it. The satchel had been looked through, likely by the Longtreaders...the Akolan administration, not her family. Its contents had been upset, sure, but few things seemed to be missing. The old purse holding her flame necklace and old Aunt Jone's tonic was still there, along with something especially precious inside. Hiding her valuables beneath Aunt Jone's tonic in the battered purse had been wise. Relief flooded her heart, and she relaxed.

Heather smiled and set it all down beside her chair, taking another drink as she glanced toward the door. She thought she had heard something.

She had, and then there was a hard knock.

Father and Mother exchanged glances. "Back into bed," Father whispered. "Don't ask questions. You feel far worse than you think you do. Quickly now," and Heather saw the fear in his eyes. She had so rarely seen her father afraid. It frightened her in a way few other dangers had. She glanced at the door and saw hanging beside it two scarves and two neckerchiefs, all dyed bright red. Mother donned a scarf, and Father tied a kerchief around his neck.

She grabbed her satchel and headed for her room. She glanced back at Mother, whose face shared the same terror, then stepped inside. She slid the satchel beneath the bed, lay down, pulled the covers up, and closed her eyes.

"Good evening, sirs," she heard her father say. "Can we help you?"

She couldn't make out exactly what the guests were saying, heard only a muted mumble, but her father's words were clear, though quiet.

"Yes, that's right," he said, "we agreed to take her in and care for her until she recovers. Then we'll help find her a permanent home."

More garbled talk.

"We understand, and we thank you for your concern. The doctor will report on her condition tomorrow. He says we should be able to bring her to the clinic tomorrow or the next day."

Heather guessed these were more Longtreaders, more of the administration's minders, checking up on her. They nearly killed her, and now they cared what she was doing?

"Yes, sir," Father said. "We will follow every protocol, of course."

She had never heard her father grovel like this, and it made her sad and sick at heart. She didn't blame him, and she was sure he was doing the best thing he could think to do to protect them, just as he always had. But she hated to see a rabbit of such learning and dignity having to bow and scrape to such creatures as these.

"We will, sirs. Of course."

The door closed. Her heart was still warmed at this unlikely reunion, intensely so, but the exchange at the door had let in a chill that cut at her happiness.

After a tense few minutes, Mother spoke. "It's okay, dear. Come on out, if you feel up to it."

Heather retrieved her satchel, settled it over her shoulder, and walked slowly back into the main room. She fell back into the comfortable chair and gratefully took the food her mother offered, along with a fresh mug of tea. "Thank you, Mother."

"My pleasure, dear Heather."

"Father, is the Commandant also my uncle?" she asked. "Hadley said he is Garten's own brother."

"No, Heather," he answered. "That's a rumor here, but it is not so. No one knows his real name, so conjecture about his family flourishes."

"He's an evil rabbit," she said.

"The very worst, for those who oppose his schemes," Father replied, his head down.

"I think Captain Vitton is worse," Mother said quietly. "He's the keeper of the dungeon and enjoys hurting his prisoners. Vit Skinner, he's called."

"A grotesque monster, to be sure," Father said, shaking his head. "But let us think of better things."

They all ate around the fire. Between bites, Father bragged about making the chair Heather was sitting in.

"It wouldn't be called a masterly job," he said, "but neither would it be called dastardly."

Heather laughed at his subtle, playful way with words. It was as familiar to her as Mother's songs. "It's very comfortable, Father," she said between slurps of soup. "I would never accuse this chair of being anything but friendly to a rabbit's rear."

"And that's high praise for such a low chair," he said, sniffing in mock self-importance.

"Oh my," Mother said. "He has missed having his collaborators at home."

"Yes," Father said. "Sween only says that it's a fine chair, yes, but it will break like all the others, and then what will we sit on?"

"And *he* says that we'll sit on the ground and talk of chairs we once knew and treasured, like shipwrecked sailors marooned on a desperate coast. Because that's the way poets talk, for some reason."

Heather smiled, but the allusion to being marooned was a little too close to home, and their playful happiness dipped for a long moment. They ate on, the meal surprisingly good to Heather's taste. "Is this potato soup?" she asked.

Her parents laughed. "I'm afraid so, Heather," Mother said. "Everything here is *potato something*. That's almost all we have."

"So the cake will be…?"

"Potato cake," they said together.

"And the tea?" she asked, sipping it with a wary scrunch of her nose.

"Potato tea," they said together.

"That explains a lot," she said, coughing through their laughter.

Settling down after dinner, they sat around the fire and talked of small details until Father stood up and took her hand. "Now, my beloved daughter," he said, smiling bright like Flint's first dawn on Blue Moss Hills, "tell us a story."

"A story of bravery?" Heather asked.

"Yes," Father said. "A story to make us brave."

She fished in her satchel and brought out a battered old purse. She reached inside and pulled out the torch pendant that had been a gift from her beloved Smalls. She put it on and raised her chin.

"It begins with this," she said, now drawing out the emerald gem on its thin strong chain. Fingering the elaborate pattern carved on the back of the gem, she held it out as Mother and Father gasped. "It begins with the Green Ember."

Chapter Eleven

A New Front

Picket lunged for Helmer, desperately dragging him back inside the slight cover of the thicket while more arrows blazed by.

"Master!" he called, stealing anxious glances at Captain Helmer and the unseen archers beyond the open glade. He crouched over Helmer, shielding him as best he could.

"Get off me, Picket!" Helmer growled.

"Master, are you okay?" Picket checked Helmer over for wounds, then saw with relief that his pack had three arrows sticking out of it. The archers had missed him, and now they seemed to be either out of arrows or simply waiting for them to move from their cover.

Helmer shrugged off the pack with a scowl and glanced inside. "My waterskin's been pierced, so I'll be thirstier than usual, but otherwise I'm fine."

"Why have they stopped shooting?" Picket asked.

"Because there's nothing to shoot that they want to hit."

"Good thing they missed you."

"The Harbone archers are famous all over Natalia," Helmer grunted. "They never missed. Your friend Jo Shanks, and Nate Flynn, of course, are the only archers Halfwind has to compare. Believe me, they hit just what they aimed for."

"But…I don't understand."

"Nor do I," Helmer said, rising up to glance around. "Or not entirely. But they don't want us to cross this glade, that's plain."

"What do we do now?"

"Stay put awhile," Helmer finished, shifting to get comfortable.

Picket reached in his pack for his waterskin, then offered it to Helmer.

"Very funny, Ladybug," Helmer said.

"So, we just wait?" Picket asked. Helmer nodded but then shook his head quickly, eyes widening as a terrific howl filled the air, followed by a raucous, rushing footfall.

Picket swiveled and froze. A massive pack of wild wolves rampaged through the glade. The two rabbits hit the ground as the pack charged by, Picket's heart thumping along with the pounding ground as the grey blur bounded past, howling with their charge. Picket saw in snatches as they passed that these wolves were barely clothed and unkempt. Spittle foamed at the edge of savage grins, and wide wild eyes darted every direction as they ran on. Picket was astonished at their number. On and on they came.

Arrows filled the air, cutting down the front line, but soon Picket and Helmer could see little of the battle up ahead. Hearing explosions, they covered their heads. Looking up, they saw that the wolves charged on. The two rabbits saw the desperate hunger of the last of the wolves, surging past their own comrades, slashing out as they did to cut ahead. They were a reckless, rash, and terrifying pack. This was no army, but a frenzied hunting party.

As the last stragglers moved past, Helmer nodded to Picket. They rose and crossed the glade, found the forest side, and slipped onto a better path than they had yet used on this journey.

"Straight now," Helmer whispered, turning back for an instant to be sure Picket was following closely.

"Yes, sir," Picket said, sword poised as he hurried along.

They dashed down the lane, Helmer straining with his aching leg. Picket had more energy, so he spun to scout their surroundings and stayed close. After they had run unseen for fifteen minutes, Picket began to believe they would make the gate of the secret citadel. But as soon as he thought it, a howling echoed along their path, and a stray section of the angry pack poured into the lane ahead of them.

The wolves stopped, tongues lolling, as surprise gave way to an ecstatic frenzy, and they dug into the ground, bounding toward the two rabbits. Picket wasn't sure if Helmer would step forward to fight them, or if he would run. He could see that his master was torn between the madness of flight with his leg hurt and the impossibility of fighting. He hesitated two agonizing seconds while the pack came on.

"Run!" Helmer shouted, diving into the woods. Picket leapt in after him.

Picket believed he could hear the husky breath of the mad pack, and feel the foaming spittle on his neck. He was terrified but kept running, sometimes beside and other times behind Helmer. His master was slower, yes, and Picket felt the desperate desire to fly ahead, but he would never leave his master behind. And besides, Helmer might have been slower than a young buck like Picket, but he was cunning and knew these woods like Picket couldn't possibly know them. He trusted Helmer.

He loved Helmer.

Forward they sped, dodging vines and leaping over ditches, hearing always the jeers of the pressing pack. The wolves were just behind them. Picket saw, with terror, that they would soon be caught.

Helmer darted down a slippery hillside, and Picket leapt down after him. The hillside was long, and they lost their footing, sliding down. Helmer rode the slide better than Picket, and, sheathing his sword, he found his feet at the bottom and burst onto another path. This path crossed back away from where they had been running, and the wolves were, for the moment, slow to adjust. Picket imitated Helmer, sheathed his sword, and scrambled to his feet. He quickly made up the distance and came up behind his master. A gap formed once more between them and their wolf pursuers. They sped on down a narrow path overhung by long vines. Picket grinned, eager for the next trick in Helmer's escape.

But Helmer turned and drew his sword.

He charged straight at the frenzied wolves.

Chapter Twelve

We Bring the War

There were six of the wild wolves, and Helmer had turned to take them on. Maybe his leg had finally given out on him. Maybe he had gone mad. Picket blew past Helmer, whose face was hard-set in concentrated fury. Glancing back at the pack, Picket reached for a sturdy vine and clung to it as his momentum took him out in a wide swing.

His mind churning a quick calculation, he rode the momentum out and arced into the forest, speeding him around again to swoop down on the path just as the first wolf leapt.

Picket's crunching kick caught the blindsided wolf with such force that he flipped in the air and smashed against a tree. Helmer surged into the gap and drove his blade into the belly of the next leaping attacker.

Two down. Four to go.

Now on his feet, Picket rebounded from his swinging kick by driving his shoulder into the next brute. The wolf missed sinking his teeth into Helmer and instead settled for a slicing claw strike as he tumbled past. Helmer winced, dipping quickly as he adjusted to the wound, but kept up his considered defense. These wolves were not disciplined in any way, Picket realized. They were only angry, hungry, and desperate to be first to the kill.

Picket spun to the path and deftly drew his sword while Helmer crouched beside him. The two rabbits worked wordlessly as the remaining pack pounced, all four at once. Helmer and Picket both dropped and rolled left to right with heavy sword swipes up across the slavering attackers' unprotected middles. They rolled on as the four fell, howling beyond them on the path.

Both rabbits sprang up, brandishing their blades defiantly at the wounded wolves. Two did not rise again.

Two more.

Now the wolves' fury was at fever pitch. To the gluttonous hunger of their earlier anger was added the fury of being bested by their prey. Their pack brothers were slain and they themselves were painfully wounded. They came on like a storm. As quickly as they came, though, Helmer and Picket cut them down.

And it was over.

Picket sagged to his knees.

"Are you okay?" Helmer managed between gulps of air.

"Yes, Master. How is your leg?"

"It's still…there," he said, smiling. "Let's get moving. You saw how many of them there are. More will come."

Picket nodded and fell in behind a badly limping Helmer as they took to the woods again, going directly for the citadel.

In a few minutes they reached the gate, a wide iron enclosure over a hole that disappeared into the earth.

"A friend of the mending!" Helmer called as they neared. Nothing happened. The gate did not budge. "A friend of the mending!" Helmer repeated, louder and more urgent. "I know it's an old code, soldiers! But we are friends and rabbits, and we're running from wild wolves, so unless you want me to strip your skin and send you to Morbin's table, open the gate!"

After a moment, the gate cranked open, just wide enough for them to slide in. They collapsed on the ground as soon as they entered the tunnel. The gate clanged shut behind them. Picket took deep breaths and felt relief welling up within. They had arrived. The first destination of their commission was reached. They had made it to Harbone Citadel.

"Why, Captain Helmer, could that be you?" asked a rabbit in an officer's uniform. The crest on his chest showed a green field, with a white tree that bloomed seven yellow stars. He was standing over them and flanked by several guards.

"None other," Helmer answered. "And you are?"

"I'm Lieutenant Meeker, and I was in your division in the last war, sir. Before the old king fell."

"Little Meeker? Meeker the Squeaker? Why, son, you were only a baby in the last war. How have you been?" Helmer asked, getting slowly to his feet to embrace him.

"Yessir, I was. I'm an officer now, though. And was made gate commander last fall."

"I am so pleased, Lieutenant Meeker. Your father must be so proud."

Lieutenant Meeker's face clouded, but he managed to smile through it. "What is it, son?" Helmer asked.

"They got Father, Captain," Meeker said, his eyes shining. "But he went out as he would have liked, charging into the pack to hold them off while a convoy of families left. The families got away and made it to Kingston in the end. But Father and some of the others..."

"You're right, son," Helmer said, taking the buck's head in his hands, "it's exactly how he'd have liked to go out. Like the ancient king and his noble old bucks on Golden Coast. May we all die so honorably."

As Helmer released him, Meeker looked down at his leg. "Well, sir, I can see you are hurt. What brings you here?"

"I need to see Lord Hewson, as soon as possible."

"And your best doctor, Lieutenant, if you please," Picket added.

Meeker looked at Picket, his gaze full of questions. The secret citadels and this long buildup to open war, breaking out with betrayals by the score, had made every wise rabbit deeply suspicious. And Picket did not begrudge the lieutenant his wary stare. But then the soldier smiled and extended his hand. "I'm Dev Meeker, and I'm pleased to meet any friend of my old captain."

"I'm Picket Longtreader," he replied, taking his hand.

The guards let out low gasps and exchanged looks. But Meeker only smiled and nodded. "Any friend of Captain Helmer's is a friend of mine. I will be happy to countermand our newcomer laws on my own authority as gate commander." He looked significantly at the soldiers gathered, and they all saluted. "Lord Hewson will want to see to you as well, so I will take you both to him directly."

"Thank you, Meeker," Helmer said.

"Rollins," Meeker snapped, and a soldier stepped forward. "Please run to the hospital and beg that Doctor Wim meet us in Lord Hewson's receiving room."

"Yessir!" Rollins said, and he spun to run into the deep tunnel.

"What brings you here, sir?" Meeker asked, turning to Picket.

"The war," Picket said. "The war brings us here."

Helmer nodded. "And we bring the war."

Chapter Thirteen

The Lay of the Land

An hour later Picket and Helmer sat with Lord Hewson's council at Harbone Citadel. They met in a plain room hung with three banners. The middle banner bore the double-diamond emblem of the cause, a white field with a red diamond set alongside a green. The left banner showed a green field and a white tree with branches blooming seven yellow stars. The right banner was green with white words in bold. *Remember. Resist. Retake.*

"Welcome, all," Lord Hewson said, rising. The room quieted, and many bowed to Lord Hewson and then took their seats. Doctor Wim was standing over Picket's shoulder, stitching the last of his fresh wounds. Lord Hewson went on, "I want to be clear in saying that both Lord Captain Helmer, my old friend—indeed possibly my oldest friend—and his friend, Captain Longtreader, have the liberty of Harbone Citadel."

The council and gathered captains pounded the table in approval. Picket knew this was no light matter, and he felt the honor keenly. It meant they could go anywhere and were above suspicion, which had not always been the case for those named Longtreader.

"Thank you, Lord Hewson," Helmer said, rising to make his polite bow. Picket imitated his master's action.

"We are deeply honored," Picket added.

"By your leave?" Captain Redthaw, master of the forces at Harbone, asked Lord Hewson. The lord nodded. "The honor is all ours," Redthaw continued, turning his attention to Helmer and Picket. "To have two such heroes here is a pleasure indeed. We regret we did not know of the battle at Rockback Valley in time to be of any aid."

"Indeed," Lord Hewson said. "We would have come at once, though the cost would have been high."

"The cost?" Helmer asked.

"Make no doubt, we would have come for certain," Captain Redthaw said. "But in order to come out in any numbers, we must engage the wild wolf pack—packs, really—who haunt these regions. They exact a heavy price for any outing. Beyond light teams of archers, we dare not emerge unless we have half our forces ready to repel them while the convoy escapes."

"I had no idea it had gotten so bad," Picket said. "We met them, of course, and I'm astonished at how many there are."

"And I'm sorry to say you could have seen only a fraction of their numbers," Lord Hewson said, shaking his head. "It has gotten very much worse in the months since the blue fever outbreak. They preyed on our weakness after that period. When Doctor Emma—I should say, the princess—left, things were tolerably under control. But a few weeks later everything changed. It seems more of the creatures have abandoned their alliance with Morbin, where they were kept moderately tame and in armies, and joined this wild pack. And it seems also, from the best intelligence we can gather—and I might add that it's quite difficult under these circumstances to get reliable information—that several other wild packs have drifted this way and joined together."

"We went out to meet them on the field early on," Captain Redthaw said, "and it went very badly."

"They fairly hem us in on all sides," Councilor Greaves said, her face bending in a disgusted frown. "I'm amazed you made it in here at all, Lord Captain."

Picket felt a clamp around his heart. What were they to do now? "It sounds like you're saying that you're trapped here." *And us with you.*

"It is nearly so," Lord Hewson answered. "We have tried to address this threat well, but so far only with disastrous results that further diminish our ability to add value to the forces fighting for the cause."

"And what of First Warren?" Helmer asked. "Any news from the old capitol?"

"Unchanged," Hewson answered. "We are the closest citadel, and so we have tried to gather all the intelligence we can about goings-on there, but it is impossible to penetrate."

"We assume the situation is as it has been," Captain Redthaw added. "We have, of course, kept up maintenance on the attack catapults and the secret arms caches, as we agreed at the Third Citadel Congress. But right now we alone could do little more than annoy them and give away our best chance of future success."

"Captain Wilfred and the prince—may he rest in the Leapers' arms—sometimes spoke of going to First Warren, and it has been the mad desire of many a rabbit since the fall and the afterterrors," Lord Hewson said. "But it is the worst of all possible ideas, and I told Wilfred that time and again."

"Wilfred knew that there's no way to truly retake what was lost if we don't start at First Warren," Helmer said, glancing at the banner on the wall.

Remember. Resist. Retake.

"We agree, of course," Councilor Greaves said, "that First Warren must eventually be retaken, and we have, as Captain Redthaw said, maintained the advanced assets in accord with the agreement. No one says we will never attack. It's only a matter of when. We at Harbone have always believed that it would be the last action of the war."

"And some of us believe it must almost be the first action," Helmer said, "including our princess, King Jupiter's heir herself."

At this the room went silent, and heads bowed all around. There was honest anxiety on every face. Picket felt his heart go out to them. "Just how do things lie at First Warren?" he asked, partly to redirect the conversation but also to see if he could learn anything new from these beleaguered rabbits, closest to the heart of the Great Wood.

Lord Hewson nodded to Captain Redthaw, who stood and went to a drawer behind him, retrieved a large map, then laid it out on the table near Picket. "We are here," he said, pointing to the edge of the large mass of forest on the page. "The Great Wood's heart holds First Warren, the former seat of King Jupiter the Great. As you no doubt know, when the king fell the wolves came and swept into First Warren, burning and murdering as they went.

"First Warren is not what it once was. But our new 'lords' rebuilt it to some extent and installed Winslow, the king's oldest son, as a puppet governor under Garten Longtreader's control. Under *Morbin's* control. They desecrated sacred sites within the city and put the rabbits under their cruel law. The seven standing stones—the largest in all Natalia—are now topped with massive statues of the Six: Morbin, Falcowit, Gern, and the rest—the leaders of the Lords of Prey. The last, well, it has another statue.

"The city always had a vast wall, but it had wide gates. It used to be a fortress that was defensive in capability but open in its orientation. First Warren was once the welcoming heart of the Great Wood, the many-gated city. But those days are over," Captain Redthaw said, frowning as he went on. "They sealed the gates, filled them in with stone cut from the slave mines far away in the High Bleaks.

"After they closed all the gates, they burned and cleared a wide circle around the city wall so the raptor sentinels could see any approach from far away. This is the Black Gap. They made the wall and gates stronger than ever.

Our secret assets are staged in the Great Wood, some distance beyond the edge of the Black Gap. They govern themselves at First Warren, in a manner of speaking, but they are under the strictest watch."

"The Preylords at First Warren," Lord Hewson interjected, "are under the constant leadership of one of the Six, a white falcon who is, some say, as wicked as Morbin himself. Lord Falcowit is the bane of First Warren, the cruel malevolence that broods over the city, infecting it with his limitless malice. Lord Falcowit is behind and above Prince Winslow, hovering there, unsettling any scheme that does not comport with his cruel designs."

"And the sentinels Lord Falcowit commands come and go in regular rotations," Captain Redthaw said. "They sit in perches on the city gates, all around the city, from our side all the way around to the waters, where the wall is a dam. These sentinels sit and watch."

"And they act," Lord Hewson added, bitter disgust showing plain. He spat.

"They act," Captain Redthaw said, "indeed. If there is the least hint of trouble of any kind, Lord Falcowit takes action. If the peace, as the Lords of Prey define peace, is breached in any way, they swoop in and…take little ones." He fairly snarled as he said this. "They take children. The monsters take children. Innocent and uninvolved? No matter. They take them."

"This breeds a mistrustful atmosphere, naturally," Councilor Tarr said, speaking up for the first time. "It turns otherwise good rabbits into informers. The secret police, under Winslow's government and the active arm of a villainous captain, take quick action to suppress any hints of insurrection."

"This was how it was years ago," Lord Hewson said, "and we suspect it hasn't changed. We assume it's only gotten worse."

"But no one has been in or out for years," Captain Redthaw said. "Even if the lunatic pack of bloodthirsty wolves wasn't blocking the way with their hordes, we couldn't get anywhere near First Warren. Outside of the High Bleaks, it is the most protected place in all Natalia and dangerous beyond all reckoning."

"It's impossible to enter," Councilor Tarr said. "Only a fool would try."

"So what can we do for you, Captain Helmer?" Lord Hewson asked.

"Can you get word to the princess?" he asked.

"It won't be easy," Hewson replied, "but we can do it. What message?"

Helmer stood up, and Picket rose to stand beside him. Helmer said, "Tell Her Royal Highness we travel to First Warren. Say that we are going in."

Chapter Fourteen

Emma's Cause

Emma was exhausted. She had slept little since the flight from Cloud Mountain, and the pressure was mounting to get everything right on her official tour of the secret citadels. It had been a hard, hurrying journey to this first destination, and she was full of doubts.

"Were we right to come here first?" she asked.

"I believe so, Your Highness," Lord Blackstar answered weakly, and Mrs. Weaver nodded her agreement.

"Vandalia Citadel is small," Mrs. Weaver said, "but its personnel are hardy and hopeful."

"Have they not been through some of the worst of the woes?" Emma asked.

Heyna Blackstar smoothed a rumpled edge of Emma's dress and then, glancing around, receded to her proper place as a lady in waiting. Jo and Cole stood back further still, honor guards for the princess at the head of a cadre of stone-faced soldiers.

"All the citadels have paid a price for opposing Morbin. Vandalia has been through a particularly awful ordeal, yes," Lord Blackstar agreed, "and so is very low indeed. But it makes them all the more eager for the rising."

"Remember, dear," Mrs. Weaver said, "that we rise as you rise. Be what you are so that we may be what we are."

"And so hasten the mending," Lord Blackstar added, leaning on his cane.

"May it be so," Emma said, breathing deeply.

Large double doors opened, and she squinted against the glare of streaming sunlight. A silhouette, thin and bent, appeared in the doorway. It was an ancient rabbit with a black medallion around his neck. He hobbled forward into the corridor.

The rabbit lord was frail. His long, wispy fur looked like swirls of smoke and his grey eyes like a candle on the verge of burning out. When he reached Emma, he slowly began to kneel. Emma's eyes widened, and she started to reach for the old rabbit, to insist he didn't bow before her. But a subtle, insistent motion from Mrs. Weaver showed her that this would be deeply insulting. So she stood, every bit the princess, as the fragile lord knelt slowly and paid homage to the heir of Natalia and the rightful bearer of the Green Ember. It didn't matter to him that the emerald stone itself was far away, with Heather, who had bravely taken Emma's place. Emma held out her hand, and the rabbit lord kissed it. Then, placing her knuckles reverently on his forehead, he softly sang.

"May she rise and reign,
Rise and reign,
May she like the sun ascend!
May she rise and reign,
Restore again,
Let this darkness not be an end.
May she rise and reign, and mend."

"Lord Booker," Emma said, "please rise."

Lord Booker, with Emma's helping hand, rose slowly and smiled at her. "Your Royal Highness," he said in a thin whisper, "you are most welcome to Vandalia Citadel. We are profoundly honored to have you here. Will Your Highness come within?" This last he said while motioning to the modest hall inside the doors. She nodded and accepted his offered arm, and they led the slow procession into the small sunlit room.

"Your Royal Highness must not hesitate to ask any service of us," Lord Booker said, breathing hard from these small exertions. "We will do all we are able for your cause."

"I am deeply grateful, my lord," Emma answered. "I admit I balk at asking more of you, for I know and honor the tremendous sacrifices your community has made for our common cause."

Lord Booker stopped and turned, looking into her eyes. "My dear princess," he said weakly, "there is no cost too high for doing what is right and no wage great enough for doing what is wrong. To believe otherwise is to surrender our liberty to lies."

"May I be faithful to your wisdom and example," she answered.

"I do not have much to offer in your service," Lord Booker said, resuming their walk, "but all I have is yours. We are small but determined. We are hard pressed but persistent. We are wounded, yet we live. We are humble but hopeful. And our hope is ignited by the sight of you, Princess Bright."

"You are truly the jewel of the world, Lord Booker," she said, her eyes glistening. "What I would give for fifty more like you."

"I am an old rabbit only," he replied, "with few days left to serve you. But my last living son, Morgan, is strong. I know he will faithfully carry on our fixed resistance to the Lords of Prey. Fear not on that account."

As Emma entered the hall, escorted by Lord Booker and flanked by her council and court, she was greeted by the sight of ten rabbits kneeling low. The one at the head, after a decent pause, looked up. Lord Booker's son. Morgan was handsome, despite the long scar that stretched from his right ear to the left side of his jaw. He smiled at her. Then, glancing back at the gathered rabbits, he placed his fist over his heart and led them in saying,

"My place beside you,
My blood for yours.
Till the Green Ember rises,
or the end of the world!"

Chapter Fifteen

High Heather

Heather told Mother and Father everything. From the moment she and Picket came back from picking berries to find their Nick Hollow home on fire and their family captured to the moment she woke up in their Akolan home. Everything. With no hesitation, she shared the bitter disappointments and the wild, exultant triumphs. She told of Picket, amazing them at how he grew from a bitter, resentful cripple to a high-flying hero, willing to sacrifice all for the cause. She told of her own low moments, the bad dreams and real-life terrors. She shared the joys of her friendship with Smalls, and with Emma, the best friends she had ever known outside of her family. She wept as she talked of Smalls and smiled when she told how Picket flew—really flew—and rescued her and Emma at Cloud Mountain. She told them everything.

"Somehow, I have become the Scribe of the Cause," she finished, "and Picket is something like its talismanic hero. The world as we knew it was shattered, and we never knew what we might be forced to find within ourselves.

In the tumult and the trials, we found our callings. And we have done some good. Thank you for loving us, Mother and Father. Thank you for preparing us for the unnumbered dangers we've faced. We had no idea that when you gave us all the light you did, you were guiding us to one day strike out at the darkness so fiercely. We have been far from flawless, but we have made a hard dart at that darkness. We have seen cracks forming and the light seeping in." She took a deep breath, let it out slowly, then leaned back in her chair.

Mother and Father gazed on at her, mouths open, expressions caught between wonder and unbelief. Tears fell down the fur of their faces, but they didn't look at all sad. They eyed one another and shook their heads slowly.

"I am…astonished," Father said softly. "I am amazed at what you say, my dear, and how well you say it."

"Yes, Heather," Mother added, slowly and hushed. "You're as eloquent as any I've ever heard. It's beautiful to hear you unravel this tale. But tell me, dear. Is it really true?"

"It's too good to not be true, Mother." Heather felt exhausted from her long story but satisfied as well, as from a hard day of healing when the sick were clearly mending.

"You are well-called the Scribe of the Cause," Father said. "To my great joy, my love, you have surpassed me."

"It's true," Mother added. "Picket has flown, Heather. But so have you. Since last we saw you, a timid young doe, you have ascended."

Heather looked down, a satisfied smile forming. She did not feel proud at heart, only glad in the knowledge that her tale had been clear. And that her story—every word true—had soared.

They talked on for a few more hours, then finally went to bed.

Heather started that night in the bed in which she had slept so far but soon tiptoed to her parents' room and slid in beside her mother.

Mother held Heather and sang her to sleep.

* * *

In the morning they ate breakfast, and Heather felt better than she had in a long time. Part of her broken heart had healed, and even though she was wounded and sore, she felt more whole.

"Shall we go into the clinic, Heather?" Father asked.

"I will do as you say," she answered. "You and Mother know what's best."

"That's a theory," Mother called from the kitchen. "Unproven, I think."

"I'll take you there," Father said. "It's not too far from my work. And if you're feeling well in a few days, maybe you can help Doctor Hendow. Our clinic in this district is short of help, especially being so close to the Lepers' District."

Mother walked in, a mild reproof in her look toward Father. "I have to go back to my duties as well. I work at Morbin's lair, as a servant," she said, smiling with some effort.

"And she listens," Father added, winking. "She's very brave."

"I would love to go with you, Father. But tell me, what are the districts?"

"There are seven—" he began. Then he held up a hand. "I'm sorry, six districts. We live in District Four. Districts One through Four are roughly the same, with some small variations. They are all little settlements, like small towns, on the outside edges of the pit. But they all represent different time periods of settlement here. We are among the last to come, so we are in the last ordinary district, District Four. District Five is the Lepers' District. It is only for—" he stopped again.

"Those who are sick and contagious," Mother finished. "It's a foul place."

"I was there," Heather said. "It was putrid. I feel sorry for them. Do they receive any care?"

"Our clinic does care for them at times," Father said, "but it works very hard to avoid contamination that might spread to the other districts. They are left to themselves almost entirely."

"When we first arrived, half of District Four, our district, had to be shifted to the L.D.," Mother said. "The disease—it's incurable."

Heather frowned. "But what is the disease?"

Mother and Father exchanged glances; then Father went on. "We aren't medics, dear. We don't know how such things work. But District Six, inside the wall, is where you saw the Commandant."

"In District Six, the inwallers live the easy life," Mother said. "At least compared to us outside. District Six is home to a privileged class, the informers and government workers. They get the best work and are exempt from the hardest parts of life in Akolan. They feel less like slaves. But they still are, maybe even more so."

"And they take our family name…my father's name," Father said, "and make it mean Morbin's stooges. The administration is called Longtreader Command and its brutal officers are called Longtreaders. It is intolerable."

"But we have found a way," Mother said, laying a gentle hand on Father's arm, "to live in this reality without losing our souls."

"Without losing them entirely," Father said, scowling.

"I must go," Mother said, "back to the heart of darkness. And I must remember to forget how to sing." She crossed to hug Heather and kissed her on the cheek.

"Please don't sing again, Mother," Heather said, clinging to Sween with worried eyes. "I can't lose you now that I have you back."

"Dear, we must live every day here as if it's our last," Mother said, gently patting Heather's cheek. "We must always be prepared to die, if duty calls for it."

"It is the way, here," Father said. "And really, it has been the same for you. We must be who we are."

"And if that means the end for us," Mother said, "then those left alive must…well, they must bear the flame."

Chapter Sixteen

Low Moments in a High Calling

After checking her satchel, securing it over her shoulder, and wrapping a red scarf around her neck, Heather followed her father outside. Ash fell in looping wafts, landing on streets, where sweepers worked to push it away. The outside of their home, and those surrounding, was much like the ones she dashed among the night she fell into Akolan. Her parents' home had a stairway cut to the roof, as did most of the other stone homes. The landscape was marked by the impossible heights of the rocky pit wall in the distance. Its massive tumbling waterfall poured into the reservoir beyond the Lepers' District. The other distinctive feature was the circular central stonework wall protecting District Six, where the false Longtreaders dwelled. Heather shuddered as she saw it—small compared to the pit wall but massive against the other structures in Akolan—in the plain light of day.

Heather heard pounding in the distance, the shatter of rocks, and the rasping shouts of angry rabbits. She and Father paused as a group of weary miners, clothes smeared with grime, passed in the street. Their faces were hollow and expressions hopeless.

"How many mines are there, Father?"

"There are fifteen mines, though only seven are in operation. Chutes seven and ten have both flooded since I've been here. I worked in chute thirteen for months before being transferred to the aqueducts."

"Is it crushing labor?"

"It doesn't have to be," Father said, "but the administration seems to design the work to rob bucks of their dignity. It exhausts your body and smothers your soul."

"Does every doe work for Morbin?"

"Almost all. Most does, like your mother, are housekeepers and servers for the most elite Preylords. Some work down here in District Six, serving the inwallers, but many work in manufacturing up there," he said, pointing past the burning acres of trash high atop the pit wall to the wooded peaks above. "We are far from home here, my dear. We are in the heart of the enemy's mountains. And the administration wants to act like that's a good thing."

Heather scowled toward the city center, then scanned the surrounding landscape.

The colors of Akolan were all whites and red-browns, with the grey ash a constant filmy glaze. A clay-colored stone dominated the surface, and many of the houses were made from it, though some were infused with swirls of white. Indeed, the massive wall was nearly all white, its gate an imposing black. But the whites were smeared by the ash, and so a drab scene met Heather's gaze as she followed Father down the street.

They walked through an orderly neighborhood and then another, finally breaking out into a small expanse that separated District Four from the Lepers' District. Between the two stood a large low stone building. Benches lay along its outside wall, and rabbits sat on them. Many were hunched over, faces pinched in pain. All wore the mark of their slavery—their vulnerability—a red cloth around their necks.

"Are they all waiting to be seen?" Heather asked, her pace quickening.

"Now, go slowly, Heather," he answered. "You have to recover."

She reached for her satchel and walked on. "Yes, Father."

"You have an appointment," Father said as they approached the curve-top door in front of the clinic.

Inside, more sick and injured rabbits waited to be seen. Heather's heart was struck by the suffering. Her father spoke to a rabbit seated at a small desk up front. When he returned, he said, "Doctor Hendow will see you in just a few minutes."

"I'll be seen before all of them?" she asked, adjusting her sling gingerly.

"You have to pull yourself out of the river first, Heather," Father answered, "before you can save others from drowning. Just don't give yourself a setback."

Heather had no wish to argue with Father, but she felt as though there was a river full of drowning rabbits, and she was confident that she was a strong swimmer. Beside her stood a rabbit with an injured arm. He was young, around her own age, and strong.

"How'd you get hurt?" she asked.

"Like all young bucks get hurt," he answered, "in the mines. Which chute you at, sir?" he asked, nodding to Father.

"I've mined most of my time here, yes," Father said, "but now they have me as a mason over at the outside reservoir, building a better wall for the aqueducts."

"Got all fancy, ain't ya?" the young buck teased. "Left the mines to the likes of me."

"Very fancy indeed, us aqueduct masons," Father said, smiling.

"I'm Heather," she said, smiling at the young buck. "Can I look at your arm?"

"I'm Jabe, and you're looking at it now," he said, winking.

"Without the wrap."

"Heather," Father asked, "what are you doing?"

"Saying yes to my calling," she said as she slowly unrolled the bandage. Jabe winced, but Heather had it off in a moment and looked at his arm intently. "Looks like it's healing pretty well, Jabe. A few days more off work might cure it all the way," she added, poking in her bag and emerging with an ointment, which she began to spread over the wound.

"That's a lark, Miss," Jabe said. "Days off work? Imagine that!"

Heather frowned. "You're working with your arm like that? In the mines?"

"Well, they have me at the quarry now," he said, "so it's a bit easier to breathe, and I can stand straight. But the work's just as heavy."

"If we don't work," Father said, "we don't get our ration. If we don't get our ration—"

"We starve," Jabe finished, nodding at a bent elderly rabbit on the corner bench who was frighteningly skinny. Heather sucked in a breath and scowled.

She rewrapped Jabe's arm, sent him away, and walked up to the attendant at the desk. "Hello, I'm Doctor Heather. Please tell Doctor Hendow that I'm here and ask him where the best place for me to see patients might be."

"But, but," the attendant stammered, "but Doctor Hendow is now busy at…right now, present," she said. "You'll have to wait your—"

Heather interrupted, "I'm not asking you anything. I'm telling you. Go and ask Doctor Hendow where I should set up."

The attendant rose and took a few backward steps toward the door. "But, but," she stammered on, "I'm not authorized to—"

"Go. Now." Heather spoke with such authority and confidence that the attendant spun and hurried through the door.

"I'm impressed," Father said, walking up. "I have to go now. Are you sure you're all right?"

"Yes, Father, I'm fine."

"Please don't work all day," he said. "Listen to Doctor Hendow and rest when you should. You'll be more use to everyone that way."

"Yes, Father. I will."

He drew up close to whisper in her ear. "Go home and sleep when you're done. There's something I want to show you tonight."

"Tonight?" she whispered back.

"Yes, after curfew," Father said. "It's a secret place." He hugged her and headed for the door.

Heather wondered what he could mean, but soon she was meeting Doctor Hendow, who examined her closely, frowned at her arm, and said she could work for a few hours. To her relief, he explained that her arm was not broken, only sprained badly. He said she could work with the injured arm in her sling, using it only when she had to.

A few hours later, she was seeing her twentieth patient and smiling wide. She was tired, but she loved healing and helping. It was odd how long, hard hours focusing entirely on the needs of others could make her feel most fully herself. It was the same, she realized for the first time, with storytelling. She had finished up a list of directions for an older doe caring for her sister when the flustered attendant burst in.

"Doctor Hendow needs you!" she shouted, her eyes wide with panic.

"Of course," Heather said, grabbing her satchel. She hurried behind the attendant and pushed past her into Dr. Hendow's surgery. There, on the table, lay a large black-furred rabbit with a white spot just between his eyes. He was massive, and he writhed in pain.

"Doctor Heather," Doctor Hendow said, his steady scholarly manner unaffected by this emergency. "Master Mills has been hurt badly, pierced with a bricksplitter. Would you be so kind as to assist me?"

"Of course," she said. She hurried to his side and examined the deep gash in the buck's middle. "Hello, Master Mills," she said, smiling at him. "I know you're in a lot of pain. Do me a favor, though, and do your very best to lie still. Everything will go quicker that way."

"Aye," he answered through clenched teeth, settling himself as best he could. He still shook all over, his fur wet with sweat.

As Doctor Hendow cleaned the dreadful wound, Heather deftly passed him all he needed and spoke calmly to Mills. "I don't know what a bricksplitter is, Master Mills. Could you tell me?"

"Aye, Missy," he began.

"*Doctor* Heather, not 'Missy,'" Doctor Hendow said flatly in correction. Heather frowned at him, but he paid no attention as he continued to work on the wound.

"Aye," Mills said, "I'm sorry, Miss—I mean Doctor. I meant no offense."

"I've been called Missy more often than Doctor, and it doesn't bother me in the least," she said.

"Doctor," Doctor Hendow repeated flatly.

"How about Doctor Missy?" she said. "For fun? Now, about that bricksplitter."

"Aye," Mills went on, his face calmer, though he winced often as Doctor Hendow worked. "Well, a bricksplitter's a tool we use…in the mines to…ah, break up stone. It's long and narrow and has a fairly…sharp point. It's heavy," he said. He paused to groan at the pain, and after an agonizing few moments he fell silent.

"Master Mills?" Heather asked, glancing back and forth between his face and Doctor Hendow. Hendow shook his head, though he worked on, and Heather worked on beside him, using her good arm to swab and stitch. She was experienced enough to know that this wound was unlikely to heal. He was hurt beyond their ability to help.

They worked hard for a long time, Heather's hopes fading further each moment. Finally, their work was done, and they made Master Mills as comfortable as possible. "He is past our aid," Doctor Hendow said as, frowning, he went to speak to the miner's family.

Heather sagged into her chair back in her treatment room, a deep sadness settling on her. After indulging the welling despair for a little while, she stood and washed her hands, cleaned her instruments, and sorted out her satchel. She had a habit of making all ready in her bag after each patient encounter, whenever she had time. And she seemed to now. The flow of patients had slowed, and she was glad of the reorganizing task to distract her from the welling woe inside.

She took everything out of her bag and topped up the ointments and oils she used most often—or those she could with the clinic's meager stores—then added more bandages and placed her now clean instruments back inside.

While Heather's hands were busy with the tasks she had grown so accustomed to performing, her mind waded through the pain. She hated all the ways the world was broken, from the tyranny of Morbin down to a wounded rabbit in the District Four clinic. Down to Master Mills. She longed so desperately for the Mended Wood, for a mending that would remake the breaking world in a wonderful way. But was that just a dream? If it was, she would go on dreaming and doing all she could to see its awakening.

She found the battered purse holding the Green Ember and drew it out, holding the emerald gem to her heart. She traced her finger over the pattern etched on the back of the gem. Putting the gem away, she took out the small bottle of Aunt Jone's tonic and glanced back at the door. "I've done it!" Aunt Jone had said. But the eccentric old doe had always said that sort of thing. Heather frowned. Then she shrugged, walked down the hall, and entered the surgery. Master Mills lay there, his breath coming in ragged, shallow gasps. His eyes were closed. No one else was there.

Heather uncorked the tonic and, after tasting a drop on her tongue, peeled back his bandages and poured a drop into the ghastly wound. After replacing the bandages, she gently pulled open his mouth and let fall another drop inside. Then she closed her eyes and laid her hands tenderly on Master Mills' head. She heard footsteps in the hallway, turned to see the clerk staring at her through the open door, and hurried back to her room.

Once back, she finished preparing her satchel for more work. In a little while, Doctor Hendow came in.

"Doctor Heather," Hendow said in his professorial monotone, "I am sorry to say that I think we will lose Master Mills very soon. But we did all we could, and I was very grateful for your assistance today. I have never seen such excellent patient care in all my years as a practitioner of the healing arts. May I congratulate you on your technique and welcome you most enthusiastically," all this with a straight, unchanged expression, "to our clinic. I am so profoundly happy to have you as a colleague."

"I thank you, Doctor," she said, smiling wearily. "I had good training. I look forward to serving with you."

"As supervisor here," he went on, his face expressionless and his tone flat, "I say you are most welcome, and we are delighted to have you here. Now go home." With that, he turned, walked back into his surgery, and called for the next patient.

Heather frowned and shook her head. *What an odd rabbit he is.* Then, taking a quick inventory of her energy, she realized she was profoundly exhausted. Her hands were shaking.

There were few patients left waiting now. She realized with some satisfaction that she had helped, but she felt keenly the failure to save that haunted her every time she worked at healing. She could save seventy but would remember most vividly the one or two for whom she could do nothing.

"I want to save them all," she whispered as she made her way home. "Why can't I save them all?"

Chapter Seventeen

Return to the Lepers' District

Heather woke from a long, refreshing afternoon nap. It was evening now, and she padded down into the main room to find supper waiting. Seared potatoes, with a loaf of potato bread. She passed on the potato tea, preferring water, which she drank in long gulps.

"I'm glad you slept," Father said, beaming at her.

"Yes," Mother agreed, "but we heard about your day at the clinic. We're so proud of you for facing such hard things with boldness."

"That's who you raised me to be," she said. "That's who we are. How was your day?"

"As good as can be expected," Mother answered. "Morbin's palace is in some disarray, which is always good to see. I didn't hear much, sadly. I did see the wolf called Captain Blenk, who has taken the place of the white wolf and is in command of the ground forces. They have an alliance that was forged with Garlackson, and they renew it when the old leader is killed. To think, it was our Picket who ended Redeye Garlackson! But I saw Blenk renew the promise, and I heard them discussing plans in council. They seemed determined to destroy Cloud Mountain."

"That would be a very sad thing," Heather said, "but our friends will be gone by now; I'm sure of that."

"I hope so," Mother said. "I don't like to think of Picket there."

"Nor I," Father agreed.

"They're gone, I'm sure," Heather repeated, thinking of all her friends and how they might fare in an evacuation. What would happen to Mrs. Weaver and the others who were older? She hoped they were all right.

"Gritch is in a panic—I'm sorry, Heather. Gritch is the appointed head of the household slaves in Morbin's Lair. He hurried me off to Stitcher's for the afternoon to help with the sewing."

"And who is Stitcher?" Heather asked.

"He's a lovely old rabbit with many gifts, among them making and repairing clothes."

"That's probably a much less trying way to make stitches than I'm used to," Heather said.

"I suppose it is," Mother replied.

"How about that cake?" Father asked.

"If you're up for it," she said, looking carefully at Heather.

"Oh, Mother," Heather said, "we must live every day as if it's our last. And we never know who we will lose. But those of us left behind must endure. We must… bear the cake."

"Bear it into our bellies," Father added, nodding vigorously.

Mother smirked and headed for the kitchen. "Potato cake, coming right up!"

* * *

A few hours later, after darkness had settled over the slave city of Akolan, Father and Heather crept out into the night. They wore dark clothing, talked softly, and took side streets and lanes.

"If we get stopped," Father said, "say you were called out for medical care to the L.D."

"Yes, Father," Heather said, her heart beating fast. "But where are we really going?"

"The L.D.," he said. "Follow me."

"The Lepers' District?" Heather asked. "Father, I don't understand. I barely escaped from there."

"Hurry now," Father said, darting forward. She followed behind, her sense of dread growing.

They skirted the edge of District Four, as far as possible away from the wall and its several watchtowers. When they reached an alley covered in shadow, Father held up a hand.

"We'll wait here a moment," he said. "It's good to avoid predictable patterns of movement. I never go the same way and never pause at the same points. They are brutal, these Wrongtreaders, but their overreliance on regulation and central power makes it possible to thwart them. At least in small ways."

"Have you ever been tempted to join them?" Heather asked, nodding toward the wall and the Sixth District inside. "For an easier life and an end to all the turmoil of resisting?"

"No," he whispered. "They do worse than even you know, Heather," he said. "Rabbits are forbidden to speak of it, but they force all our little ones into their school, which is nothing less than administration propaganda, and they turn them into their informers."

"That's vile," Heather said, "and must sicken you as someone who values schooling so much."

"It does, Heather. I still dream of the academy I always intended to begin at First Warren. But we are far from First Warren, and I haven't told you everything about what they're doing here." He scowled, and the edge of his lip curled. "It gets much worse. About five percent of the students disappear each year, and their parents are told they have been taken to another prison camp to serve out their time. But before they go, I've learned, they give these younglings a special diet, a better diet, with fruits and varied vegetables, for the weeks leading up to their disappearance." Father nodded and moved on. Heather ducked behind a low wall, then followed Father up the stone stairway on the side of a house at the edge of the District Four. Father lay down on the roof and gazed into the moonlit night, all around but with particular attention to the L.D. "We wait here a bit," he said, slumping down low.

She imitated him, getting as comfortable as possible with her injured arm and other pains. She did feel much better than she had earlier. The nap must have set her up amazingly well.

"What does the diet have to do with where they go?" she asked.

"They don't go anywhere, Heather," he said with real anger. "They are fattening them up."

"No!" Heather gasped.

"They end on Morbin's table, as food for his dark rites," he said, disgust twisting his mouth. Heather flushed and felt a sickening lurch in her belly. She was ready to vomit, but she swallowed hard and shook her head. He went on. "I'm sorry to tell you this, and there's much more I could say. But I told you so you would know this and know it well. I never think of betraying the hope of the Mended Wood, where such things shall not be so. I never have, and I never will. I'd rather die than take sides with those whose cause is so drenched in innocent blood. And I'm heartbroken that any rabbit can turn a blind eye to it."

"But what can we do?" she asked.

"Come and see," he said, peering over the edge. Then he hurried down the steps and into the street. He motioned for her to follow and took off across the large gap between districts.

He ran into the Lepers' District. She followed.

The reek met them. Mother had said that faint whiffs of the tremendous stench sometimes wafted as far as the middle of District Four. As they jogged into the streets of the Lepers' District, right into the ramshackle huddle of hovels, Heather gagged at the horrific odor. Father fought off a throaty cough and pulled up his red neckerchief to cover his mouth and nose. Heather raised the red scarf at her neck to her mouth.

It helped a little.

She witnessed again the tents pitched indifferently all around, the battered shacks all askew and caked in ash. She marveled at such a significant contrast to the neat rows in the other areas of Akolan. And something about it felt wrong. She shook her head, inwardly scolding herself for her overly intense observation. *What's wrong is that these rabbits are ravaged by disease, and they need compassion.*

She followed Father farther in, weaving between canvas homes and fighting the urge to retch at the disturbingly awful smell. No one would willingly come here unless they absolutely had to. That was plain. She held her satchel tight and inwardly recited her vows as a medic. Her mind filled with the memory of groaning noises and her heart raced.

"We're almost there," Father said, waving her forward toward the edge of the camp, where the shacks and tents were pitched awkwardly against the high pit wall. She nodded and hurried behind him, kicking up the grimy grey remnants of the falling ash.

Footsteps sounded behind her. Heather stopped and twisted to see several rabbits staggering through the street, one carrying a bright torch. Their faces were pinched in pain, and they groaned loudly as they stamped toward her. Mottled fur showed through ragged holes in their threadbare clothing. The torchbearer spotted Heather and pointed a shaking finger at her, and they all began stamping her way. Alarmed, she stepped back, tripping over a tent peg. She leapt up and turned around and around, scanning the streets. The mottled band of rabbits surged forward, but she could not find her father.

"Father!" she shouted. Her terrified cry echoed off the pit wall and resounded in the putrid air above the Lepers' District.

Chapter Eighteen

No Way

Picket stood by Helmer as the gathered leaders of Harbone Citadel tried to talk his master out of his plan to enter First Warren. When it was clear that they wouldn't be able to move him from his determined course, they gave up, breaking into several different murmuring conversations.

"If you are thus determined," Lord Hewson said, holding up his hands for silence, "then I call for us to rest this night and to each reappear in the morning with ideas on how we might aid our allies in this…this adventure."

Helmer nodded, and Picket could see that he was grateful.

"Till the morning, then," Captain Redthaw said with a bow before turning to retire.

"I'm sure you need sleep, friends," Lord Hewson said. "May I show you to your quarters?"

"Thank you," Helmer replied. Picket followed the two old friends as they walked down the narrow tunnels of Harbone, reminiscing as they went about their childhood together and the mischief they got into as young soldiers.

"Remember when you and Airen dropped rotten pumpkins on those sailors in their dress uniforms," Lord Hewson asked, smiling, "just as all the pretty does arrived?"

Airen. Helmer's twin sister. Picket wanted to hear more about her, but at the same time it made him think of Heather, and his heart grew sad.

"The pumpkins were *your* idea!" Helmer answered. "But when the deed was done, you were off courting Lynn."

"We had a great view of the whole thing from the pavilion, as did most of the officers. How we laughed! I think she was impressed that I knew the rabbits who'd done it."

"Her father was in the army, wasn't he?"

"He was," Hewson said, "so she loved seeing the sailors get blitzed like that."

"I didn't want to go through with it," Helmer said. "I was concerned about my rank and getting disciplined. Plus, our ancestor and my namesake was in the navy! But Airen, she wouldn't hear of it. She called me every form of coward you could think of and teased me mercilessly until I agreed to join in."

"Oh, Airen," Hewson said, smiling, "what a corker! I've never met her like again."

"Nor I," Helmer said. They walked on in silence, a heaviness descending on them.

Picket spoke up. "Were the sailors and soldiers at odds?" he asked.

"In those days," Lord Hewson answered, "we could afford a petty rivalry. The truth is, they had dominated the water for so long that they had little to do, so we poked at them for their ceremony and for missing out on many of the battles."

"But they were a brave bunch, that's for sure," Helmer added. "When we did need them, like in Kingston and Two Rivers, they showed their mettle."

"Indeed," Hewson said, unlocking a door and pushing it open. "Here we are, bucks. Pull the bell if you need anything at all. We have servants on call through the night."

"Fancy," Helmer said. "You know we're both lowborn, right?"

"I couldn't help but notice," Hewson said with mock severity.

"I've almost been afraid to ask," Helmer said, his face turning earnest. "But Lynn, Lady Hewson, is she okay?"

"She has been unwell for some time, but she is alive," Hewson said. "We have seven children, Helmer. Four are here, and the other three are at Blackstone."

"You must be very proud of them."

"I am. They are good children, all. The oldest, Gantlin, is an officer here, and the next two, Gwen and Perry, are medics. The youngest buck, whom I would particularly like you to meet, is in school here."

"I would love to meet him," Helmer said.

"Then I'll bring young Helmer by tomorrow," Hewson said. Helmer looked down. "I'll take my leave," Hewson went on. "I shall see you both in the morning. Captain Picket, it's an honor to have you here."

"Thank you, Lord Hewson," Picket said, bowing neatly. "I am so grateful for your generosity and kind welcome."

"Helmer," Lord Hewson, said, but he didn't continue. The two bucks embraced, and Picket looked down, eyes shining. He touched his black scarf, thought of Jo and Cole, and hoped they and the princess were all right.

* * *

After breakfast the next day, at which young Helmer met his namesake, another council was called. This one had a more martial air than the previous day's deliberation. Uniforms, most with some sign of rank and the Harbone arms, dominated the room. Picket liked the Harbone arms, the white tree with the seven yellow stars. He liked these rabbits. Emma had brought back a good report of them from her time there during the blue fever outbreak, and Picket had so far found that all she said was true.

Lord Hewson called the room to order. "Well, bucks," he said, "you have been briefed on the objective. We must get these two into First Warren. I know. You will say it cannot be done, and that is what most, if not all, of us believe. But we must find a way. Lord Captain Helmer?"

"Thank you, Lord Hewson," Helmer said, rising while his friend sat down. "We are grateful for your offer to help, even though you dislike the decision. We have ideas for how we might enter First Warren, but we need your operational intelligence. We know the city is surrounded by the reinforced old wall, that the gates are all closed and the ground around the wall is charred and burnt and cut back for some great distance—the Black Gap, as you call it—making it impossible to cross without being seen by the raptor sentinels."

"We know," Picket said, "that where the woods aren't cleared back around the wall, the river and lake run against it. There are stout sentinel stations at nine points around the wall, full of wolves and with at least nine raptors, commanded by Lord Falcowit. We know the main station is above the dam, where the river enters the city by way of the levy. The double wall there regulates the flow and helps avoid flooding. We know this levy and the river entrance are heavily guarded and that most of the wolves are housed there in the main fort."

"If I may," Lord Hewson said, "Captain Picket, you are right about those details, and the Black Gap has been burned again recently. But the last intelligence we received suggested that the main fort above the dam is the only place where the wolf army is garrisoned."

"Thank you, Lord," Picket said, bowing his head quickly.

"So," Helmer went on, "we need to run our ideas by you to look for weaknesses, just as Lord Hewson now has corrected our understanding of the target. We welcome any and all ideas you have. I'm sure wise minds in this place have been mulling this for years, and we need your help."

Helmer sat down, and a quiet settled over the room. As the silence stretched on, Lord Hewson spoke again.

"Perhaps it would be best if you shared your ideas, for feedback from the council?"

"Yes," Helmer said, rising. "Well, assuming we can get past the wild wolves—"

"A very generous assumption," a captain murmured.

"Assuming we can get past the wolves," Helmer repeated, staring hard at the captain who had interrupted, "we thought of creating a distraction in the far woods, a fire perhaps, while we sneak in, covered in black to pass unseen through the Black Gap. We could then use harpoons to clear the wall."

"Gendo Bavinson," Captain Redthaw said, shaking his head.

"Excuse me?" Helmer asked. "What does Gendo Bavinson mean?"

"He's the last rabbit who tried that, though several did before," Captain Redthaw said. "He and his team are dead."

"We could hide in barrels and float through the levee and into the city," Picket suggested.

"Bill Tollers," Captain Redthaw said. "Didn't work. Couldn't work."

"We could dump trash in the Black Gap," Picket said, "and hide among it, hoping to be tossed in the waste hole inside the city."

"Lieutenant Frale and Jorn Lin," Captain Parn, sitting beside Redthaw, said. "The raptors dropped a blastpowder bomb on them."

All around the room, heads went down. Helmer frowned and tried again. "We could use fake uniforms and take boats into the city from the lake to the river, trying to pass by the guards."

"Emery Dann," Lord Hewson said, shaking his head. "That was our last attempt. Lord Falcowit swept down on him and his team, tearing them apart while we watched from a distant hill. Horrific day."

"There must be something!" Helmer shouted, striking the table.

"There might be nothing," Lord Hewson whispered to Helmer. "We have been at this problem for years, old friend."

"We have to get in," Helmer said. "We absolutely must."

"I have a suggestion." A soft-voiced rabbit from the far side of the room stood up. He wasn't sitting at the table but in a chair along the edge of the room, with other attendants to the captains.

"What is it, young Emerson?" Lord Hewson asked. To Helmer and Picket he said, "Emerson is one of our young engineers," then to the timid buck, "Speak up, lad."

"Just this," Emerson said, stepping forward. "The principal problem has not been that the distractions don't work. They do, in fact. And we have great resources for a deliberate and effective distraction. It's only that once these distractions are made, there has been no way to get the penetrating team inside with enough speed."

"That's true," Captain Redthaw said, nodding. "So how do we overcome this dilemma?"

"I'm not certain," he said, "but last night I heard some rumors about the battle at Rockback Valley that gave me an idea."

Helmer and Picket looked at each other.

Picket smiled. Helmer sighed.

Chapter Nineteen

Emery's Son

After the meeting broke up, Picket found the shy buck whose counsel had carried the day.

"Hey," Picket said, "thanks for what you did in there. Emerson, right?" he asked, extending his hand.

"Yessir," Emerson replied, shaking Picket's hand. "I'm honored to meet you, Captain."

"And I, you." They walked along together. "Where are you headed now?"

"Back to work, sir. I have so much to do."

"I don't want to keep you from your work," Picket said, "but I wonder if you'd ever have time to show me some of what you're working on and maybe catch me up on the story at Harbone."

"It would be my honor, sir," Emerson said, smiling.

In a few minutes, they were descending into wide passages in the depths of the warren. Picket saw rabbits at work inside room after room on this low level.

"How many smithies does Harbone have active?" he asked.

"Fifty at present," Emerson answered, "and they are the best of rabbits, led by Master Hame, who is as wise a rabbit as I've ever known."

"I'd like to meet him."

"I would be happy to introduce you sometime, but may I show you my own work first, sir?"

"Certainly."

Emerson led him into a cavernous space crammed with tools and equipment, including large complex pieces, many half-finished and others covered in canvas. Picket turned, his mouth open as he gazed at the amazing room. He thought of Heyward and longed to get these two bright rabbits together.

Emerson pointed at one of the canvas-covered objects, off in a far corner, and they moved through the room toward it. "I am honored to have taken part in the team creating this."

"I bet your family is proud," Picket said. The buck's face fell at his words. Picket grimaced. He should have known, in this world of a thousand orphans, how painful comments like that could be. "I'm sorry," he said.

"No, sir. It's all right. Mother was proud," Emerson said, smiling through his tears. "Her name was Myrtle Dann. She died last week, in an attack from the wild wolf pack. She was trying to get much-needed medicine for the hospital." He coughed and wiped at his nose and eyes. "I miss her."

Picket put his hand on Emerson's shoulder. "My family's gone too. I don't know if any of them are alive or dead."

"I'm sorry to hear that, Captain."

"Call me Picket, please."

Emerson nodded as they reached the corner of the room where his project lay covered. "I threw myself into this work after Father died several years ago. He was Emery Dann, and Lord Hewson told you how he was killed trying to get into First Warren. Falcowit, that tyrannous villain, did it. Father was a good rabbit."

"A hero," Picket said. "It will not be so…"

"In the Mended Wood," Emerson finished.

"Quick come the day."

"Yes. And since Father's death, even though I was and am young—like you, Picket, if I may say so—I've dedicated myself to the cause with everything I have. I've been working on trying to get rabbits inside First Warren. I'm glad that Lord Hewson is willing to try again."

"Me too. Lord Hewson and my master, Helmer, are old friends."

"Lord Hewson has been a wonderful leader. Following in Lord Hews' steps, he has done so much: prepping and maintaining the assets in our battle burrows, helping find workarounds when the smithies don't have all they need, supporting the innovative engineers, and working tirelessly himself for the cause of the Mended Wood."

"What are the battle burrows? And what assets do you mean?"

"The battle burrows are underground caches, positioned as close as we dare to First Warren. They're bunkers stocked with weapons and other assets. Harbone hasn't been on the front line of the recent battles, but neither have we been idle. May I show you one of those weapons?"

"Please," Picket said.

Emerson pulled off the cover to reveal a large bow, its stout string drawn back by a smaller catapult crank and held by taut cords. There was a mount for easy loading of the large arrows that were stacked neatly on the weapon's platform base. The impressive device stood twice as tall as an ordinary rabbit.

Picket whistled and grinned. "Does it work?"

"Yes, though we've never tested the bowstrikers in battle."

"A bowstriker? It's incredible," Picket said, stepping onto the platform to get a closer look. "The range must be unbelievable. How do the arrows work?"

"We call them blastarrows. The arrowhead is basically a hard jar packed with blastpowder—"

"Blastpowder?"

"Yes," Emerson said, smiling. "It's an encased arrowhead, and the tip is fitted with a flint kit, so when the impact comes—"

"Boom!" Picket finished, eyes wide.

"Exactly."

Picket shook his head. "This is a breakthrough! I've been in many of the recent battles. We need these in the field!"

"We don't have many, yet. But we're doing all we can."

"Your father would be very proud of you, Emerson," Picket said. "Your mother, too."

"I believe you're right, Picket," he said, smiling through fresh tears. "I have only one desire in these painful days, to see my work matter for the mending. I know I help invent things that destroy, but they are aimed at the darkness. And I hope that, when they have blown a hole in that darkness, the light pours in."

Chapter Twenty

In Harbone's Heart

They rested and planned for days. Picket, guided by Harbone's old librarian, Mistress Gilfersnodden, studied the best maps and read the most reliable intelligence reports Harbone had on First Warren. He read the Third Citadel Congress report wherein the task of staging arms for an eventual assault and retaking of First Warren was accepted by Harbone's then leader, Lord Hews. As Emerson had said, Lord Hewson had carried on his father's scheme with diligence, seeing to the routine maintenance of the larger assets, prone to moldering in their battle burrows, as well as the continual manufacture and supply of new arms. Harbone's fifty smithies churned out weapons by the hundreds each day. They had run low on supplies of late but had found workarounds and carried on, waging their quiet war of preparation.

Though reluctant at first, and still gravely doubting the plan would succeed, the Harbone Citadel's personnel and resources were now fully committed to the scheme of getting Helmer and Picket inside.

Helmer spent much-needed time resting his leg, which he grudgingly allowed Doctor Wim to treat. Picket also rested, and he took several pleasant walks around the warren. It was like Halfwind, though it felt more old-fashioned. The warren was dark and deep, dirt-lined, with little stone. It was like going back in time to their ancestors' communities. But inside many of the dens, amazing work was being carried out. He saw potential innovations for the battlefield that made him wish to spend a month there, learning. He again wished Heyward could come there. His inventive friend would fit right in with these Harbone engineers.

Picket thought of all his friends, of Heyward, Jo, and Cole. Of Heyna, and Emma. He thought of Captain Frye, Mrs. Weaver, Gort, and Master Eefaw. He missed them all and hoped they were okay.

And Heather. Where was she now? Would he, like Master Helmer, be separated from his sister for years? Would he be left to wonder what had happened to her without ever having an answer? He missed her intensely. He loved her very much and was proud of what she had done to save Emma. She had traded her life for the hope of the cause. For the Mended Wood.

Picket would gladly trade his own life to see her safe now.

* * *

On the second day, Lord Hewson introduced him to the master smith of the Harbone forge, Hame.

"I am very pleased to meet you, Master Smith," Picket said, bowing.

"And I, you, Captain," the smith said, returning the bow. He was a large rabbit with strong arms and coal-black fur. "My wife tells your stories to our littles at night. Tells them how you defeated Redeye Garlackson, and now we hear of higher feats still."

Picket bowed again. "May I ask what you're making, sir?"

"An ordinary sword," he said, "though it'll be a strong one."

"Master Smith is modest," Lord Hewson cut in. "He makes no ordinary swords. He is the best swordsmith in all Natalia. In fact, I understand he made the sword at your side."

Picket blinked and looked from the sheathed weapon, a gift from Prince Smalls, to the smiling smith. "The prince?" he began, absently feeling for the black scarf at his neck.

The smith nodded. "Aye. He and I were friends, as odd as that may be. The best of rabbits, he was."

Picket's head hung low. "We'll never see better."

"He sent me instructions for that one," Smith said as Picket drew the blade out and laid it in his hands, "and I see it has had some use. That's good. I hope it holds up well no matter at what heights you fight."

"Master Smith comes from a long line of the finest crafters in our history. His ancestors were making arms for the last kings of Golden Coast," Lord Hewson said.

"Aye," Master Smith said. "We go way back. But the prince, he was kin to the original smith."

"The original smith?" Picket asked, puzzled.

"Aye, Flint was the first smith," he answered, rubbing his chin. "You know of Flint's stone sword?" Picket nodded, and he went on. "Some say it came to him that way, and Fay's book the same. Some say they fell from the sky—that it came from the stars. But in our craft lore, we remember that Flint forged the first sword. It did come from the stars, but it came as a falling star made of unbreakable steel. Well, some say that Fay herself believed it might one day be broken. But of this substance, the sky sword was made—the stone sword of legend."

"If it was forged from this falling star," Picket asked, "and it was supposed to be unbreakable, then how was it forged into a sword? Perhaps our First Mother was right."

"It's a matter unsettled in our lore," Smith answered. "Some say Fay herself dreamed a way, and Flint followed her counsel. Some say the sword was there from the fallen star, and Flint merely broke away the rock around it. Some say he was so strong he broke the unbreakable steel and made the blade through fire unknown to any forge before or since."

"And what do you believe?" Picket asked.

"I don't need to know every detail of how," the smith said, smiling as he handed Picket's sword back. "I know that Flint forged a sword and that he fought the first foe with it. I know it was handed down for generations and that all those who follow our craft see Flint as our father, in more ways than one. To us, he is doubly father. I am a smith, and Flint was a smith. That's enough for me."

Picket nodded. "What became of Flint's sword?"

"It was lost sometime after the crossing," Lord Hewson said. "We know Whitson had it and that Lander saw it. But I never heard for certain where it landed. Many say it's in the bottom of the river, that after Whitson's wreck they never recovered it. Some say it was carried off by Lord Grimble and held in his followers' warren, then lost when their renegade settlement failed. Others say Lander hid it with the dragon seeds, though none know where."

"What do you think happened to it, my lord?" Picket asked.

"I believe it was lost," Lord Hewson said, "and we don't know where. So we made up stories to comfort ourselves."

"The smiths believe it was recovered by Lander and stored in the dragon tomb," Master Smith said, "so that it might never be lost again. And the heirs have the key."

Picket felt again for the scarf at his neck and thought of Smalls, then Emma, and all that was lost when their father fell.

* * *

On the third day, on one of his long walks, Picket ventured near the school. There he found rabbits his age playing a game called hoopvolley. He watched as two players stood on opposing sides with a hoop in between so they could see one another through its opening. Picket smiled as the first player rolled the ball gently with the bottom of her foot from a starting point ten steps away from the hoop, then attempted to kick the ball through with her second touch. Once the ball was through the hoop, the opposite player tried to kick it back through in two touches or less. Picket watched them try and fail, then succeed, back and forth. He tried to determine the score, but they seemed to be adding their points in a strange way.

"Who's winning?" he asked, walking up as they took a break.

"We play together," the doe answered, "and we try to beat our last high number."

"I see," Picket said. "It looks like fun."

"Come and join in," the buck said. "I'll take a break."

"Oh, thank you!" he said, itching to try it out. "I'm Picket, by the way."

"You're famous, Picket," the buck said. "We know who you are."

"Yes," Picket said, "I'm famous throughout Natalia as a wrecker of games and interrupter of conversations. I butt in with legendary rudeness."

"I'm Harmon." The buck laughed, shaking his hand. "And we're thrilled to have the world's most celebrated game-crasher ruin our perfect afternoon!"

"I'm Dalla," the doe said, smiling. "Let's see if you're as good as everyone says."

"Well," Picket said, stretching dramatically, "I'm not famous for being good at games, only for interrupting them."

"More of a negative force," Harmon added, grinning.

"Exactly," Picket replied.

After a little more playful banter, he joined in. He began to get the hang of it and found his heart growing lighter as he forgot his worries in the midst of the fun of the game. He and Dalla had a good score going when a messenger ran up.

"Captain Longtreader," the breathless messenger said, "I'm so sorry to interrupt."

"You ruined the hoopvolley game!" Dalla called. "And he only just now stopped stinking!"

Picket smiled, turning to the messenger. "Yes?"

"Lord Hewson and Captain Redthaw want to see you as soon as you can come."

"What is it?"

"Sir, they say a window has opened."

A window has opened. It's time.

Picket spun to thank his new friends for the fun, then jogged behind the messenger as he hurried off.

In a few minutes, he was back in Lord Hewson's receiving room, trying to catch his breath.

"Ah, Captain Picket," Lord Hewson said. "Our scouts say the wolves have shifted northwest, taking the bait we set a little quicker than we had hoped."

"How long do we have?" Picket asked.

"About three hours to get everything in place."

"Do I need to tell my master?" Picket asked.

"No, he's already on the move."

"Then I'll meet you at the first gate, my lord," Picket said, and he hurried back down the hall toward his room.

Picket's heart was pumping hard as he ran. He was eager to get on with their mission, but he hated to leave this place. He thought of how this citadel was much like the game they played, hoopvolley, where seemingly opposing sides came together to act on a shared goal. Though they had disagreed with the decision, they were doing their best to help. He was heartened by his stay at Harbone and hopeful their preparations would bear fruit.

"Now for the hard part," he said, dashing into his room to recover his pack and strap on his sword.

Chapter Twenty-One

We Died Like Heroes

Picket stood in the Great Wood. Through a distance glass, he could see the walls of First Warren. Between his own position in the woods and the city lay a black wasteland of charred ground, newly burned again. The Black Gap. Beyond the Black Gap lay the city that had been founded by and was once home to King Lander and to every king of Natalia since. That is, until the fall of King Jupiter.

As the sun rose high over First Warren, Picket thought of Smalls. In the list of kings Smalls would never be mentioned. He would be glad to see Emma's coronation, if the war could be won and rightful rule restored, but his heart broke to think of Smalls missing what he had worked so hard to create. Picket felt for the black scarf around his neck and sighed, then focused on the task at hand.

For Smalls' sake, for Emma, and for the hope of the mending, I have a job to do.

"This is insanity," Helmer mumbled gruffly beside him.

"Then it's perfect for us," Picket answered.

"Maybe," Helmer said as he peered through the glass. "I'd rather be leading a full assault than this."

"It'll be fine." Picket glanced over at Helmer. "Is that buckle still giving you problems?"

* * *

On the other side of the woods, Lord Hewson watched through his own distance glass. He gazed at the wall, then up toward the place where Picket and Helmer lay in wait with their small team.

"Keep an eye on them," Lord Hewson said, passing his glass back to Lieutenant Meeker.

"Yes, my lord," Meeker said, carefully training the glass on their friends.

"Is everything ready?" Lord Hewson asked as Captain Redthaw jogged up, accompanied by several other officers.

"It is, my lord," Captain Redthaw replied. "We're ready when you give the signal."

"We'll stick with the plan," Lord Hewson said. "We will wait for the moonrise."

"That could be a few hours, my lord," Captain Redthaw said.

"Yes," Lord Hewson replied, and both rabbits glanced back at the woods behind them.

Three bowstrikers were mounted on makeshift platforms as soldiers loaded them under the operators' instruction. The large hybrid catapult-and-bow devices were now hidden on the edge of the forest.

"Are they operational?" Lord Hewson asked, nodding at the bowstrikers.

"We believe they'll do what we want," Captain Redthaw replied. "Though they've never been tried on this scale."

"It is quite a distance," Lord Hewson mused, staring at the city wall. "Who are the gunners?"

"They're all soldiers, my lord," Captain Redthaw said, "chosen by me. We have young Emerson on number one, as he knows the operation of these weapons like few others. He's their primary inventor."

"This was also his scheme," Lord Hewson said.

"And he's the son of Emery," Captain Redthaw added, "who was lost in one of our last attempts to get in."

"Of course," Lord Hewson said, nodding. "An apt choice, to be sure."

"On number two, I chose Harmon. He's a young soldier but a good one. He volunteered straightaway for this duty. On number three—"

But Captain Redthaw didn't get to say who was firing number three, for they heard a hundred angry howls, as the woods suddenly teemed with wild wolves.

Lord Hewson snatched the glass from Lieutenant Meeker and spun to scan the woods. "Curses! The villains haven't fallen for our trap. I hope you're ready, Helmer, old friend." Then, loudly, he called, "Fire now!"

Hewson saw Emerson's wide eyes take in the coming storm of wolves, then thin to slits as he turned back to his target and trained his weapon.

There stood the wall surrounding First Warren.

Emerson sighted again, then calmly flicked his switch. The large long arrow leapt from the weapon with stunning force. It soared straight and true in a long, elegant arc, finding the city wall just beneath a sentinel station. The stone blew apart in a terrific explosion that rocked the wall and sent a tremendous plume of smoke to cloud their vision. The raptor that sat atop the station beat his wings to fly aloft, spinning to survey the source of the unexpected blast. But he seemed to be looking within the wall.

Lord Hewson pumped his fist as the next two bowstrikers fired in quick succession, one finding the base of the far curve of the wall in another impressive explosion and the third falling just short of the wall, failing to ignite.

"Reload!" Lord Hewson called, though the order was unnecessary. Emerson's bowstriker was already reloaded and nearly cranked ready again. Without waiting for new orders, Emerson fired again, sending his blastarrow back into the same crater he had made with his first shot. Another incredible blast, and the sentinel station gave way and tumbled down as the stone beneath it blew apart.

"That's another crack shot, Emerson lad!" Lord Hewson cried, joining in the triumphant shout along with most of the gathered rabbits. But he spun around, seeing Captain Redthaw was turned toward the coming wolves. "Archers, release!" A team of twenty archers had formed a line behind the bowstrikers and their operators and now fired, two arrows each, into the rushing pack.

Lord Hewson was shocked to see how close the enemy had gotten. The archers were dead-eyed as always, and the first wave of wolves went down. But the pack didn't even slow. They scrambled over their fallen with maniacal glee. Hewson drew his own bow and fired, dropping the new lead wolf.

Still they came on. Hewson glanced back across the valley as he nocked another arrow. "Come on, Helmer!" he said, then turned and fired again. The archers were buying them precious time, but he could see they would soon be overwhelmed. Then he saw that Harmon, operating bowstriker number two, had swiveled it around. With a defiant cry, he pulled the switch and unleashed a blastarrow aimed right at the heart of the surging wolf pack.

It blew apart in a deafening blast as the rabbits dived for cover. The archers were knocked back and scattered. Lord Hewson fell to the ground not far from Emerson, who was cranking number one for another volley. Harmon was reloading and scanning the bank of smoke behind to see what damage his shot had done.

In the deafening after-blast, Lord Hewson found his glass and trained it on the far woods. *Where are they?* To his delight, he saw two forms launch and sail through the air toward the wall. His eyes widened, and he found them in his sights. He smiled wide and laughed aloud. "Go!" he said, urging them on.

One of them, reaching a good height, had activated his glider and was deftly swooping toward the city. The other, to Lord Hewson's alarm, was dropping. Helmer's glider was not engaged, and after the early momentum of the catapult launch, he was dropping fast.

Lord Hewson swallowed hard, keeping his eye on the dropping rabbit. "Engage!" he cried. "Engage it, you old fool!"

Then he saw Picket swoop down and grab hold of Helmer, turning him upward in a deft dive and swoop. Helmer's glider engaged, and he swept upward in an uneasy arc. Hewson swept his glass to the left, where the distraction they had made was paying off. The sentinels swooped around the opposite side of the wall, and there was a busy hive of activity among the rubble. He saw the massive form of the white falcon glide in, screeching furiously as he came. Lord Falcowit was there.

Sweeping his glass back to the flying rabbits—they were actually flying through the air!—he saw that Helmer's path would take him dangerously close to the wall. Picket banked back and caught a current of air so he swept around the edge of the wall while Helmer rose in a ragged passage.

Hewson cringed and made every physical effort to will Helmer over the wall. The telling moment came as he soared near the lip of the wall. Hewson gasped as Helmer's glider dipped dangerously near the wall, but he rose again, clipping the brick and tumbling inside the wall. Picket banked and glided easily over, and both disappeared from sight.

Hewson shouted, "They're in!" and the gathered rabbits gave an answering cry.

Then Hewson turned back and braced for the wolf assault.

"Should we send a runner, my lord?" Captain Redthaw asked, gasping as he gazed at the clearing smoke and the regrouping wolf pack, surging forward again with savage energy. "We have only three more blastarrows, and we need to get word to the princess that they made it in. And we don't seem likely…" He trailed off, gazing at the wolf pack.

"Send Emerson," Lord Hewson said. "His family's had enough tragedy. Maybe he'll get through."

"Emerson!" Captain Redthaw called as Lord Hewson shouted urgent instructions for the rest, "take a message to Harbone. Tell them they are inside the city."

"Sir," Emerson called, "I want to fight here with you and Lord Hewson! Please, sir, send Harmon. He's twice as fast as me, as everyone knows."

"You'll both go," Captain Redthaw said, moving toward the bowstriker. "Go now, and no argument!"

Harmon sagged, then nodded, saluted his captain, and tore off into the woods without a word. Emerson trotted after him, a last backward glance at his captain and lord.

"Tell them we died like heroes!" Lord Hewson called. Then he pointed his drawn sword at the advancing wolves. "Tell them we did our duty!"

A shout from the defiant rabbits echoed through the forest.

"Let fly!" Lord Hewson cried as the operators released the last blastarrows to fly at the attacking pack. "Tell them," he whispered to himself just before the explosion, "that we were brave."

Chapter Twenty-Two

First Warren Horror

Picket loved the feeling that came with flying. Though danger pressed at him from every side, he couldn't deny the wild surging joy within. He smiled, baring his teeth in the wind as he sailed high. When he reached the summit of the catapult's range, he stretched his arms out to engage his glider. The device answered beautifully, and he thought of Heyward, blessing him in his exuberant joy. Then he saw, with a stab of panic, that Helmer was dropping. He banked and dived, twisting his wrists to disengage, and sped toward his master, who luffed and spun as he fell to earth, well short of the wall.

Picket reached him halfway to the ground. "Master!" he called, slapping Helmer hard in the face. The older rabbit woke, eyes wide, then threw out his arms to engage the glider. Helmer recovered, steadily rising in a wobbly curve, while Picket banked back to see if his master could clear the wall. It was a tense few seconds, but Helmer dipped, then rose and roughly cleared the lip of the wall, taking several broken bricks in with him.

Picket smiled, sighed, then circled around and glided over the wall himself. He didn't have time to stay high and stare at the scene that spread out beneath him. He was afraid of being seen. But he stole a moment to gaze across this legendary city, home to so many noble rabbits over the years.

It was vast, unlike anything Picket had ever seen. The massive wall dominated with its several starlike points, and the river ran from the dam wall levee, carving through its middle. And there was the massive square at the city center, with its grey-white buildings all around. In the center of the square stood seven tall standing stones, high and imposing like a spine. Atop them, though, were massive statues of Lords of Prey. He snarled and looked away. Glancing down, he saw Helmer crash awkwardly into the woods outside of town. He dived after him.

Picket glided to a slow landing, found his feet, and disengaged the taut wings. He bent to a knee, unfastened the glider cape, and folded it all down into his pack. Then he helped Helmer, who was speechless and gasping. Picket unfastened and folded the rods, then wrapped all with the sturdy black cloth. Helmer staggered a few steps and fell to his knees beneath a tree.

"Are you well, Master?"

"Just don't talk for a minute, Ladybug," Helmer answered, holding up one finger.

Picket drank from his waterskin and checked his sword. He walked the immediate area, assessing possible routes for them. If they had been seen, it wouldn't be long till scouts found them. Three small rockets exploded above, followed by a blast of trumpets. A signal.

"Master," he said, jogging back. "We're in First Warren. I've never been here before, and I don't know where to go. They've just sent some sort of signal to the town. We don't have much time."

Nodding, Helmer turned and got to his feet. He took some water from Picket, drank, and then coughed. "I'm sure much has changed since I was last here, but I know where we need to go."

"Where?"

"To Airen's house," Helmer said, and a spark of hope lit up his eyes. "I want to find my sister. And she'll be in the middle of any resistance—I'm sure of it."

Picket nodded, thinking of Heather.

They cut through the small forest and came to the river, where, peering out from the cover of trees, they saw several rabbits rushing toward the city center. All of them wore red scarves, or kerchiefs, at their necks. It was an arresting sight. Picket hid and listened as two passed close by the wood.

"They've gone too far," one haggard old rabbit was saying, weeping as she leaned on a young buck's arm and they hurried along. "Much too far. A bomb at the wall? Several bombs on the wall?"

"Yes," the younger buck agreed, "we will feel their fury now. I don't mind them keeping alive a memory of the old days, but to act so rashly, to invite such retribution from our masters? It's criminal."

"Oooh, they took five younglings on the last Victory Day," she said, "and what shall they do now?"

"Take them all?" he answered. "It's a wonder we have any left."

When the pair had passed by, Helmer motioned for Picket to follow him deeper into the cover of trees. "We've done a dangerous thing," Helmer said.

"They will take revenge for what we've done?" Picket asked.

"Yes. They believe it was insurrectionists within the city."

"At least we know we might find allies," Picket said.

"True," Helmer answered, scratching his chin, "but for now I'm worried about what they'll do at this assembly."

"But why do they all gather? Why not just stay away?"

"I'm sure they go to the city center, to the square," Helmer said. "And no doubt they must account for each rabbit, making absence unthinkable."

"And they will punish them there?"

"I'm afraid so," Helmer answered. "I hate to think of it."

Helmer nodded for Picket to follow, and they cut along the edge of the forest. They found a high tree near the square and climbed up quietly as the sun set. Torches broke out, and the square was soon packed with red-throated rabbits.

Picket could see the faces of the nearest rabbits by torchlight when they turned his way. They were hollow-eyed, careworn, and fretful. At least, those most alive were fretful. The more frightening thing by far was when he saw some rabbits wearing a look of abject indifference, like nothing that would happen mattered, just as nothing that had happened mattered. They stared off, like those with broken minds, and moved wordlessly with the crowd.

"The red at their necks, what does it mean?" Picket asked.

"I'm not sure, but I think it's a reminder of what they are to the Preylords."

"Prey?"

"Yes. But some haven't given up entirely," Helmer whispered.

"It's awful so many have," Picket answered.

"I'm not surprised to find that," Helmer said. "I had just about given up as well, in my own way, until you came along."

Picket smiled sadly, then gazed back at the gathering crowd. The rabbits stood around and among those high standing stones, so sacred to the rabbits of Natalia, honoring Flint and Fay and the Leapers. But as he had seen on his gliding approach, these sacred standing stones had become platforms for giant statues of Lords of Prey. Picket saw there were six birds immortalized in stone, while on the farthest standing stone perched a statue of a kneeling rabbit.

"The statues, who are they?" Picket asked.

"Those are the Six, I think," Helmer said bitterly. "The Lords of Prey are said to be ruled by a cadre of six warlords, with one being their chief. Morbin has been their king for a long time. It's their ancient way. These six have a feast every year and reaffirm their lord in dark rites."

"The Rule of Six," Picket said. "I heard something of this at Halfwind. The white falcon they warned us about at Harbone, is he one of them?"

"See the second statue?" Helmer asked. Picket nodded. "That's him, I think. Falcowit, terror of First Warren. He is in the Rule of Six."

"All the other sentinels come and go, year by year," Picket said, "but he stays to watch over and carry out his cruel domination of First Warren. Why?"

"I think there's history for him here," Helmer answered. "I don't know it all, but he has special cause to brood over the ruin of our old capitol."

"I suppose the kneeling rabbit is my uncle," Picket said with disgust.

"I'm sorry, lad," Helmer said. "But remember, you're not responsible for him."

"Forgive me, but we're always responsible for our family name," Picket said. "And it will be hard to rest until his backstabbing schemes are ended."

"I understand that, son."

On the platform, raised high on the other side of the square, robed rabbits, clearly leaders, were gathering. They whispered anxiously among themselves as servants lit torches and placed them across the stage. A tall thin rabbit with a silver crown emerged on the stage, and the gathered lords hurried to him, arms extended in worried gestures, as he did his best to calm them. His clothes were fine, and he wore a sparkling red scarf at his neck, which glittered in the torchlight.

"Winslow," Helmer said with a bitter rasp. "The governor, under Morbin, of the Great Wood and First Warren. What vile scum."

Picket gazed at the lean rabbit. He could see some resemblance to Smalls, though his fallen friend's oldest brother was much taller. There was something familiar in the face, and it hit Picket like a blow. "He looks terrible."

"He ought to," Helmer grumbled. "This treachery ought to have eaten away his bones."

For a moment, Picket felt something he didn't expect. Pity. But the moment passed, and First Warren's leaders came to the front of the stage. Winslow motioned for silence. A large rabbit, clad in black and flanked by a cadre of guards in the same dark garb, loomed behind him. On one shoulder, the guards wore a feathered epaulette that looked like a small wing.

Thousands of rabbits quickly quieted.

"We were warned of the cost that would come if we allowed those discontented fools among us to act on their rebellions," Winslow said, his voice brittle and sickly pretty. "Our masters have dealt well with us, and this is how we repay them?"

"It wasn't the resistance!" someone shouted from the crowd.

"Silence!" Winslow screamed, his eyes wild. "It wasn't the royal guard who did this. Not the palace staff. It wasn't Captain Daggler," he said, motioning to the black-clad captain over his shoulder. "It was not Lord Falcowit! It *was* the resistance, curse them all. And now you know what we must do within the hour. Within the hour, or we are all doomed."

The crowd made way for weeping parents, who pushed their younglings to the center of the square, by the stage. Picket started, his heart beating wildly. "Helmer," he said warily. But Helmer was staring into the square himself, a disgusted frown forming on his face.

The rest backed up, though some had to be dragged, and the children were left alone at the front of the stage, their necks draped in red. The younglings wept and extended little arms toward their sobbing parents. Picket stared, disbelieving, as thousands of rabbits stood still and let their children, by the hundreds, be exposed.

A huge white falcon swooped over the crowd and landed deftly on the stage beside Winslow. "You were warned, redthroats," Falcowit called in a breathy, scraping scold. "We will discover the cause and culprits of these attacks, and they will be dealt with swiftly, but you know the law. We have communal justice here. The young pay for what the old do. Victory Day is near, and you will feel the full wrath of these foolish acts then. But tonight," he said, relishing the tension in the assembly, "a taste of what's to come."

He screeched, and birds swooped in, the sentinel raptors bellowing as they swept over the crowd and aimed for the center of the square.

Aimed for the younglings.

Picket leapt from the tree and landed roughly. Rolling over, he sprang to his feet. He reached for his sword and began to rush to the square. But Helmer dropped down and tackled his apprentice. Picket struggled to free himself, but Helmer held on, his strong arms pinning Picket in place. "Not yet, son!" he whispered roughly into Picket's ear. "Not yet! We'll have our chance, but this isn't it. You'd squander the lives of those who risked so much to get us in here. I know it's awful, son, I know." Picket fought on a moment, then rolled over and sobbed into Helmer's shoulder. "I know, son. I know. It is stark evil. Your rage is right, but we must pick the time of our answer. Bottle it up, for now. And when the time is right, we'll break it open on their heads."

Chapter Twenty-Three

Deep Darkness

The groaning lepers, ragged in their tattered clothes, limped quickly toward Heather. Instinct insisted she run, and run *right now*, but she waited, eyeing the approaching rabbits warily. Their mottled fur and swelling sores unsettled Heather, but not in the way she expected. She was puzzled, her mind working over the diseases she knew, both firsthand and through her studies. Then several more lepers surged in from connecting lanes, sending up a plume of ashy soot, and came for her. Her heart raced, and she coiled to leap into a run.

A hand darted out from a nearby tent, grabbed her hard, and dragged her inside.

It was dark within as she stumbled inside. She was about to scream when she felt a hand over her mouth.

"Quiet, Heather." It was Father's voice. "Follow me."

Her heart still beating wildly, she lay a hand on his shoulder and followed as he walked ahead. Taking deep breaths, she fought back the urge to be sick. The smell, putrid and potent, was overpowering. She gagged beneath the scarf that covered her mouth and nose. Soon her eyes adjusted to the darkness, enough at least to see the vague form of her father directly before her. He spun and whispered through his kerchief, "Down on our knees," and he crouched down, moving ahead with evident caution. He turned and whispered back to her. "Are you okay?"

"I am," she replied softly, "but you gave me a fright."

"I'm sorry. I had to secure your safe conduct."

"Safe conduct? Where are we going?" she whispered.

"You'll see soon enough. I can't tell you yet, my dear," he said. "Do you trust me?"

She thought of the many times her faith in her father had been tested, when the evidence she knew and the testimony of others seemed to indicate that her father was a traitor. She thought of how her uncle Garten Longtreader, who had worked so closely with Father for years in King Jupiter's service, had turned suddenly to Morbin's side. She remembered the painful rejection she experienced because her name was Longtreader. *Longtreader.* This name that had been a heavy chain around her and Picket's necks in Cloud Mountain and that stood for Morbin's awful allies here in Akolan's privileged District Six. The name she had gotten from her father. Longtreader. She squinted at him in the dimness.

"I trust you more than any other soul in the world," she said. "Lead on, Father."

"Then follow me in, and say nothing until I say it's all right." He turned and crawled on. Lifting a flap, he entered a narrow opening. Heather felt for the edges of the hole, finding they were solid rock. As she crept inside, she reached out to touch the top and sides of the tunnel. All hard rock. As the tent flap snapped shut behind her, she was plunged into total darkness.

Heather's breath came in fast panting gasps. She tried to breathe slowly, to quiet the manic beating of her heart. Her air felt short in this cramped black passage. She could see nothing and could hear only the sound of her father hurrying ahead. She reached forward and felt the empty air of his absence. He was moving quickly. She needed to move, one way or the other. She wanted to back out in panic and run home. Fear surged inside her, rising like a high tide. *I can't do this.*

Heather forced herself to think only of breathing, forced herself to slow down and name her fear. *I feel afraid because I can't see. I am afraid because it's dark and cramped in here, and that's normal. I'm sick from this smell and have had a harrowing time lately.* Father had told them what he most regretted in his life was when he had said to fear, "You are my master." She was determined not to give in to this insistent twisting imposter within. She said no to what she felt desperate to do, ignored as best she could the welling panic, and crawled ahead.

At first it was slow going, especially with her arm still twinging with every motion. But soon she was moving faster. Panic remained agonizingly present, but she tried to focus on what was true. She hurried ahead for several minutes, though it felt like an hour. While she went, she told herself over and over that she could go for one more minute, and she counted the seconds down again and again. She tried to drown out the panic she felt at not being able to turn around and how far the entrance was behind her. Farther and farther with every counted-off second.

Finally, she saw a light ahead. It was only a little bit of light, and it was far, far ahead. But even a little bit of light meant the world to her in all that darkness. She smiled, breathed deep again, and hurried ahead. She realized, with relief, that her most recent deep breath had much less of the sick, mephitic air of the Lepers' District. She was amazed at how grateful she could be for a very little light and clear air.

As the light grew at the tunnel's end, she saw Father squeeze through a light-soaked opening, displacing the canvas flap that covered it. Heather crawled forward and came to the bright cover. Carefully, she pulled it back and crawled through. She squinted at the bright fire. Stretching her injured arm slowly, she gazed intently around the room.

It was a rounded hollowed-out rock room, a little bigger than Lord Ramnor's ready room at Halfwind Citadel. The main chamber looked like it could hold fifty rabbits packed tight, and thirty or so were in there now. She caught a glimpse of openings above, where she saw forms looking down on this gathering. But those around the fire looked down, stealing wary glances at her. Most wore the ordinary clothes common to outwallers, those Akolan rabbits who lived outside the Sixth District. But the red at their necks was gone.

Father motioned for her to follow him, and she got to her feet and stepped carefully around the fire. She imitated Father as he loosed his preymark and secreted the kerchief into his pocket. She stuffed her red scarf into her satchel as she walked forward and sat beside him. The fire was circled several times by neat lines of rabbits, making a kind of widening circle, like an archer's target, with the fire as its center. They all sat close together, except for the area Heather thought of as the head of the fire. There, flanked by gaps on either side, sat an old rabbit in simple brown clothes, white eyes gazing at the flames. He sat cross-legged, his shoulders hunched with age and years of labor. Laid across his lap, his gnarled hands were folded over a pickaxe. He seemed to be blind, his milky eyes reflecting the bobbing orange of the fire.

The old rabbit rose slowly, tottering as he balanced, and stood as straight as he was able. Then he struck down on the stone with the handle end of his pickaxe. The rest also rose at this cracking call. Heather got to her feet, following the motions of the assembly. The blind old rabbit raised the tool high and said in a hoarse, shivery voice, "I am the Tunneler, and I am the Truth. Hear me and help me, and our children's children shall be free."

The gathered rabbits solemnly answered in a low chant. "We will hear and help and free our heirs."

Heather glanced up at her father, whose eyes shone as he reverently recited these words.

Then the blind old rabbit tilted his head Heather's way and in his fragile tones said, "Welcome to the Seventh District."

Chapter Twenty-Four

The Truth in the Tunnel

The assembled rabbits turned to Heather. She nodded in a quick, graceful bow.

"You are Heather Longtreader, daughter of Whittle and Sween Longtreader," said the blind old rabbit. Heather nodded. "It's all right, young doe," he said. "You may speak."

"Thank you, sir," she said. "I am who you say I am."

"I am the Tunneler. I am a brittle rabbit—yes—but a strong link to Akolan's past and rabbitkind's future. We are the sons of those who never settled for slavery. You are brought among us, this sacred council, based upon the testimony of Whittle Longtreader, your father. He has vouched for you, that you will never do us harm or reveal our secrets—secrets that have been protected for generations."

"I could never betray the cause," she answered.

"Anyone could betray our cause," a rabbit called from above. The voice sounded familiar to her, though she couldn't place it. It sent shivers down her spine as he continued. "We all could. We all *can* betray. The question is, *will* we?" A murmuring approval followed these words. It was clear that many present thought it unwise to invite her here.

"Aye," the Tunneler answered, "and you do not yet know what our cause is."

"It has been the tradition here for a very long time," Father said, "since before any of us were born, to invite only those who have lived among us for many months—years, usually—those tested and approved in a hundred ways. I have asked for an extraordinary exception, and the Tunneler has granted it."

"With the stipulation," said one of the rabbits in the inner circle, "that the usual penalties apply."

"The usual penalties?" Heather asked.

"Aye, Heather Longtreader," the Tunneler said. "The council will vote at the conclusion of our meeting."

"Vote about what?" Heather asked, feeling a slow panic rise.

"Whether you live or die."

Father laid his hand on her arm. "I have no doubt you will all see what I know," he said. "That Heather, known all over Natalia as the Scribe of the Cause, is invaluable to our aims in many ways."

"I hope it may be so," said the Tunneler, his milk-white eyes still reflecting the fire. "We shall see directly.

We have never used this rare, terrible, and necessary last resort, not in all my many years as the Tunneler. But your father has insisted that the protocol be enacted in order that we might hear from you sooner. Have you anything to say, young doe?"

Heather's panic began to twist into indignation. She thought of the suffering she had experienced for the cause, and she was tired of the atmosphere of distrust among those who should be allies. Her mind understood the desperate need for caution, for the necessity of these desperate rabbits to keep their doings secret from the enemy, but her heart was grieved and angry.

"I'm not certain what you want to hear, but, begging your pardon, nor do I care," she said, looking around defiantly. "If you were a thousand partisans of Morbin's murderous horde, I would say what I believe. I love Natalia and the cause of the Mended Wood. Since I first heard the name of King Jupiter, my heart has been with him. I have lived among and loved his heirs with deep and unbreakable devotion. I have risked everything, lost everything, in service to the rightful bearer of the Green Ember. If this is treason to your cause, then I do not ask your pardon. I would rather die fighting for the Mended Wood than live pretending to be free. So examine me, torture me, do what you want. Question me a thousand times. The answer will always be the same. I am meant for the mending, and I'll do nothing against it, come any calamity or the end of the world."

She sat down.

After a moment, the Tunneler sat down too, and so did all the others assembled. "Would you tell us about the world outside, Heather?" the Tunneler asked. "We have had no word for some time, since shortly after your father and mother came to us."

She looked at Father, and he nodded. "Tell them," he said, smiling. She could see he was proud of her, and it made her swell with confidence.

Heather stood again and moved closer to the fire. She bowed her head and breathed in deeply. Then, closing her eyes, she began. "There was a rabbit named Smalden. He was young among his brothers and sisters but wise beyond his years. His father early saw his gifts, knew his gentleness, wisdom, and deep strength. He saw all this and gave him a gift." Heather reached in her satchel and drew out the Green Ember. She held it up to gasps, and it glowed in the firelight. "His father gave him the token of his future rule, even though he was very small. In fact, he never grew tall. His friends called him 'Smalls.' After his father's betrayal and murder, the prince was bundled away by a covert council seeking, in the fouled and fallow ground of the broken world, to plant the seeds of the mending. He was agreed upon as the undisputed heir and given to the guardianship of the brother of his betrayer. His sister, newborn, was designated as the second heir and, never told who she was, raised by a loyal lord. So the prince's early years were marked by hardship, fleeing from secret citadel to hidden hideout, always moving and ever shrouded in mystery. His mentor and friend, one Wilfred Longtreader, guided and guarded him as he grew up in the hostile world dominated by his father's murderer. You know all this," she said, walking around the fire. "You know of Jupiter Smalls. You know of him. But do any of you know him? I knew him. I loved him," she said. She paused with her head down. She went on, emotion choking her words. "I loved him...would have given anything to see him crowned as our longed-for king. And so he should have been. But he gave his life trying to save lives, trying to save slaves like...like us.

"Prince Smalls was the noblest rabbit I have ever known, and if his sires were half the rabbits he was, then they are deserving of all the honor we give them, from King Whitson Mariner himself down to Jupiter the Great. But these are all gone, and now only the princess remains. Princess Emma is a worthy heir to these heroes, and she, though never eager for the crown, will fill it with grace and strength. I came here in her place. I am her herald, and I bring you the news that this war, like it or not, is right now being waged. The battle is joined. We, rabbits of the ground, heirs of Flint and Fay, have risen to the heights and fought in the skies with the raptors. I have seen it with my own eyes. We fight. We fly. We will—we must–overcome. If you are faithful to Whitson's heir and Whitson's way, then this is your war, and it is being fought right now. Morbin's fall draws near, and the Mended Wood waits—on the other side of this fight."

"It cannot be," a rabbit said, among a chorus of gasps. "It's not possible."

Heather turned on the rabbit, at first in fury, eyes squinting tight. Then she took another breath, and her face loosened into a smile. "I will tell you all about it," she said. "And you will believe me. For I have nothing to lose now and no reason to lie. The Green Ember rises," she said, holding up the emerald gem. She saw its reflecting glints flicker all around the room. "The seed of the new world smolders."

Chapter Twenty-Five

Between Life and Death

When Heather was finished telling all she knew, she sat down. She was exhausted. She was barely aware of the pregnant pause that followed her harrowing tale. Heather closed her eyes and breathed in deeply, feeling satisfied at the honest telling of her story. Though it hurt, she spoke often of Smalls. The pain of his loss was acute. But she felt a fire kindled in her soul at the memory of his light. In her own heart, she made a decision. Heather vowed there, in that deep cave in the heart of Akolan, that she would live to honor his memory and die fighting for his cause. Heather would live on as if she were what she knew she could never be, the widowed wife of Jupiter Smalls. She knew she could never have that honor, but she would live as if she did. At least in her heart. She would never marry another. She would tell his story, in a book if she was able, and carry him in her heart like a fire.

She would bear the flame for his cause, and for him, as long as she lived.

"Is it true?" she heard someone ask into the silence.

"It's too good," Heather said, almost to herself, "and bad, to not be true."

"We will speak of these things further, at our next meeting and beyond. But we have been here a long time, my fellows," the Tunneler said. "We will vote in a moment. Is there anything else for tonight?"

For a while the silence held, as if no one dared compare their offerings with the weight of great import that lay in Heather's story. But after a heavy pause, someone spoke up.

"Bandt and I keep working on the Old and Infirm Community scheme in District Four," said a rabbit in the second circle. She was a young doe, little older than Heather. "If we can get them close, we can bring them in without suspicion. They are vulnerable to disease, after all."

"The Wrongtreaders won't stand for it," another rabbit, an older doe, said. "The Order of Utility bars special care for the infirm and aged. They'll fight it."

"I know it will be difficult," the younger doe replied, "but we can't just wait and do nothing."

"We never do *nothing*," the Tunneler said. "We must not give in to the desperate demands of the urgent when our project is for the generations."

"I understand, Master Tunneler," she said, "I really do. But if we let the old suffer and die simply because they aren't useful, how can we be who we want to be? We already let them take the younglings in the school, only to be fattened for their feasts!" At this heads dropped, and Heather felt the burden of collective shame. The doe went on. "Who knows what fresh villainy they have planned for this year's Victory Day sham? What fresh horrors will we silently witness? When freedom comes, will we be strangers to goodness? And if we are strangers to goodness, then should we even be free?"

"Do not lecture the Master Tunneler, Harmony," said an older buck sternly. "He has been working for this cause since before my father was breeched."

"And where is your father, Master Timmons?" Harmony asked. "Do you want him to wither and die without dignity? My father is..." She paused, looked down, then back up fiercely at the Tunneler. "I lost my father long ago," she said bitterly. "My mother is dead, as are my brothers, and now my...my sister too. I only want to see our oldest cared for. We have avenues available—"

"Say no more, Harmony," said the Tunneler, emotion choking his words. "It is for another time. The time has now come to close our meeting."

"So says the Tunneler," a buck called. "He is our father. Let it be so."

"Take a moment to consider carefully. Our project is a project of life, and of preservation, though the lives of many will be lost while we pursue it. We never shall seek to destroy, only to preserve, persevere, and rescue. Our brother has asked for the trial of Heather Longtreader, and we have heard his request and granted it. You have heard her. Now, be sober and decide. If any say that Heather Longtreader threatens our project, speak now and let it mean death."

Heather realized with a pang that the old rabbit meant that if any spoke against her, anyone at all, she would be killed. She looked around, terrified to find that a few had their hands raised. The Tunneler called on the nearest.

"What have you to say, Leeyo?"

The buck stood and spoke. "I believe we should welcome Heather into the first circle of the Seventh."

"Hear him!" many said, and they stamped their feet on the rock.

"Do any oppose her?" the Tunneler asked. There was a noise from the windows above, and then all was silent. "Then your journey begins, Heather. So hear these words. I am the Tunneler and the Truth."

"He is the Tunneler and the Truth," they all, except for Heather, repeated.

"We have kept this hallowed hollow since Whitson's day. The first Tunneler was snatched from the deck of *Vanguard* in Ayman Lake when the raptors first attacked on their way to level Seddleton. And they did level that first Natalian settlement, carrying off scores, who were brought to be slaves in Akolan. Among them, him who became the Tunneler. The Tunneler dug this tunnel and cave for fifty years, and he died. The next Tunneler did the same, and he died. The next, and he died. They all died, but I am alive. And I am the Tunneler. I will never stop until we all are free."

"We will never stop," they called in response. "Until we all are free."

"Go, friends," the Tunneler said, raising his arms high, "and fight in your quiet ways, until the day we shall all cry out and come out, leaving our chains behind."

The gathered rabbits broke up, many heading for the tunnel. As they left, they replaced their red scarves and kerchiefs.

Father put his arm around her and whispered in her ear. "I'm so proud of you, Heather. You don't know how badly we needed your words."

She smiled up at her father while the outspoken doe from the council came over. "Hello, Heather," she said, taking her by the hand. "I'm Harmony."

"I'm pleased to meet you," Heather said, smiling. "I was glad to hear of your scheme for the care of the aged and infirm. I'm a doctor, and if I can ever help, please let me know."

"That's very kind," Harmony replied. "And you can rely on me. Your cause is my cause, and the sooner we act on it the better."

Heather felt her father's hand on her arm. Looking back, she saw he was smiling, but he was also looking around cautiously. "We all agree there, Harmony," he said, "but let us obey the Tunneler now and go our way."

Heather glanced around and saw many eyes staring at them. Some wore wary looks, and others beamed. Only perhaps a quarter of those present crowded around the passage back to the L.D.; the others milled around in small groups, speaking quietly.

"I would never contradict you, Master Longtreader," Harmony said, glancing at the exit, then back at Father. "But you and I both know how much over-cautiousness costs us."

"And you know, young Harmony," Father answered, "the price of hasty acts of defiance."

Harmony hung her head. "She was foolish, I know. But she loved the cause and was very brave."

Father put his arm around her in a consoling embrace. "I'm very sorry about Melody, dear. She was indeed a sweet, brave doe. And your brothers were very brave bucks. You are right to say we need some haste here. I hope Heather's tale will push the council to decision. Give it time to work. But we must do what is effective, not what is desperate."

"I understand, sir."

Heather followed her father with a hug of her own for Harmony. She didn't know the exact circumstances yet, but it was clear that Harmony had lost someone she loved. Melody must have been her sister, the one she said had died recently. "I don't know your story," Heather said, "but I know the pain. I'm ever so sorry for your loss."

"You know it well," Harmony said. "I heard it in your story. You are mourning for the prince, as should we all, and the wound is widest for you."

They hugged again, then Harmony, with a final squeeze of Heather's hand, turned to the tunnel entrance. Father followed her, and Heather came last of all.

The return trip wasn't nearly as awful, as Heather knew better what to expect. Still, she was oddly relieved to smell the strengthening odor as she neared the L.D. The stench was horrid, but it comforted her to know they grew closer to the end of the tunnel.

Soon she and Father were slipping into District Four, sliding along darkened walls. They paused in one shadow, crouching down while Father listened. "Let's stay here a few minutes," he said. "It's always best to weave an unpredictable pattern of return."

Heather nodded. "I liked Harmony."

"She is a good one," Father said. "Mother worked with her sister, Melody, and was there in Morbin's lair when she was killed."

"It must have been awful."

"It was. She and Melody shared a deep concern for the younglings they so wickedly prime for their vile purposes."

"You said they give them special food for weeks, and then they disappear?"

"Yes, fruits and vegetables—I mean vegetables other than potatoes. So that the younglings believe they have a rich reward ahead. An adventure. But it is only Morbin's table that awaits them. Harmony and her sister were committed to ending this grotesque preparation."

"How? I share their disgust, of course," Heather said, "but what could possibly be done?"

"You hit upon the problem. Melody got herself assigned to work in Morbin's lair in order to uncover more and try to figure out the best course of action. But in the end, it was too much for her. She wasn't cautious enough."

"And what did Mother think?"

"She believed that Melody's ideas about the problem were right but her solutions were brash and wrongheaded."

"What did Harmony mean when she talked about how there was over-caution on our side?"

"Rabbits have been here since the first days of King Whitson. Since the first attack of raptors at Ayman Lake. There has been a Tunneler here, leading a secret scheme of escape, since before First Warren was ever founded in the Great Wood."

"They really plan to escape one day and make it all the way to the Great Wood? It's impossible! I was taken from Cloud Mountain and flown here over the vast mountains. How could they ever hope to escape this place, here in the heart of the High Bleaks? First Warren is so far away."

"It is," Father agreed. "But as your stories show, what seems impossible can happen, if we are bold."

"You believe they are too cautious?"

"The Tunneler's conclave has been so long at work in Akolan that it has become an institution. Unbelievable work of preparation has been done, and I mean truly remarkable things I am sworn to keep secret, even from you. But preparation can be a great obstacle to action. I have seen it in scholarship, in matters of state, in family life. And it is here, too."

"So, you and Mother are caught between the brash actions of some in the conclave and the over-caution of the institution itself?"

"That is the situation exactly," Father said. "But we are not alone. There are others who stand in the middle with us. It is the time for action, I think. It's the time for considered, deliberate, and wise action. The big challenge, rightly diagnosed by Harmony, is institutional inaction. It's always preparing and never going. It's packing for a trip we will never take. I think if we can show movement of any kind, the brash, undisciplined party will come along."

"What will you do?"

"I believe I have struck a subtle blow against the institutional inaction of the conclave. I have employed a deft stroke that will be, I think, impossible to defend."

"And what is that?"

"You, of course," he said, smiling wide in the moonlight.

"Am I only a piece in your game of battleboard?" she asked, smiling back.

"Not only that," he answered, taking her hand in his, "but I do like to win. And I truly believe that winning this battle against inaction may one day matter in the true war."

"What you say gives me great hope, Father," she said. "I want to hear more."

"Tomorrow night," he said, signaling for her to follow.

They crept along an alley, then darted through an empty street. Reaching their own lane, they stayed close to the walls, dark with shadow, until they came to their own door. Slipping inside, they saw two silhouettes by the lit fire.

"Jacks!" Heather cried, rushing to him. She smothered him in a hug. "I have missed you, brother!"

She looked at him. He had grown so much. Jacks was no longer a baby at all but a very young buck. Seeing him in his red neckerchief and uniform disturbed her intense happiness.

"Say hello to your sister," Mother said, smiling warily. Heather saw that she and Father exchanged nervous glances.

"Hello, Heather," Jacks said. "I don't remember you. But I'm glad you have finally come to us. Where have you been all this time?"

"Jacks, I've been fighting for—"

"She's been away, son," Father interrupted. "But now she's home, and we're very happy."

"Where were you tonight, Whittle?" Jacks asked their father. Heather was confused at her brother's use of Father's first name. "You and Heather were out after dark. Teacher says I must tell her if you go out at night."

"Please don't do that, Jacks," Mother said. "Why not just enjoy that your sister's home?"

"I want to follow the rules especially well, Sween," he said. "I've been picked for a special program."

Heather's breath caught as dread seized her heart. Heather saw that Mother was fighting back tears, and she dared not look at Father. She looked down at Jacks. He was beaming. He pointed to the kitchen, where a basket of fruits and vegetables sat on the table.

"I've been picked! I'm supposed to eat these special foods. And, very soon, I'm going on an adventure!"

Chapter Twenty-Six

Emma's March

Emma had wanted to stay longer at Vandalia Citadel. Though small and less strategically important than the citadel they were journeying toward now, she had enjoyed her time there. Lord Booker had been a perfect host, and his son, Morgan, was a charming guide with whom a blossoming friendship had begun. They were also loyal at Vandalia, intensely loyal.

Not so at Blackstone.

Of course Lord Ronan and the Blackstone Citadel council would be civil, but they were seen as the last holdouts, uneasy about Prince Jupiter Smalls' close connection with Wilfred Longtreader and the Longtreader family at large. Would they oppose her, argue with her, or worse? Lord Ronan was cunning and experienced. How could she impose her will?

"Your Highness," Heyna Blackstar said, appearing at her side.

"Heyna!" Emma said, hand over her heart, "you startled me!"

"I beg your pardon, Princess," Heyna said, backing away, ashamed.

"No, no, it's fine," Emma said, smiling. "What is it?"

Heyna smiled back formally, and her eyes flitted from Emma to their surroundings. Emma was in awe of Heyna, for the black doe's startling beauty and tireless vigilance. She had saved Emma's life at Halfwind Citadel during the wolf attack, receiving a terrible scar, then watched over Emma throughout the battle of Rockback Mountain and ever since.

"Your Highness," Heyna said. "I believe we should change our route plan and travel on through the night."

"But your father and Captain Frye," Emma answered, "said they believed we should camp here and carry on in the morning."

"I honor them, of course. But it is my duty to serve you first, and I believe I do that best by advising you as prudently as I am able. They are the best of rabbits, to be sure, and I honor my father above all other bucks in Natalia. But they are both older and grow more easily tired. They want you to be fresh for your encounter with Lord Ronan at Blackstone," Heyna said, momentarily locking eyes with the princess, "and that is wise. But I fear they don't know your strength. I know that the visit to Vandalia was not a drain on you but rather the opposite. You loved spending time with Lord Booker, and his son. You feel energized and eager."

Emma looked down, smiling. "Go on."

"I see that, but they do not. And, if we rest soon, then our passage tomorrow will take us across open land by daylight, with no cover from raptor scouts."

"It seems to me to be a choice between two equally worthy opinions," Emma said. "How can I decide?"

"Consider this last factor, Your Highness, if you will," Heyna said. Emma nodded, and Heyna went on. "If we march on through the night, then we will arrive at dawn instead of dusk, many hours before they expect you at Blackstone. I know you would not like to do anything to annoy Lord Ronan..." She trailed off, returning her attention to the woods.

"If we marched through the night and showed up early," Emma said, eyes alight, "then we could wrong-foot him from the start and begin with him unbalanced."

Heyna nodded. "It is worthy of consideration, Your Highness," she said, bowing.

"Lieutenant Shanks," Emma said, motioning for Jo to come over. He jogged up, his quiver bouncing at his back and his bow at the ready.

"Yes, Your Highness?" Jo said, bowing neatly.

"Jo, would you advise pressing an advantage in a delicate negotiation or to let it pass in favor of more civil and modest aims?"

Jo scratched his chin and exhaled heavily. "Well, Your Highness," he said after a moment, "I look at it like battle archery. Always aim for the heart. If you hit something else, then that's still okay. But, aim for the heart."

"Thank you, Jo," she said. "Would you please ask Lord Blackstar to step up?"

"Yes, ma'am," Jo answered, touching his eyes, his ears, and his mouth. He backed away until he was far enough distant to spin and jog back toward Lord Blackstar. In the silence that followed, as they waited for Jo to return, Emma's mind turned to another matter.

"Heyna," Emma said, "will you be truthful with me now?"

"Always, Your Highness," she answered, her face showing a hint of hurt.

"I don't mean that you haven't been honest in the past," Emma said, taking her by the hands. "I only mean I want you to be honest about what I'm asking and to hold nothing back."

"If I can, with honor, I will," Heyna said.

"Why did you learn to fight and defend?" Emma asked. "Your mother wasn't like that. I met her some years ago, and she was lovely. A perfect and courtly doe was Lady Blackstar, like all her honored ancestors. I know you have all that training as well, and I can see you know the ways of court, far better than I do. So why did you learn to fight?"

Heyna's eyes thinned to two slits, and she made as if to turn away, but Emma held her hands tight. She lowered her head. After a moment, she raised it to reveal damp eyes and a vexed expression. "I will tell you why, Your Highness," she said, her voice hoarse. She cleared her throat. "My mother was, as you said, a lady unmatched for grace and charm. She was the most hospitable and generous hostess and never lacked for poise, no matter the guest or setting. Even during the very darkest days, she persisted in her dignity and always modeled a positivity I recall with some wonder. These are her known qualities, seen by dignitaries and friends within the cause over the years. What fewer knew was how funny she was," and Heyna smiled sadly at her brother, who was standing close by. He came closer still at Emma's nod. "Remember, Cole, how Mother made us laugh?"

Cole nodded. "She was a distinguished lady," he said, "but she was relaxed and natural with us. And very funny."

"We had the best of her," Heyna said.

"That's true," Cole agreed, putting his arm around his twin sister. "She had, still has, even now, a reputation for her excellence at court, but she spent most of her time with us. And we were very happy, even in the troubles."

"We were," Heyna said, "up until that day."

"I'm so sorry, Heyna," Emma said, taking her hands again. "You don't have to tell me. I was wrong to ask."

"You weren't wrong, Your Highness. And I want to tell you," Heyna said, looking up through streaming eyes. Cole Blackstar was also losing his battle to stop the tears from spilling down his face. "I was trained," she said, "like every doe at the Kingston court, in the etiquette expected of the heirs of our ancestor Lady Lucianne Blackstar, wife of the second Lord Blackstar and daughter of King Whitson and Queen Lillie. She had all her mother's graces and was a friend always to her brother, King Lander."

"So the friendship between our families goes back a long way," Emma said.

"Indeed," Heyna said. "So I learned all that a young doe ought, and this included hard work of many kinds. But not war. That was reserved for the bucks of Kingston. My brother," she went on, looking at Cole, "was schooled at court, like me, but he did his shifts in the mine and with the army, as all bucks must. So he was trained to fight, and to defend, and excelled at both beyond any at Kingston. He was such a keen warrior that no one dared oppose him, though he begged for partners to spar with him. They had to come at him in packs, for he could only be overcome if at a tremendous disadvantage. So he did his schoolwork, learned the ways of court, did his shifts in the mine, and became a warrior prepared to lead and defend both Kingston and those he loved. But he was not there when they came for Mother."

Cole hung his head, and Lord Blackstar walked up, with Jo at his side. Emma motioned him over, and he came between his two weeping children and extended an arm around each. Jo stood some way off, silently guarding their privacy from beneath the bending boughs.

"It was no one's fault but mine when your dear mother died," Lord Blackstar said. "You were only children."

"Still," Heyna said. "I was there. And from that day, I begged Father to allow me to train to defend so that I might never be so helpless again if the worst happened.

So that I might do some good in the service of some highborn lady. I trained for years to serve as I now do. And I will do all I can to see you safely to your throne, Your Highness."

"I am honored, Heyna," Emma said, "by your devotion. By that of your legendary family. I'm so new to this life, but I am happy to learn that our families are connected by bonds of the past. We are cousins, dear Heyna!"

"We are that, Your Highness," Heyna replied.

"Then we have a good excuse for you to call me Emma, since we are family."

Heyna smiled. "I couldn't do that, Your Highness."

"Will you, or won't you, obey me?" Emma said, a smile playing at her mouth. "I insist on it, at least when we're alone," she said, then, nodding at Lord Blackstar and Cole, "or among the other cousins."

"As you wish…Emma," Heyna said.

"That wasn't so hard, was it?"

"It wasn't easy."

"You'll get used to it. Take my counsel, as I have taken yours," Emma said. Then she turned to Lord Blackstar. "We will march on, through the night, and so arrive early to Blackstone."

"Yes, Your Highness," he said, bowing as he backed away. Cole did the same after a last squeeze of his sister's shoulder. They turned to relay the change of plans down the small caravan.

"I'm so pleased to have a cousin," Emma said, turning back to Heyna. "I have never known my family. My mother is far away, and I do not know when I might see her. My living brothers are all traitors. My sisters too, for all I know. Heather is gone, and Picket is on a perilous mission. I'm glad you're here, Heyna."

"My blood for yours," Heyna said.

They marched on, toward Blackstone Citadel.

Chapter Twenty-Seven

The Teller Hears

Clouds covered the moon over First Warren, and the rain fell down. Picket walked in darkness, his heart as heavy as the soaked pack on his back. Helmer led the way, picking their path carefully to intersect with the fewest rabbits. They saw no one for a long time. The assembly had broken up, though the terrified cries of the younglings still echoed in Picket's ears. They had been taken, many of them. He and Helmer heard the report in the hopeless conversations of the rabbits leaving the square, and saw it in the faces of the pacified bucks, the mothers' vacant eyes. Picket felt a vast heaviness descend like a millstone, a great weight of shame, covering all the rabbit inhabitants of this forsaken place. But for him, the shame gave way to outrage.

This tyranny was worse than death, he decided. And he recommitted himself to the cause for which he fought. He knew, in that moment, that he would eagerly trade his life to strike a blow against Morbin and Falcowit, and against Winslow.

In the middle of this recommitment, as the rain fell on First Warren, Picket saw a light. He stopped and touched Helmer's shoulder.

"What is it, son?" Helmer asked. Picket pointed to the fire, dim in the middle distance. Helmer nodded. "There are caves over there. Let's see what it is."

They crept around to come at the caves from some cover and saw a small band of bedraggled rabbits gathered around a fire. Picket looked up at his master with a question, and Helmer whispered, "I think it's okay, but let's leave our things here, hidden in these bushes."

Picket set aside his sword and pack, then followed Helmer into the edge of the firelight.

"Who goes?" a nervous rabbit called as they came into sight.

"Travelers only," Helmer said, hands up and open. "We seek only the hospitality of your fire for an hour."

The nervous rabbit glanced around, then said, reluctantly. "Come out of the rain and warm up."

Picket followed Helmer to the fireside, where they both knelt, extending their hands. "Thank you," Helmer said. "These are unpleasant days to be out."

"Unless you serve the prince loyally," said a thin brown rabbit, nearest the cave entrance, who seemed ready to flee at the slightest provocation, "as we all do." Picket glanced around, measuring each of these bucks for how they might fare in a fight, a skill he had been forced to acquire. He guessed almost all of the seven were weak and incapable of opposing him and Helmer together, but the eighth was somewhat stronger. That shaggy rabbit squatted in the corner of the cave, his hood low while he snacked on dried beans. There was no red at his neck.

"True, true," the first, nervous, rabbit added. "We are Prince Winslow's bucks, all of us."

"We aren't," Helmer said flatly. "I'd like to take his head off."

An awkward silence followed. Then the hooded rabbit laughed, choking on his snack. "Don't you know," he asked, clearing his throat, "that it's death to say such things in First Warren?"

"It'll be death to him when I meet him," Helmer said, without a hint of worry. "Listen, I know what sort of rabbits you are. You're outside of their attention—barely. But you're too cowardly or lazy to join any formal resistance. So you skulk around the caves and just try to survive."

The hooded rabbit laughed again, and the others nervously joined in, though without sincerity.

"What about you two?" the thin brown rabbit asked. "You look like soldiers, all muscular and well-fed. You have to be in the Black Band."

"We're from outside the walls," Helmer said, "and we're here to liberate this city."

"Outside the walls?" the thin brown buck asked, astonished.

"He's joking, Mo," the nervous rabbit said. "No one's come in, or out, for a long time."

"What about the Herald?" another rabbit asked. "They say he brought the story in."

"Yeah, but he was killed that night. Arrow in the back."

"What story?" Picket asked.

"You ain't heard the story?" Thin Brown asked. "I never met someone who ain't heard the story. About Picket Packslayer?"

Picket glanced over at Helmer. "And what happened to the story?" Helmer asked.

"Well, the Herald handed it to the Teller, a rabbit who goes from home to home sharing the story. That's how come everyone knows about Packslayer. The Teller tells them. But the Teller's also dangerous hisself, and they say he's half-mad."

"Sing the song, Rand," Thin Brown said to a bright-eyed rabbit leaning against the back of the cave. "Rand here used to sing at the old C.O.D., in the way-back-before days. Sing it for us, Rand. C'mon."

"I'd rather not," Rand answered, his eyes flitting from the fire to their guests.

"Go ahead, Rand," the nervous rabbit said. "I'll share my portion with you again if you do."

Rand smiled, revealing several missing teeth. He nodded, then crawled forward to the edge of the cave, where the firelight fell full on his face. He closed his eyes and breathed deeply. Then he opened his eyes and looked around, now full of lively expression. He began to drum out a beat on his leg and soon launched into his song.

"Listen, my bucks and my does, lend your ears,
I'll tell you a tale that will quiet your fears.

There was a buck who once flew in the sky
And fought fifty falcons in wars way up high.
And when he landed, he rolled up his sleeves,
Then killed all the wolves just like swatting at fleas.
From his fell deeds all the birds that are dead
Help him sleep easy on his feather bed.
And there in his warren, he walks over
Carpets of conquest made from wolf fur."

The rest joined in on the chorus.

"Whose shadow is crossing the moon?
Picket Packslayer, Picket Packslayer!
Who is coming to rescue us soon?
Picket Packslayer, Picket Packslayer!
Picket Packslayer!"

"Listen, my bucks and my does, hear me well,
When you're afraid here's a story to tell.
Of Picket Packslayer, who stands twice as tall
As the ten tallest rabbits that you ever saw.
As for his food, he's never tasted defeat,
Each meal in his warren is served with wolf meat.
His eyes are gentle and his heart is so true,
But if you fight him, he'll cleave you in two.
So friend, share the story and go spread the word
Of Picket Packslayer, bane of the birds!"
"Whose shadow is crossing the moon?
Picket Packslayer, Picket Packslayer!
Who is coming to rescue us soon?

Picket Packslayer, Picket Packslayer!
Picket Packslayer!"

Picket had no idea what to say, and Helmer seemed about to burst out laughing. "Well, I'd hate to meet this Picket Packslayer in a cave on a wet night," Helmer said, unsuccessfully hiding his smile.

"You're wrong to snicker at the song, stranger," the hooded rabbit in the back said. "It's an exaggeration, sure, but it gives us hope."

"An exaggeration?" Helmer asked. "It's an absurdity."

"I don't think it is." The shaggy rabbit stepped forward and drew back his hood. He was old and wise-eyed, and his fur hung down in long grey shocks.

"It's the Teller," Thin Brown said, and he seemed caught between reverence and terror. He stammered out a few incoherent words, bowed to the Teller, then darted into the rain. The rest of the rabbits followed him, and Picket and Helmer were left alone with the old rabbit.

"Is it true that you saw the Herald?" Helmer asked. "And that he gave you a story?"

"Aye," the old rabbit answered, reaching deep into the folds of his cloak and drawing out a thin bound book. "He gave me this."

"Is it like the song?" Picket asked.

"No. It has the ring of truth to it. It's about a rabbit prince named Smalls and his friend, Picket, who really have fought birds and wolves and have begun the battle back against Morbin. I tell the tale straight as I move through the city and the surrounding country inside the wall, but the story outruns me. I can't quite correct them all. And anyway, like I said, it gives them hope to think of a rabbit who defies Morbin and fights birds and wolves."

"Do you think it's true?" Picket asked. "I mean, what you read in the Herald's tale?"

"It inspires us anyway, whether it's true or not," he said. "But I believe it's true."

"You *believe* it is?" Helmer asked.

"I know it is," the Teller said. "Because when I read these words, my heart is on fire."

Helmer smiled and nodded.

"So you travel around and...bear the flame?" Picket asked.

The Teller frowned. "Have you two heard the story?"

"We've lived it," Picket said.

"He's the rabbit who flew, Teller," Helmer said. "He's Picket. And you're right about the Herald's tale. It's true. It's all true."

The Teller's mouth opened, but he seemed unable to find speech.

Chapter Twenty-Eight

Too Late

Picket and Helmer spent an hour with the Teller, updating him on all the events that had happened since Heather's story had gone out into the world. Picket was pleased to see that her story had broken into an unbreakable place, and had somehow spread even here.

They took their leave of the Teller, who hurried out into the night with renewed vigor.

After that respite from the sad events of the evening, they walked on, falling silent as Helmer led the way. Despite the encouraging meeting with the Teller, Picket thought of the younglings in the square and felt again the weight of woe in this place. He hoped to pierce it with more than words. The rain fell harder still and chilled Picket again.

"Not far now, Picket," Helmer said, the first words spoken for a while. The rain had stopped. "Our family home, which my great-grandfather built, is just over the next hill."

"It will be dawn soon," Picket said.

"It can't come soon enough."

Dawn did come. The sun rose behind the home that Helmer pointed to, his family's farm since the founding of the city. Sunlight crowned the house and spread stretching beams around as the two weary bucks hurried toward it. Picket noted the silence and saw, as they neared, the air of disrepair that hung about the place. The grass was long, except for a small patch around the house itself. Out of the house and onto this lawn came a wary young doe with a bow, arrow nocked and ready.

"Turn around," she said. "And head back where you came from." Helmer walked on, raising his hands. Picket imitated him. "I won't warn you again," she said. "Not another step."

Helmer took another step, and she fired. The arrow found the narrow gap between Picket and Helmer, sinking deep into a tree behind them. They stopped, Picket whistling in wonder.

"Is Airen home?" Helmer asked.

"Who's asking?" She nocked another arrow.

"Her brother," Helmer said.

"Not possible," the doe said, her face fixed in worry as she stared at them, glancing nervously at the swords at their sides. "Her brother's dead."

"I'm not dead, girl. Who are you? Where's Airen, and where's Snoden?"

"Father's dead," she said. "Been dead for years. How could you not know that and say you're Mother's brother?"

"I've been gone a long time. I'm very sorry about your father," he said, and Picket could hear the sadness in his voice. "Sno was a good rabbit." She seemed to relax at this, her anxious face less tense.

"Father told me about a time you two got in trouble," she said. "Did a thing that nearly got you booted from the army. What was it?"

"We swam to Forbidden Island." He smiled at the recollection. "Airen was furious for a month that we didn't include her."

"You really are my uncle," she said, lowering her bow. He crossed to fold her in a hug. Picket smiled at this reunion. It made him all the more eager for more like it.

"Now, child, where's Airen?" Helmer asked.

"Where she always is," she answered, "inside, sitting and knitting."

"What's your name?"

"I'm Louise, but they call me Weezie."

"All right, Weezie," Helmer said, "I'm going to see your mother."

She nodded, and Helmer hurried up the front steps and entered the run-down house.

Picket stood in silence for a little while, unsure what to say.

"Where are you from?" Weezie asked.

"I'm Picket. And I'm from a place called Nick Hollow," he answered. "Up northwest pretty far."

"Picket?" She laughed. "Like the song? You think I'd believe you came from the outside? Nobody's come from the outside for a very long time. You tell some stories, don't you?"

"I can also fly," he said, smiling as he set down his pack. "Do you have any water?"

She laughed, shook her head, and motioned for him to follow her inside.

They walked down a corridor and entered a small room with a wide window. Picket stopped and gazed out at overgrown fields leading up to a riverbank. "It's lovely," Picket said, accepting a mug of water dipped from a big pitcher.

"It used to be," Weezie answered. "Now I can barely keep the lawn around the house tame."

"You don't have any help?" Picket asked. But before she could answer, he heard loud weeping. Weezie frowned and hurried from the room. Picket followed her through a hall and into a wide space, where Helmer knelt in front of a thin fragile-looking rabbit whom he held tightly in his arms. She stared off, her eyes wide and distant.

It was Helmer who wept.

"Are you the only ones here?" Picket asked quietly.

"Have been for some time," Weezie answered, "since they killed Sissie."

"You had a sister?" Picket asked.

"My twin," she answered. "They took her on Victory Day, almost two years ago. Mother's never been the same since. Now all she seems to do is worry they'll come for me."

"Airen," Helmer said tenderly, "I'm going to take care of you. We'll make this right."

"They've taken Layra, Helm," she said, her voice flat and emotionless. "It can't be made right. First Sno, and we survived. But Layra too. Just a child."

He held her tight, his eyes overflowing with tears. "I'm home now, Sis."

"You're too late," she said, and Picket's heart felt as if it had been harpooned. "You're too late."

Chapter Twenty-Nine

Flicker in the Eyes

Picket went outside. It was too much to listen to the weeping and the regret, the sad weight of grief that hung in the house and on every soul inside. But looking around outside, from the nearest farms in disrepair to the tops of the buildings in the distant square, he saw a city sick with sadness. It seemed to drip from the buildings and ooze through the fields. Since his naive childhood ended when his family was attacked in Nick Hollow and he became aware of the truth of the broken world, he had felt the collective despair at the heart of rabbitkind. But now he saw how different life at the secret citadels was compared with the sullen slavery of First Warren. Compared to this city, Halfwind Citadel was teeming with hope. As was Cloud Mountain, the bright bastion of the heralds of the Mended Wood.

He missed those places then, thinking again of the rabbits who, for him, belonged in each place, following their own callings and sharing life. He had not realized how good he had it. Had not realized what a privilege it had been to be there among free rabbits. To have been free himself.

I'm still free. And I'll die fighting to free the rest. For Airen, for Weezie. For Father, Mother, Jacks. For my dear Heather.

He heard the door open behind him, and soon Weezie was at his side. "You hungry?" she asked.

"I don't feel like eating," he said, turning away to hide his face.

"Lots of bucks leaking from the eyes today," Weezie said, punching his shoulder. "Someone should call a doctor."

Picket smiled, turning to her. "How do you keep your spirits up?"

"You really from the outside?" she asked.

"I am."

"Well, outsider," she said, motioning vaguely around. "I've never known anything but this. I get that it's a sad situation, especially since my sister's been gone and Mother's gone to pieces, but that's how it is here. That's normal life."

"It's not normal," he said. "And I'm so sorry that it feels normal to you."

Weezie took his hand and squeezed it. "Thanks, Picket," she said, smiling. She pulled him toward a path, and they were soon on a walk around the farm. They said nothing for a while, and Picket examined the old place and all the signs of its fading fortunes. What had it once been? It was easy to imagine the pleasures of life here in simpler, safer days. Freedom and a farm, surrounded by loved ones, sounded like the pleasantest dream he could right now imagine.

"Maybe we should tell them where we're going," he said.

"You're probably right," she answered. "Mother'd lose all connection to the world if anything happened to me." They stood within sight of the house but didn't turn back.

"What happened to her—to your sister?"

"The secret police took her. Prince Winslow's Black Band, his own private death squad. It's operated by his lieutenant governor, Daggler, a handpicked assassin whose life is spent making sure there are no disturbances."

"Disturbances?"

"Like yesterday. That's what Daggler does. He keeps that sort of thing from happening. Wait," she said, as if struck by a new thought. "Was that you? The bombs?"

Picket nodded, frowning. "It's how we covered our entrance. If we had known the cost, we wouldn't have done it."

"You couldn't have known," she said, patting his hand. "They will take any excuse to reinforce their control."

"So your mother has been ill since your sister's disappearance?"

"She was so strong for so long." Weezie sighed. "And it was understood that she was being watched by the Black Band and that if she stepped out of line there would be severe consequences. She was on their list from the beginning. Rabbits of Extreme Interest. She didn't do anything. She never stepped out of line. But they took

Layra anyway, the villains. They took her from us, while the three of us were on a walk, and she was just gone."

"Maybe she's still alive?"

Weezie shook her head. "Mother went to the governor's palace, pleaded with them for any news of Layra. She got nowhere. On her third visit, it was represented to her, in brutal clarity, that her Layra was dead and that Layra's twin would join her if she came asking questions again or if she made the slightest move that seemed to support the resistance."

"So this hangs over your family—this warning."

"Yes. And I'm all she has."

They walked back to the house and tiptoed inside. They found Helmer bringing Airen some food and trying to coax her to eat. Picket signaled to Helmer, indicating they were taking a walk. Helmer nodded, his face twisted in an anxious expression. Picket put his fist over his heart. Helmer nodded, gratefully returning the salute.

When they were outside, Weezie grabbed her bow and quiver, then led Picket down a new path away from the house. "You love my uncle."

"I do. Very much. He's my master but also a dear friend. He's been a father to me while my own has been absent."

"Did your father abandon you?"

"No, he was taken. I hope he's still alive."

"I'm sorry."

"You know, I'm from a place kind of like this," he said, bending to pick up a twig. "Far away from the hurry and worry, a slow place with wide fields, ample orchards, and good neighbors. I thought I only missed the ones I love, but I miss the place, too. The way of living."

"And here I thought you were some exciting soldier with tales of adventure," she said, laughing.

"I have those," he replied. "But it's no way to live."

"Adventure is no way to live?"

"Not always, Weezie," he said, tossing a stick into a thicket. "You want rest at some point."

"You don't seem like you're ready to rest."

"Not yet," he answered. "Not while the world's as it is."

They moved through an overgrown path, then into a fence-lined field, over which continued to climb the sun. Weezie smiled at Picket and nodded at the sun. "The world as it is," she said.

"Dark as it gets," he said, gazing at the light breaking over the fields, "there's always a dawn."

"And always another night looming," she mumbled.

They were quiet for a little while, enjoying the modest glory of the country sunshine. Picket breathed in deeply. He felt, even amid the pain behind and ahead, that this was a moment to savor. He closed his eyes and breathed it in once again. He felt the sun on his fur and listened to the whisper of the swaying grass, bending gently in the easy breeze. It felt so familiar. It was a little like going home. He felt if he opened his eyes he might see Heather streaking past him to grasp the starstick. He might at any moment hear Mother call them in for dinner, and Father would be there with his stories, while Jacks played at his feet. How old was Jacks now? He must be walking and talking and reading and writing by now. Where were they all? What had happened to them?

And what would happen to him? Would he ever have a home again?

"I know they took your daddy, but do you have any other family?" Weezie asked.

He opened his eyes and saw Weezie staring at him. He had almost forgotten her for a moment, thinking of his family. Seeing her leaning against the fence, he sensed her intense connection to this place. Picket nodded, then swept his gaze once more over the stretching fields, down to the river, and back to the forest behind them.

"My family. Yes, I have more. Father and Mother and my little brother, Jacks, were taken by Morbin's wolves. My sister, Heather, was taken more recently. So, other than my Uncle Wilfred, Helmer is the closest thing to family I have, along with Emma—and Jo and Cole."

"It seems you have quite a band of family substitutes," Weezie said, smiling at him. "Tell me about Emma."

Picket laughed. "Well, that is a long story."

Weezie looked down, then out across the fields. "I have no friends," she said. "I have only these fallow fields, this empty sky, and a mother whose soul is broken beyond repair."

"I'm sorry, Weezie."

"It is what it is," she answered.

"True. But it's not normal," he said, "and it's not right."

"It's normal here. It is what it is."

Picket took her hand and said, "It is what it is, but it is not what it shall be."

"You believe the stories about the mending?" she asked.

"We're living those stories," he said. "And it's time you saw your part."

"What will we do?" she asked. "What can we do against such powers?"

"I'm not sure, Weezie. But we will never do nothing, until the mending comes."

He looked at her face, saw the sun reflected in the deep green of her eyes, and saw there a flicker of a fire that seemed certain to grow. She, like her mother and uncle, was not naturally meek and yielding to this evil regime. She needed very little, Picket thought, to burst into fiery resolve. He saw it smoldering there.

"It feels wrong, but I want to leave her, Picket," she said. "I want to go with you and join your cause."

"We are bringing the cause here," Picket answered. "And you are welcome to it."

They heard a snapping limb behind them. Glancing quickly at each other, they burst away, rushing up the path back to the house. Picket ripped free his sword, and Weezie nocked an arrow as they ran.

Picket saw ahead the narrow path between thick brush on both sides and called to Weezie, "Is there another way?"

"No!" she shouted, and they sped on, rushing into the dense thicket's path.

Weezie was just ahead of Picket, so he saw the black-clad rabbit dart from the brush. She loosed her arrow, but it missed as she was tackled, rolling into the brush on the other side of the path. Picket leapt in after her but was himself tackled, his hand pinned to the ground and his sword knocked free. Seven rabbits at least, all dressed in black with black masks covering all but their eyes, had them subdued in seconds.

Before they could cry out, gags were forced around their mouths. Picket looked at Weezie. Her eyes were wild in terror, then slowly sank in grim resignation. She had expected this for a long time.

It was normal here.

The fire in her eyes was gone.

Chapter Thirty

No, Escape

Picket was dragged—gagged and bound—down a slim forest path. He saw Weezie's face and felt a keen stab of guilt, knowing well what fresh wreckage this would bring to Helmer's home. He saw Weezie's withered look, the beginnings of the hopelessness that had so seized her mother. Then a black bag was forced over his head, and he could see nothing. He felt the agony of helplessness added to his mounting guilt. He was dragged down the path, forced along by firm hands. At first he fought back, making everything hard on his captors, but after a while he tired and surrendered to the reality that they, in fact, had him.

Picket remembered his training then and tried to calm his head to find a solution to this situation. The greater part of his mind insisted that none was possible, that there was no real tactical solution available. But he pressed on, thinking of what small openings there might be to effect an escape.

He became docile then, walking without resistance, needing no further prodding as they hurried along. He would pick his moment. He would save his rage. They would think he had surrendered, and then, when they least expected, he would lash out with savage fury.

Picket listened. He pretended to stumble, feeling with his bound wrists the equipment with which his nearest captors were armed. He did this several times, pretending to be nursing an injured leg so that they came closer and aided him more. He set his mind to work. After a march of fifteen minutes, they turned left, and Picket could feel the air change. It was cooler now. Perhaps it wouldn't be long before his opportunities were gone. He affected to weep beneath the bag over his head, and the grip on his arm loosened ever so slightly. It was now or never.

Picket lunged hard to the right, knocking into the nearest bandit, whose grip had loosened. He felt the crunch and separation as the bandit fell away with a startled curse. Picket balanced against the blow and stood steady, gripping in his hands the bandit's belt knife. He made quick work of cutting his wrists free while running hard to his right. He hoped there were no trees immediately in the way. He tripped into a thicket, low limbs scraping against him as he freed his hands and tore the bag off his head.

They were coming, of course. Black-clad bandits tore after him. He couldn't just run off and leave Weezie, but he had to make them think he would. It was one of the few advantages he had. They didn't know what he would do and would have to base their tactics on obvious expectations. He would have to counter those with his own precise schemes. Taking in the scene before his eyes in a fraction of a second, he leapt away, tearing off the gag as he ran.

Holding the knife tight, he planned as he ran, arcing back toward the group in a seemingly frantic flight. Picket could not, would not, leave Weezie to these thugs. But he had to be careful. Everything depended on his execution of a perfect plan. The scene he had just left, and was carefully bending back toward, was set in his mind. Several black-clad bandits, perhaps three, surrounding Weezie and gripping her arms tight. The rest, maybe four, tearing through the woods behind him. He marked the location of the limbs, the play of the sunlight through the trees, and a thousand smaller details that fed into the machinery of his mind.

In a minute he had almost made his way back to the scene of his sudden flight. Ducking and dodging through the forest, he found Weezie much as he had left her, but now only one bandit held her, and one other stood guard.

Picket sped toward them, securing the knife in his own belt. After leaping over a leaning branch, he ducked beneath another, then darted hard at the guarding rabbit in black. The guard gripped his sword and pivoted back and forth, ready for the attack. Picket made as if to dodge around, as if he were surprised to find he had returned to this spot. Then he sprang up, reached for a low limb, and, taking it in his hands, swung forward with tremendous force to find his enemy's chin with his powerful sweeping feet.

The bandit's head snapped back, and he buckled, falling in a heap. Picket landed, spun on the guard who held Weezie, and charged in wild fury, ripping out his dagger as he came.

"No!" the bandit cried. "You're not—" but he couldn't finish his warning. For Weezie, sensing the situation, drove her elbow into his middle. Picket slowed as she spun on the bandit and kicked him hard to gain separation. Picket sliced her bonds and took her hand, leading her into the thicket nearby as the other bandits pursued from behind.

Weezie tore at her own mask with her free hand, but Picket charged on, frantically searching for a path. He realized that she would be far better than he at routing their escape, so he let go of her hand and slowed to help her with the bag and gag. He glanced back and saw the pursuit was very close. "This way!" Weezie shouted, leading Picket on into the forest.

Now they ran more freely and gained a small gap between themselves and their pursuers. Picket could hardly believe they had done it. But he kept his rising relief down as he trailed Weezie through twists and turns of her native terrain.

"Fools!" he heard a rabbit cry from behind, and they ran on.

Picket grinned. The evident frustration of the following bandits made his heart swell. He followed Weezie through a snarl of trees, into a descending path that bent beneath a gnarly grove all tangled in overgrown vines and briers.

"I think we're losing them!" Picket said.

He was sideswiped by a leaping tackle from a black-clad rabbit. His head whipped back, and he smacked against a rotting stump, shattering the brittle wood in a spray of splintered shards. Rolling over, he reached for his knife. But his hand was pinned once again, and several stout rabbits hovered overhead. He saw Weezie being dragged from the thicket, her eyes full of terror as the black bag was once more placed over her head.

I've failed again.

"I'm sorry!" he called to Weezie as the gag once again was fitted round his mouth. The black bag descended to make all as dark as night.

Chapter Thirty-One

The Miner Who Forgot

Heather was reeling from her reunion with Jacks. What she had hoped would be an occasion of tremendous joy had proven to be its farthest opposite. Jacks, hardly recognizable as a member of their family with his disturbing devotion to the Akolan administration, had been chosen for what he called "an adventure." But Heather knew better. She knew that her youngest brother had been picked to be fattened up with special foods and become part of a meal for Morbin's table. She lay motionless in her bed, dark thoughts descending.

When Jacks was asleep, Father and Mother crept into Heather's room for a hasty council. She shot up in bed.

"What will we do?" she whispered.

"We knew this day might come," Mother said, patting Heather's hand. "It has come for many others. We have a little time."

"I will go to the Tunneler," Father said, running his hands through his fur and pulling at his ears. "I will ask that they be brought into the Seventh District."

"He won't allow it," Mother said, her eyes wet with tears. "You have overreached already in asking for Heather to be admitted on trial. To ask for Jacks, or for him and all his class, to be transitioned—it's impossible."

"We can't just let them take him!" Heather said. Her swelling anxiety made it hard to breathe. "Not just when I've found him again."

They sat in silence for a while, each uncertain what to say.

"We didn't know how to say it, Heather," Mother said after a while. "And we didn't want to upset our reunion, which has been so sweet. But Jacks really is one of them now. He's been trained to be."

"You can't think of giving up on him?" Heather asked.

"Of course not," Mother said. "I'm only saying that he would likely resist any effort at rescue."

"He's been so carefully cultivated by the dogmatists in the Sixth District," Father said, shaking his head. "We tried, Heather. We tried to subtly counter what was happening. But he's one of them."

"What if we tell him everything?" she asked.

"He would go to Longtreaders High Command and inform on us," Mother answered.

"He wouldn't," Heather said, her mouth hanging open.

"I think it likely," Father said. "Almost certainly he would."

Another long silence. Inside, Heather felt the familiar turn of her world as it slid sideways in a sickening shift.

"Let's try to sleep," Father said, "and maybe hope will come with the dawn."

They hugged, clinging together, tight and united in their anxiety and devotion. Heather felt grateful for this moment but couldn't help but think of the two members missing in this family embrace.

* * *

Heather did manage, at last, to sleep for a couple of hours. And she dreamed.

She was in a dank, dark cavern, as so many times before. But this time she was talking to someone in the dim, slick bottom. She carried on a conversation, one that pleased her, but all the while a voice in her head said over and over, *Unsettle the foundations. Unsettle the foundations.* She awoke perplexed.

She still felt groggy as she made her way to the table. She came fully awake at the sight of the special food Jacks had brought with him from school. Her face formed a snarl, and her heart beat faster. Her anxiety and sadness of the night was turning to anger in the morning.

"What makes you so angry, Heather?"

She turned to see Jacks standing across from her, his sleepy-faced gaze set in a questioning stare. Heather's eyes went wide, and she exchanged her scowl for a smile.

"Good morning, Jacks!" she said, moving close to hug him. He patted her back, then squirmed away from her embrace.

"Why were you frowning so mean?" he asked again.

"I was, um," she began, "a little angry because you have all this good food, and I'm jealous of the adventure you get to have." Her stomach turned at the words.

"Teacher Len said that would happen," Jacks said. "I'm supposed to be polite but to firmly insist that these rations are for me only. And I am to report any unauthorized reassignment of rations."

"I see," she said. "I suppose I'll have to be content with potatoes then."

"We should all be grateful for what the administration provides," he said.

"Of course. Of course."

"What's your favorite thing about what the administration gives us?" he asked, squinting at her with a penetrating glare. She was so unsettled by this encounter that she wasn't sure what to say or do. She felt as if she were moments away from being informed on by her little brother. It was so different than the reunion she had hoped for that her heart sank.

"Why don't you tell me your favorite thing," she said calmly, "while I think of mine."

"For me, it's the games at school," he said. "Oh, and my adventure and the adventure food."

"For me, it's that I get to see my family again," she said. "Do you remember, Jacks, that I used to tell you stories?"

"No."

"Well, I did. Can I tell you one again?" she asked.

"I guess," he answered, yawning into his hand.

"Thank you, Jacks. Shall we walk?"

He nodded, and they crossed to the door and went outside. They walked through the neighborhood, silent for a little while as ash drifted around them.

"Do you have a job, Heather?" Jacks asked. "We must all do our part for the community."

"I do," she answered. "I'm a doctor, and I help the infirm and ill."

"If they can be healed and put back to assigned jobs," he said casually, "then that's a good work. But we must protect our resources, and too many rabbits mean depleted resources."

"I always do everything I can to save and serve every life, no matter how small or inconvenient."

"You need to visit the school, I think," he said.

"I would certainly relish that opportunity," she answered, clenching her jaws tight.

"You'd better hurry up with your story," he said. "And I hope it's not too long."

"It's short," she said, breathing in deep. She stopped, looked at Jacks, then bowed. Upright once more, she began. "With what art and skill are mine, I will this humble tale unwind." Her face became animated, and she whispered the beginning of her tale. "Our story starts with a rabbit who mined for coal. His name was Flitch. Now Flitch was wealthy, had a sprawling warren for his large family, a beautiful wife, and children who all loved him deeply." Jacks frowned and started to speak, but Heather held up a finger. "Let me finish my story, please, brother?" He nodded, and she went on. "Flitch was rich, you see, in many ways, and he went to work every day whistling in his joy. One day, while Flitch was digging in a seam of coal, a great rock came loose and fell, striking him on the head. He was dazed, swooned, and fell over, senseless. When he awoke some hours later, he had a great pain in his head and…he didn't know who he was." She paused a moment, breathed deeply once again, and bowed a second time to Jacks. She went on. "Whether hence through fire or flowers, what has been mine will now be ours."

Jacks frowned at this strange ritual. Heather continued.

"Flitch staggered from the mine and looked around for some clue as to who he might be. But he could find none. He wandered off and took the wrong road, for he could remember nothing. He wandered so far that he came to a different town from his own, one called Newton. No one knew him in Newton, and he soon settled in as a laborer on a farm. For years he worked and wondered about his past. He didn't even know his own name. Now, Newton voted on every matter in the town hall, but he always stayed silent during the votes. But one day, when a great controversy had split the town, it came down to a close vote. Half the town wanted to elect a council, and half wanted to simply appoint a mayor. The division was so strong and close that the vote really was evenly split. Then everyone looked at Flitch and said, 'Stranger, your vote will decide the matter. What say you?'

"Now Flitch was upset, but he rose, and the hall fell silent. 'I can't say what I should do, for I don't know who I am,' he said. And he walked out, leaving the hall in a wild uproar. He walked out of Newton that day and took up again the lonely road that split in a hundred different directions. He traveled the road for years, wondering who he was." Heather fell silent for a moment, then closed her eyes and breathed deeply a third time. She bowed once more and said, "My tale is told, the seed is sown, what grows from it will be your own."

They walked on in silence for a little while longer.

"Did he ever get home again?" Jacks asked.

"Well, now. Lots of folks say you should never explain a story," she said, thinking of her Storyguild master back at Cloud Mountain.

"But I want to know," Jacks said.

"I'll tell you this much. He had to remember who he was first," she answered, "before he could find his way home."

Jacks frowned. "We'd better get back to the house," he said. "You shouldn't be late for work. The administration is counting on us all to do our part."

She nodded, looked away, and quickly wiped at her eyes.

* * *

Not long after, Heather was at the door of the District Four clinic. She could smell the faint foul wafts of the fumes of District Five. She worried about the Lepers' District. She stared at the pit wall and thought of the secret chamber within that held the Tunneler and his council. What could she do to help Father bring on the action needed? And how much time did she have to save Jacks? Could he even be saved? She didn't know whether he was moved by their encounter this morning and the story she told or if he would report her to the administration. She sighed as she entered the clinic.

"Doctor Heather!" the clerk called, rushing up to her. "I have such wonderful news. Please, come back and see Doctor Hendow at once."

Heather smiled, astonished to find this welcome from the surly clerk. She was walking toward the inner passage when, following a rush of footsteps behind her, the clinic door was thrust open, and she turned to see guards clogging the clinic entrance.

"You!" their chief called, pointing at Heather. "Come with us!"

Chapter Thirty-Two

The Warning

Heather's heart sank. *Jacks, what have you done?*

"I have patients to see," she said without moving.

"And Captain Vitton has no patience at all," the chief said in a snarl. The clerk and several nearby patients gasped at the hated name of *Vitton*. Vit Skinner, Mother had said. "Come along now, or we'll get rough with you and some of these other loafers."

Heather frowned and turned to the clerk. "Please express my regrets to Doctor Hendow and say I will be back by—" She turned to the chief. "Do you know when I may return to work?"

"That's for Captain Vitton to decide," he said, grabbing her arm. It was her injured arm, and she braced for the pain. But to her surprise, it didn't hurt too badly. With a backward glance at the clinic's waiting room, she was shoved outside.

In the street stood a tall lean rabbit, about Father's age or a bit younger. He wore the uniform of the Longtreader administration, with four golden bands around his upper right arm and the single birdwing epaulette on his left shoulder. Somehow his uniform looked neater than the others, as if the most careful attention possible was paid to its perfection. He brushed at the ash that settled on his pristine uniform. She recognized him from her ordeal with the Commandant. He was one of those officers who watched as she was beaten and struck off the roof. She particularly remembered his sickening sneer of delight, frozen in a frame of her memory, when she was plunging off the edge.

"Young Miss," he said without looking up, "I see you have reported for duty as a doctor in this clinic?" His voice was slippery and sweet, like he was speaking to a youngster who disgusted him but whom he wanted to deceive.

"I had," she said, then checked her defiant attitude. *That will only lead to more trouble.* "I have, sir. And I'm grateful for the assignment. I can do much good here."

"You think so?" he said, glancing up to squint at her. "Come along." He smiled at her, and she saw that his teeth had been filed to points. He began to walk away. Heather hurried to come alongside him. "I like to welcome some newcomers with my own introduction," he said, his lips pursed and his nose high in a disgusted expression. "I have not had the pleasure for some time and have missed it."

"I appreciate your attention," she said, though this was far from true, and they both knew it. He smiled a disingenuous smile, never losing that permanent expression of smug disgust and superiority.

"I'm sure," he answered in his prim tone. They walked on, and Heather could see he was leading her toward the great gate of the wall surrounding District Six.

"I am Captain Vitton," he said, "and everyone hates me."

"Surely not, sir," she said, trying to sound believable.

"They do, they do," he said, delicately taking off a glove and swatting the air in dismissal. "I assure you, even the set inside the wall do not like me, nor the things I do. But," he said, stopping to gaze into her eyes with his sickly stare, "they approve of the results."

"And what are the results?" she asked, though she was afraid to know.

"That peace is kept," he said flatly, "and our authority is maintained."

"I see."

The gate was opened, and they passed inside in silence, Captain Vitton strolling breezily along, Heather walking nervously at his side. They passed the place where she had been dragged and held and walked through a lane that led to an area of industry. Rabbits, most well-dressed with elegant red scarves or kerchiefs, were working at various jobs in a corridor. They walked past chandlers and coopers, barbers and an armory. He stopped at a smithy and then walked within, while the several smiths slowed in their work and bowed to him.

"Captain Vitton," said a large blacksmith, "we are very much honored to see you." The massive rabbit's voice quavered in the saying.

"Master Smith," Captain Vitton said, not looking up, "is it possible you spoke to me before I spoke to you?"

The blacksmith flinched at this rebuke. "I beg your pardon, Captain," he said, dropping to his knees. "It will never happen again. I will never speak until you desire it, sir!"

"You're doing it now," Captain Vitton said, nodding nonchalantly to his guards, two of whom came and led the perplexed blacksmith away. "Continue your work," Vitton said dismissively to the rest. The wide-eyed smiths continued, each hurrying to outwork the next. Vitton motioned for Heather to follow him up to the departed blacksmith's work area. There she saw his anvil, massive hammer, iron tongs, and a glowing rod fresh from the fire.

"Do you believe this work valuable?" he asked.

"I'm sure it is, sir," she answered. "Yes."

"We bring in the dregs from the outer districts to do the work we inwallers don't wish to do," he said, "but I suppose it must be done, and having outwallers here is the price we must pay. However, I am only concerned with my work." She felt a tremble beginning in her legs, but she fought to hide it. "This is where you ask me what my work is," he said flippantly.

"What is your work?" she asked, barely keeping the tremor out of her voice.

Captain Vitton's air, so recently nonchalant and disinterested, changed in a moment. He lashed out with lightning speed, taking Heather's arm and pinning it down on the anvil. He reached for the tongs and took up the blazing orange rod. She felt the heat as he brought the blazing hot metal close to her face. "My work is this!" he said, bringing the orange rod down on her arm.

Agony. Burning, searing anguish. "If you step out of line," he said in a frothing cackle, while the fur and flesh of her arm smoked. She could barely keep her jaw clenched against the excruciating pain, "I will burn you. I will burn everyone you love!" He laughed again, his wild eyes reflecting orange.

"Please stop!" she cried. He pressed harder.

"The Commandant may not acknowledge who you are publicly," he said, "but I have my own sources among Ambassador Longtreader's inner circle—or should I say, Uncle Garten? I know who you are, girl! It was I who picked your little brother for the…adventure he's going on. And I will see you sent on a similar journey. Nothing will stop me."

He released her at last and stepped back, breathing heavily, eyes still lit with depraved delight at his craven act. She fell to her knees, squinting against the searing pain.

"I hope young Jacks is enjoying his meals," Vitton said, resuming his expression of aloof disgust. "On Victory Day, he becomes one himself!" He spat at Heather, then twisted and walked languidly away, carefully smoothing his coat and brushing the ash off.

Heather was left on the ground, clutching at her wounded arm, while Captain Vitton and his guards disappeared around the corner.

Chapter Thirty-Three

LOST IN THE DARKNESS

Heather's arm was burned badly. She knew it would result in an awful scar. She sat on the ground, right there in the blacksmith's shop, and dug in her satchel. She carefully applied a dressing to her wound, then tried to bandage her arm. She looked around for help, but no one would dare step forward, even though Vitton had disappeared. At first she was angry about this cowardly inaction, but then she thought of the many horrors they must have witnessed and what risks to their families might be involved in seeming to help one whom Captain Vitton had so publicly threatened.

Heather used her teeth and finished the bandage as best she could. Then, while she put away her supplies, she contemplated her next move. Her heart was still racing when she stood and walked slowly out of the corridor and down the long street toward the center of District Six.

She noted again the neat rows of homes and the exactness of the town layout. Sweepers were everywhere, dealing with the accumulating ash. Reaching the large central square, she saw the preparations for Victory Day.

A huge banner, bearing the same symbol that stood out on the door of the Commandant's quarters, was being raised against the long wall of the tallest building. The thick banner was visible all over the square and far beyond. A silhouette of a black bird was perched over several rabbit skulls. In his hand, a sickle; upon his head, a crown. Heather, a sickening twist in her gut, hurried away.

Heather first went to the aqueducts, looking for her father, but she couldn't find him. So she ran toward home. As she neared the house, she saw a rabbit pacing back and forth out front. She ducked behind a wall, then peeked again. The rabbit was a doe and clearly agitated. But Heather couldn't make out her face, as her back was almost always toward her. Heather was shifting to get a better look when she saw Jacks emerge from the house, an ear of corn in his hand. She dived back behind the wall and peeked out again, listening intently.

"What are you doing here?" Jacks asked. "Shouldn't you be at your assigned duty?"

"Listen, Jacks," the doe said, and Heather recognized her voice. It was Harmony. "I'm looking for Heather. Is she home?"

"No," Jacks said, his face showing suspicion. "She's at her assignment, just like you should be. I think I'll have to report this."

"Listen, you little snotbag," Harmony said, "I know you get fed a bunch of special food for your mouth and a bunch of special dungrot for your tiny brain, but listen to me. I need to see Heather!"

"She's at the clinic," Jacks said, displaying a disgusted face that reminded Heather, sickly, of Captain Vitton. Her burn seemed to flare as she recalled his face. "And you should know that I'll be reporting you both to my teacher at tomorrow's Victory Day assembly."

"You do what you have to do, Jacks. But one day you're going to realize what they are," she said, motioning with her thumb toward the wall and the Sixth District within, "and you're going to remember who you are," she finished, poking him in the chest.

Heather had no idea how to feel about this. Harmony was saying so much of what she wanted to say, and that felt good. But she was also provoking Jacks to inform on them, and it seemed he needed very little prodding. Heather began to understand how Harmony's sister, Melody, had acted so rashly and met a bad end.

Jacks turned back into the house and slammed the door. Harmony spun and groaned, slapping her forehead.

"Hey!" Heather called, motioning to Harmony. "Over here."

Harmony hurried her way. "I've been looking for you!" Harmony whispered as they huddled behind the wall.

"I noticed," Heather answered. "Snotbag?" she asked. "What's wrong with you? He'll inform!"

"It doesn't matter," Harmony said. "You have to come with me," she said, pulling Heather's arm as she began to run off. It was Heather's injured arm, and her fresh burn throbbed at the tug.

"No!" Heather answered, breaking free of Harmony's grip. "You're going to explain this to me, now! I'm not going to go storm Morbin's fortress with you calling everyone snotbags and saying their brains are dungrot boxes!"

"I'm not proposing we do any such thing!" Harmony replied harshly. Both were managing to whisper as if shouting. "I'm not so rash as that!"

"Not rash? Not rash! You just unsettled a very delicate balance in my home," Heather said, pointing angrily back toward her house.

"You sound like my father. Listen, O great Scribe of the Cause," Harmony huffed, "we have bigger problems."

"That's my brother!"

"I know."

"Well, I don't want to lose him!"

"I didn't want to lose mine either!" Harmony said, taking Heather's hands and speaking more softly. "I'm on your side, Heather. I want to save Jacks. I want to save him and all the others too. Will you come with me?"

"Where, Harmony?"

"The Seventh District."

"I have to find my father, Harmony," Heather said, settling down a little. "Captain Vitton said they're taking Jacks tomorrow. Tomorrow, Harmony!"

"At the Victory Day celebration," Harmony said, nodding. "I know. That's why I want you to come with me. We have work to do."

"It isn't rash, is it, Harmony? I want to follow my father's way and do what's best. Not what's desperate."

"I understand, Heather," Harmony said, "but the two are quickly merging. I have to follow *my* father's way, and that's why I want you to come along with me."

"Who is your father?" Heather asked.

Harmony turned and walked a few paces away, but Heather caught the agonized expression on her face. "You said you lost him long ago," Heather said, placing her hand on Harmony's shoulder, "the other night at the meeting in the cave in District Seven. You said you lost him."

"I did lose him," Harmony said, turning back with tears in her eyes, "but he's not dead. The rest of my family *is* dead, but he was lost to the cause in a different way. When he became father of the community, he couldn't be mine anymore."

"Your father is the Tunneler and the Truth?" Heather asked, amazed.

"He is. I am his youngest, and last alive. Melody and I were twins. But he has had, and lost, seven sons. My brothers."

"My dear Harmony!" Heather said, folding her in an embrace. "I cannot imagine your grief. I am so sorry."

"Thank you, Heather. Now will you come with me?"

"I will."

The two rabbits walked swiftly through the lanes, carefully avoiding the streets and every avenue that had line of sight with the wall surrounding District Six. They made the edge of District Four and walked quickly across the ash-piled gap between Five and Four, entering the Lepers' District. Its vile odors met them as they came, and they slipped past rough shanties and into the dilapidated lanes. Heather followed Harmony as she dodged through a swirl of confusing paths, past nauseating neighborhoods and finally into a long, low tent that was caked in ash.

Inside, she saw a fire fixed and over it a pot, similar to the one she saw her first night there. Its noxious fumes filled the tent and spilled out through a large hole in the top. On benches in the corner sat several rabbits dressed in rags. Their fur mottled and sores plain, they sat still and nodded to Harmony. She pulled Heather toward a flap at the tent edge that covered the rock wall side. Harmony pulled at a long belt that wound several times around her waist, unwrapped it for several turns, then secured it again. She handed the long loose cord part to Heather.

"Don't let go," she said as she pulled back the flap to reveal a tunnel, different than the passage of the previous night. They ducked inside.

It was dark within, and Heather felt the panic rise again as she followed Harmony closely, holding on to the slender cord. It was completely dark, the ceiling was low, and Heather struck her head from time to time as Harmony turned suddenly right or left. Heather would carry on, then feel the tug of the cord, leading her to back up to follow Harmony's course through what soon seemed to be a labyrinth.

This wasn't the single tunnel to a single room that she had traversed the previous night. This was a series of complicated paths that no one who didn't know them well could possibly navigate. Heather wondered where Harmony could be leading her. They crawled on and on, finally getting to a place where a quick whisper reached Heather's ears. "You can stand." She stood slowly, reaching up with her free hand and finding the cave roof just above her ears.

They walked on and on, Heather growing weary with the long jaunt in the darkness. She was reaching the point where she would need to ask Harmony to stop a moment so she could rest. She had had very little rest the night before, and she felt overcome by the urgent events pressing her. Just before she spoke, she heard Harmony's voice say faintly, "Trust me."

Heather walked forward a few paces, and the cord she had held for the entire dark journey grew slack. Panicking, she pulled at the cord and, her heart racing, found the end of the rope in her hands.

She was all alone in the darkness, inside an impossible maze within an endless mountain of rock, with a limp cord that led to no one, and nowhere, in her hands.

Chapter Thirty-Four

A Window into Hope

When desperation rose inside Heather's heart and she felt the alarm within her growing, she heard a voice and saw a light.

"I'm sorry," Harmony said, coming into view with a lantern held aloft. "It took me longer to get this than I expected. Come on." She turned and led the way through the now lamp-lit passage, and Heather, mute and wide-eyed, followed.

Soon they reached a large flap, and Harmony paused before the door. "He's tired, Heather," she said. "But he wants to see you."

Heather didn't ask who. She knew. Harmony pulled back the flap, and Heather walked into a warm cave. It was sparsely furnished. A desk was covered with papers and recently extinguished candles. A fire flickered in the corner. There was a modest table and a bookshelf holding many well-worn volumes. A lute leaned against the bookshelf. A large canvas covered the wall on one side, and beneath it was a small bed, on which sat the Tunneler. He looked very old here, feeble in a way she hadn't realized in her first encounter at the council.

Heather turned to see where Harmony was, then noticed she was alone with the old rabbit. Harmony had never entered.

"Come in, Heather Longtreader," the Tunneler said. "I would rise, but I'm sorry to say that I am pitifully old and weak."

Heather moved toward the bed, noticing as she did the large map that featured across the canvas covering. She could make out a scheme of tunnels and then lines across parts of large open areas. Was that water?

She bowed to the Tunneler.

"Heather, I asked you here so I could consult you." He coughed, and she bent to take his arm and feel his back as he wheezed painfully.

"May I listen to your chest, sir?" she asked. Not waiting for an answer, she placed an ear against the old rabbit's chest. She listened to the ragged passage of air with a frown he couldn't see. "Deep breath, sir, if you please?"

"This is all I can manage," he said, his milk-white eyes open, though unseeing, "and I want to say what I must while I still have breath."

Heather was concerned. With breathing as bad as this, she knew he might not last another month. But she smiled at him. "Of course, Master Tunneler," she said, touching her eyes, ears, then mouth.

"Do you touch your ears, eyes, and mouth?" he asked.

"I do," she answered.

"Ah," he said, "you practice the very old ways. The path of Flint and Fay. It is well."

"I revere all our honored foreparents," she said, "including you."

"You have the scent of Fay about you, and I am told you have a light in your eyes as that of a seer. Do you dream, Heather?" he asked.

"Yes, sir."

"I dare say you do. And more than ordinary dreams, I'd guess. They are true, as they were for her."

"I am no Fay."

"For your Flint is gone," he said, his face formed in a sympathetic smile. "Quite. And for that I am sorry. For a blind old buck, I have some sight, but I do not see all. I am given to see what is needed, I hope, for this community. And it is about them that I must speak with you."

"I am your servant."

"But no one's slave," he said.

She nodded, said, "Yes, sir."

He stood then, slow and unsteady, and Heather helped him. He began to slowly walk around his bed, toward the rock wall where hung the edge of the canvas hooked to a peg. "They speak of you, Heather. Already they speak of you. The council. The community. You have moved them with your story. It spreads throughout the six districts, and even here in the seventh. They call you the Oracle of Akolan. They say you are a healer, that your hands hold miracles. They say you are the herald of our freedom. That freedom follows you like a silver trail tracks a falling star."

"I am only a simple doe, sir."

"Let us be honest with one another," he said, frowning at her.

She nodded. "Yes, sir."

"What do you want to see happen?"

"I want us to take in all the younglings destined for Morbin's table."

"And the ones Morbin takes to replace them?" the Tunneler asked. "For he must have his feast. It's in the old code of their cult. What of them?"

"We must save them all," she said, but now she was unsure.

"Perhaps we can," he said. "I'm an ordinary rabbit, with an extraordinary task. My honored predecessors, all the way back to the original Tunneler, all did the same thing. They all preserved the project and carried it forward. None ever initiated the final protocol. If we take in these younglings, then it sets us on an inevitable course to action."

"Isn't that good?" Heather asked, not knowing what the project actually was. "Isn't that what we want?"

"Many do, yes. I thought I would live out my years, finishing by handing over that heavy pickaxe to my successor and going to my grave with a good conscience. It is, if I may be honest, a terrifying prospect to be the one who launches it all."

"Launches what?"

"Only this," the Tunneler said, reaching weakly to unhook the peg holding the large canvas and letting it fall. Heather gasped.

The wall was a window, wide and high, showing a massive cavern deep inside the mountain. It was lit with sunbeams from holes high above and with torches all around. She saw rocky land split with a massive lake, into which flowed a river. This river also issued in a dammed stream on the other side. And there were ships, large ships, on the lake. Another was being built at the long dock.

Hundreds of rabbits were at work, some at smithies, others at archery, and all over the cavern a fantastic array of vocations was on display. She saw bucks training in a far corner and a council of others at table in the near distance. It was a humming hive of activity and life. She was astonished.

"We've been working for a long time here in the Seventh District," the Tunneler said, a tired smile forming on his wrinkled face, "for that day when we will quit this despicable pit and, like our honored ancestors, sail away to freedom."

Chapter Thirty-Five

The Edge of Doom

"It's staggering," was all Heather could say. She was speechless at the massive scale of the preparations and had no idea how to express her awe.

"We've made great gains since the first slaves dreamt of escape," the Tunneler said, coughing. "Finding the cavern and lake unlocked a new world of possibility. We have done our best with what we've been given."

"Can they get to the river below?" she asked, pointing at the ships with eyes wide.

"We have prepared for that for over fifty years," he said. "For defending them, we have had far longer to ponder." Heather strained to hear him, stepping ever closer to catch the wheezing words of the old rabbit. "The first Tunneler made only the council chamber to which you came last night. But we've had incredible mineralogical discoveries since then, discovered and made tools and resources of which we couldn't have dreamed. We've carried out schemes sketched out over more than a century. And in the last twenty years, we've made a series of dams that will, we think, when blown, make a swift escape that may give us a chance. It isn't perfected, of course, but the dedication of hundreds of brilliant rabbits has made it possible." He paused to catch his breath.

Heather's mind was beginning to take in the incredible scale of this undertaking and what pressure it meant for a single rabbit to stand at the center of it, directing all. "How have you managed to..." she began. "How could I ever consult with you, sir?" she said, reverently turning from the grand project seen through the great window to the bent, blind, humbly dressed rabbit before her. "You are a lord, sir. Of the greatest secret citadel in all Natalia."

"I am the Tunneler and the Truth," he said weakly, "and a dying old rabbit."

"I can't believe what I am seeing. This scheme, it is ready to carry out?" she asked.

"It will never be ready, Heather. That's the problem. Nothing ever is. But it's close enough to perhaps try. Many—thanks to you—are now willing to try. Still, for that rabbit who says 'Now is the time,' it's a grave and heavy weight." He seemed to bend lower still under the burden of those words. "We've known preparation for so long. And preparing, though hard, is nothing to the *going*. To the acting. To the carrying out of that moment when one says 'Go' and an undertaking of generations is set in motion."

"You are afraid?" Heather asked gently.

"I'm not afraid of dying," he said, his words coming in a dry, airy speech that alarmed Heather. "Not afraid of Morbin Blackhawk, or Garten Longtreader—your cursed uncle—or the Commandant, certainly, or the wicked Captain Vitton. I am afraid of failing when so many have hoped for this. I have become a father to this family of rabbits. If I fail, I fail not only all who live now but all those who died making this way. I fail all of our fathers and squander our inheritance. I become a failure as father."

"You are our father, sir. And, if you will allow your daughter to advise you," she said, "it's the first duty of a father to protect his children, especially the most vulnerable."

"Aye, it is too true. Your story of what's happening in the world outside has inspired our council. I have the support now to move forward. My most likely heir as Tunneler is against it and favors the slow evolution of our preparations over ages. He sees our work as an institution to be guarded more than a project to be realized."

"So you are eager to act?"

"I am," he wheezed, bending as another coughing fit gripped him. Heather was at his side, helping him balance as he recovered. "But my likely successor, the rabbit in my shadow, will halt all. So it's important that I stay alive."

"I see," she said. She was realizing now, with some embarrassment, that she had been called here not to consult about the scheme but to advise as a doctor. She touched her satchel and led him back to his bed, laying him down gently.

"It's rumored you are a healer of uncommon gifts," the Tunneler wheezed. "I would be deeply grateful were you to give me the gift of another few days."

"I will do my best," Heather said, pulling open her satchel and reaching for her best tonics. "Though it's an uncertain art, as any medic will tell you."

"My dream is not to live on and on, Heather," he said, breath ragged, "but only to die defending the ships as they go, like King Gerard on Golden Coast, standing side by side with all the brave old bucks of our community to trade our lives for their liberty."

"It's a noble dream," she said, tears in her eyes, "and you are a noble rabbit who will be remembered for centuries." She opened his mouth and poured in some of Emma's mixture. She had considered Aunt Jone's mix but wanted to be on surer footing with this crucial case. "Swallow that, my lord. And drink as much water as you can. And please, rest."

"My body cries out for rest," he said. Then he took a long drink from the cup she set to his mouth. "But my mind tells me there's work to do."

"The work will be there when you awaken," Heather said, smoothing the creases on his brow. "Until then, dream of that day when you'll stand with your pickaxe and hold back the enemy's attack." After a few minutes of her soothing words and kind caresses, the old rabbit fell asleep with a smile on his face.

She stood and again looked out the massive window, staring open-mouthed at the incredible project in motion below. The cave roof reached high, forming an oval cavern wherein the many activities were being carried out with military efficiency. The ships alone were astonishing.

She had never seen such large vessels and thought they must be like those of Whitson Mariner's days. She watched as a team of bucks a hundred strong across from the lake went about martial exercises in perfectly synced rhythm.

"He's asleep, then?" Harmony asked quietly from behind her. Heather turned to see the young doe standing side by side with another rabbit. He was older, small of stature, but his eyes were big and bright and kind.

Heather nodded.

"Can you save him?" Harmony asked, worry plain on her face.

"I don't know. I've given him the best I know to give him."

"They say you can heal even the worst cases," the other rabbit said. "I'm sorry," he added with a short bow, "I'm Edward."

"I'm pleased to meet you, sir," Heather said, nodding respectfully.

"Let's go to the council chamber," Edward said, leading the way out of the room. Heather followed, along with Harmony, who gave a last worried glance back at her father.

Heather followed Edward's lamp through the labyrinth until, after many winding turns, they entered the council chamber. There were four rabbits within, all wearing nervous expressions.

"What's the news, Stitcher?" a tall thin rabbit asked, hurrying up to Edward. So this was Stitcher. Mother had spoken so highly of him.

"He's still alive," Harmony said, "for now."

The four visibly relaxed. "Heather," Edward, who they were calling Stitcher, said, "this is Stretch. And those three are Wisp, Dote, and Gripple."

"I'm pleased to meet you," Heather said, nodding. She remembered their names from her first night in Akolan. They had been looking for her. She wished they had found her instead of the accursed Wrongtreaders and their Commandant.

They bowed in turn, eyes widening with some awe. "The honor is ours, lady," Stretch said. And the three in the background whispered to one another.

"What news from your side?" Harmony asked, cutting through the awkward quiet that threatened to settle in.

"It's bad," Stretch said. "We think Vit Skinner's informers have detected our increased activity because they're planning a memorable display. We learned today that they will take the younglings they already picked tomorrow at the Victory Day festival. In the square, in front of everyone, they'll take them." Heather lurched, her stomach dropping. "But that's not all. They're going to take *all* the younglings. Our buck inside says that Morbin's council is looking for a show of force across all their locations, in every slave camp and at First Warren. They will gather the crowds for the usual Victory Day assemblies, and they will take every youngling. They will slaughter them all."

Heather staggered back, and Harmony held on to the wall. Edward groaned and put his hand over this mouth.

"This intelligence, Stretch—?" Edward began.

"From the top, sir," Stretch answered. "There is no doubt."

"I have to get home!" Heather said. "My brother...he will be taken, killed. I have to bring him here."

"Garlen Canton, the likely heir to the office of Tunneler," Stretch said, "is passing word among the council and others that we are not to panic. He says the Tunneler is gravely ill and that he must help us through this time by urging calm and a commitment to the long-term strategy. He says we mustn't be hasty in this panic and undo the progress of generations simply for the sake of some children."

Harmony cursed. Heather wheeled on Stretch. "Did he say that?"

Stretch nodded. Dote spoke up. "I heard him myself, lady."

"Then he must be stopped," she said. "He is *no* leader."

"But he likely has the council's support, if the Tunneler passes away," Stretch said.

"I will speak to as many councilors as I can," Edward said. "Harmony, you go check on your father."

"I've got to go," Heather said, heading for the tunnel.

"Where?" Harmony asked.

"I'll try to find Father, then home," she said, knocking the flap aside and disappearing into the tunnel.

Heather hurried ahead, a new kind of panic pushing her forward. She noted, with passing curiosity, that her arm felt better than it had in a long time. Much better. Only the burn still hurt. The sprain seemed entirely healed. She emerged from the edge of the tunnel and into the Lepers' District tent.

She marked the foul boiling brew but hurried on, ignoring the rabbits clustered around. She ran through the streets of the L.D., not stopping to see if she was being watched. She ran for the aqueducts, hoping to see Father. She felt panic pulsing within her, intense worry about every single young rabbit in Akolan, and beyond. But she was in agony over Jacks.

That Jacks might be killed was horrible enough, but that he would become food for Morbin in his dark rites was abominable. Worse still, the poor young buck didn't even know who he was. He had no idea what criminal abuse had been visited upon him in the indoctrination he'd been subjected to. She felt ill but ran on.

Arriving at the outside aqueducts near the pit wall, she saw only the few workers she had seen earlier. No one knew where Father was. She was frantic, frustrated, and beginning to feel that the thin door of hope was closing and there was nothing she could do.

Angry over the lost time, she ran toward home.

Heather sped through the gap between Districts Five and Four, cut through several lanes, then hurried down the street where her family had made their home.

Bursting through the front door, she found Mother sitting on the floor, her face in her hands. Mother looked up and, seeing Heather, burst into fresh tears. "Oh no. I had hoped you had gotten away, Heather!"

"Mother," Heather said, hurrying to her side. "What is it? What's happened?"

"Jacks has informed on us," Mother said. "And they have him. They're keeping him there until the feast tomorrow…on Victory Day. They're taking them *all* on Victory Day."

"Mother, we have to get out of here!"

"Captain Vitton is searching for you and your father. He came here earlier. They ordered me to stay. Said they will keep a watch out on the house. There's nowhere to run, Heather."

Steps, urgent and hurrying, on the doorstep.

Loud pounding at the door. Heather stood and reached for Mother.

"Hurry, Mother. Around back!"

The front door burst open, and they turned. Stretch ran in, gasping.

"The Tunneler…" he said, breathing hard, his eyes wild with fear, "is dead."

Heather barely had time to register all that this meant, the certain doom that followed such news, when they heard more footsteps, louder and more urgent than before.

They all turned to see Captain Vitton, flanked by a party of guards, hurry through the door. He smiled sickly and pointed at Heather as his guards surrounded her and Mother. Others dragged Stretch through the door, and Heather heard awful screams in the street, which were suddenly silenced. Hopelessness fell on her heart like a smothering smoke.

"Now, Miss Longtreader," Vitton said, "the real burning will begin."

Chapter Thirty-Six

Emma's Rending

Emma emerged from her tent, worn out but satisfied with what they had accomplished so far on this mission. *So far.* With the aid of Mrs. Weaver and Lord Blackstar, she had rallied rabbitkind to the cause, including several reluctant citadels. She was hopeful. But the greatest test, with the most to gain and lose, lay ahead.

Kylen of Terralain.

Emma had been dreading this meeting. She and Kylen had a lot of bad blood in their history, even before she learned they were close cousins. He was the son of Prince Bleston, the Silver Prince, the ruler of the land of Terralain. And she was the daughter of King Jupiter the Great, Bleston's younger brother. Bleston was furious when their father chose Jupiter instead of him to succeed him as king, and he had left First Warren with a band of malcontents. They had found Terralain and fused the culture of that settlement with the bristling ambition of Bleston. Years later, Kylen was sent to unsettle things in the wider world and pave the way for his father's return. He had done this by betraying Smalls and nearly costing him his life.

Emma had never forgiven Kylen.

And she had heard that Kylen and the Terralains now blamed Picket for Bleston's death. The rumor had gotten back to Kylen, through Tameth Seer, their advisor, that Picket had betrayed Bleston.

Emma knew Picket was innocent, but Kylen had not been there and had only the word of his father's most trusted advisor.

She walked out into the moonlit night, following the path deeper into the Great Wood. She turned to be sure that no one was following her. This would be a secret meeting.

In a few minutes, she saw a white-handled dagger stuck in a tree, and she turned right. Following a seldom-used path, she came to a small clearing and saw a fire. Kylen sat by the fire on a stool. He looked haggard and unwell, and the part of Emma's heart that made her a healer felt compassion. But the princess side of Emma had less sympathy, and the young doe at Cloud Mountain who had a hundred times clashed with Kyle—as he was called then—had less still.

"Kyle," she said, walking into the firelight.

"Hello, Emma," he said, looking up at her with worried eyes. "Are you alone?"

"Yes. Are you?"

"I am alone. Only Tameth Seer knows I'm here."

Emma's heart lurched. That wasn't good, she knew. She had told no one.

"And only Lord Victor Blackstar knows I'm here," she said, though it wasn't true.

"Good," he said, and a long silence followed.

"Why did you want to meet?" she asked. "I got your message, and I'm here. What is it you want?"

"I want peace," Kylen said, getting to his feet slowly. "I want this war to be over."

"It'll be over when we defeat Morbin," she said.

He turned on her with a fierce expression. "That would be a lot easier if rabbitkind wasn't filled with traitors!"

"That's true," she said, trying to stay calm.

"Where's Picket?" he asked.

"He's carrying the war to the enemy, just like always."

"Don't play dumb, Emma," Kylen said, stepping toward her. "We both know he murdered my father. I can't believe you're standing by him. His whole family is made up of traitors!"

"You can't possibly believe that!" Emma said, snapping back. "Heather? You think Heather's a traitor? After the chance she gave you. I can't believe you would—"

"Where is Heather now?" he roared, interrupting her.

"She's at Morbin's palace—" Emma began, indignant to express how heroic Heather's action had been. But Kylen interrupted her.

"Exactly!" he cried. "You see, she works for Morbin in his lair, and Picket works for Morbin out in the field. It's a devious scheme!"

"Kylen," Emma began, feeling her heart beat faster and her face grow hot, "I don't know what's wrong with you, but you're not thinking clearly. Heather and Picket are the most loyal rabbits I have ever known. You need to get things straight!"

"You always were a scold, Emma. I know what happened. The eyewitness account of rabbits from both Terralain and Cloud Mountain confirm it."

"I was there!" she cried. "I was there! I saw your father betray us and try to seize me in order to trade me to Morbin for a small slice of bread from his table. I saw it happen! I saw him try to murder me, and I saw Lord Rake, the only father I've ever known, lose his life to save mine. I saw your father try to murder Picket, and I saw Picket defend himself, and, yes, that resulted in your father's death. I saw it all! Picket is a hero, and your father betrayed us!"

"Lies!" he shouted, his eyes wild and frenzied, and he lurched toward her. "I've been given the facts by many witnesses! Many reliable witnesses!"

"They are false, I assure you! Who? Who from Cloud Mountain accuses the Longtreaders?"

"Captain Pacer, for one!" he cried. "And others!"

"Pacer has betrayed us?" she asked. "I can't believe it."

"Believe it, Emma!" he said, pointing a quivering finger at her. "Your allies are...all lies." He gasped and stumbled back to his seat.

It was a blow to hear that Pacer, Lord Rake's trusted friend, had betrayed them. And she was furious at Kyle's baseless claims of treachery and accusations of her friends. But beneath her anger, she was beginning to see just how unwell Kylen was. He was more than wounded. He was ill.

"Kylen," she said, "you need help. You need medical care. I'm not sure you're getting what you need. Can I help you?"

He looked up at her in confusion, almost like a youngling looks to a parent in a panicked confusion. Then his features hardened again. "I could never accept help from you. You're a usurper. The throne is mine." With this, he fished inside his vest and pulled out the amulet on the end of the chain that hung around his neck. It was a large red diamond—the Whitson Stone. The Ruling Stone. The rightful bearer of this token was, by ancient rights, the ruler of all of Natalia.

The hot anger returned to her, and she clenched her teeth. She was indignant. "I wish you could take the throne! I don't even want it! I have *never* wanted it. I have only received this inheritance as the grimmest duty. I wanted to be a healer. I wanted to help sick rabbits like you be well. I wanted my little work to fit together with thousands of other little works to make a great mosaic of hope. I didn't want to be responsible for the whole thing! I never have!"

"Well, you don't have to," he said weakly. "You can lay it all down. Just bow your knee to me, and you'll be free."

For a brief moment she considered how much easier everything would be if she did. She thought of the weight of responsibility passing from her to him, and the thought was delicious. But she thought of Picket, of Heather, of Mrs. Weaver and Lord Blackstar. She thought of those who had died when Kyle betrayed them at Cloud Mountain and the soldiers left vulnerable by Bleston's betrayal at the battle of Rockback Valley.

"I cannot bow to you, Kylen," she said flatly, "because your throne would be built on lies. I will have to be what I am."

"And go to war against Morbin *and* me?" he asked hoarsely.

"If I have to. But just remember whose side that puts you on," she said.

Emma turned to leave and walked out of the glow of the firelight. Then she remembered, with some panic, that Tameth Seer knew of this meeting. She half-expected a bolt from the dark to take her down. She knew she must be in grave danger.

But she wasn't the only one.

Everything within her screamed out for her to run away as fast as she could, but she turned at the edge of the clearing. "Kylen," she said softly, "don't take the medicine they give you anymore. Pretend to, but don't swallow it." He scowled at her, and she hurried off into the darkness.

Emma passed by the tree with the white knife-hilt driven in. She pulled the blade free and hurried through the forest. She heard a rustling behind her and turned to see only shadows playing at the edges of the brush.

She walked faster, then burst into a run. The forest felt full of active shapes, and soon she heard whispers and muffled shouts. Then they were on her. Several large rabbits in black, with bright silver stars showing on their chests, grabbed her and held her against a tree.

Terralain soldiers.

Emma was gagged, and ropes were thrown around her head, shoulders, and legs to secure and pin her against the tree.

A cackling laughter echoed through the forest, as a bent shape emerged from the trees. *Tameth Seer.*

"The little sister of the little prince," he said in his high metallic shriek, "pretended heirs of all Natalia, both dead, along with their pathetic cause." She could answer nothing with the gag in her mouth, but she glared back with defiant eyes. "So brave, little one. But now your pretensions are ended. King Kylen will rule this land, and our alliance with Morbin will secure his place. You will be forgotten," he said, stepping close and peering into her eyes. His breath was foul, and the strange beads braided throughout his fur rattled in her ears. His wild eyes shone in the moonlight, and his deranged cackle distressed her deeply. He drew a long crooked knife from his side and raised it high so that it glinted in the moonlight. "It's time for you to die, Princess Emma!"

He brought the blade down, but a black form darted in front of Emma, blocking the blade arm and kicking the brittle old rabbit back.

Heyna!

The nearest Terralain soldier swiped at Heyna with his blade, but Cole appeared, blocking the sword strike and returning his own with deadly effect. Arrows swished through the air, dropping several soldiers as they tried to reach Emma and her friends. Jo dropped down from his perch atop a nearby tree, and nocking two more arrows, he scanned the path for more foes.

Heyna freed Emma and wrapped her in a quick embrace.

"Let's go!" Cole said, and they followed him back down the path.

Emma was glad to be alive and glad Heyna had somehow found out about her meeting. But she was certain she had made a grave error and set back the cause by her folly. How could they hope to unite rabbitkind and finish their mission with her in command?

Chapter Thirty-Seven

Descent into Darkness

Picket knew he had squandered his one chance to escape. They had almost done it, he and Weezie. They had almost gotten away. But the black-clad band had them again. With gags in their mouths and bags over their heads, they were being led far from Helmer's old homestead and the last link of support Picket had in all of First Warren.

They marched for half an hour. Then, after a series of indistinct whispered conversations, they began to descend. Not the slow descent of the gentle fall of a field but the sudden drop of a cavern. Soon there were steps, and they plunged farther still, down and down the winding drop, always gripped by strong hands. Picket listened carefully and imagined what his surroundings looked like. He began to contemplate trying to wrestle free, possibly sending one of his captors plunging over a precipice. But he couldn't be sure he wouldn't knock Weezie in as well, and he could see no way now to escape. He would have to wait to see what fate awaited them in the deeps.

As if reading his mind, one of his captors whispered, "There's no reason for escape here, lad. Just hold on." The voice was hard to make out through the bag covering his head, but the use of the term "lad" sent a pang through his heart. He nodded.

They descended farther still. Then a door of some kind opened, and they walked forward, taking several turns so that he grew dizzy with all the twists.

"Wait here," the same captor said, ushering them through a thin doorway Picket had to squeeze into, then onto a bench to sit. "And don't try anything, lad."

The bag over his head was raised, and his gag was cut loose. His hands remained bound, but he watched in the dim light as Weezie was also freed of her bag and gag. She worked her mouth, stretching her jaws. Picket imitated her and gained some relief. The guard whose white fur Picket saw beneath his black mask left a lantern within and backed out, his comrade locking the door after him.

They were in a small cell. The dirt floor met walls of brick, thick by the look of them. To dig free would take days, or weeks. And they would have to get their hands free.

"Mother won't survive this," Weezie said, shaking her head. "It will ruin her."

"Helmer will..." Picket began, but he realized he didn't have any answers, and he didn't feel like politely lying about their chances. "I'm sorry," he said at last.

They sat in silence then, the weight of this failure settling over Picket in a familiar invitation to despair. Resentments rose, injustices clamored for a spot in his heart. He had so often been in positions where the most intense bitterness felt justified, and here he was again. The catalog of unfair calamities paraded through his mind, beginning and ending with his own family's misfortunes. They were all gone. Father and Mother, little Jacks. He had promised his baby brother protection, that he would never let him down. But he was taken, and Picket had no idea if he was well or ill, alive or dead.

And then there was Heather, the last connection to his past, his dearest friend and beloved sister. She was gone too. Likely dead. *How did this happen to her?* He fought against the hopeless tale of a wasted life and a meaningless death. But Heather didn't die—if indeed she was dead—for nothing. She believed in the cause. She was its prolific, prophetic herald. Heather had traded her liberty for the hope of the Mended Wood. He would do the same. He would die, if dying was his duty, determined to do all he could for the cause.

"If we can get our hands free," he said, "we can tunnel out of here."

Weezie laughed. "You are some kind of crazy, Picket."

"It's not impossible," he replied. "Our ancestors tunneled massive warrens."

"You think so?" she asked with a mischievous smile.

"What?" he asked, frustrated at her coyness.

"Don't you see, Picket?" she asked, pointing her chin all around. "We're in one of those warrens. We're in the depths beneath First Warren. We're in the *real* First Warren. This is the place King Whitson built and King Lander ruled.

This little prison area likely held such celebrated traitors as Baltrane and Gamson."

Picket glanced around as the reality dawned on him. "Of course! How could I not have realized?"

"Bucks are usually pretty slow-witted," Weezie said with an intense expression of sympathy. "It's not my opinion. I read it in a thick book by a very learned scholar."

"Oh, the book was thick?" Picket said, skeptical.

"This book was as thick as your skull, Picket," she said, nodding seriously, "so, pretty hard to argue against."

"Who am I to argue against such a thick book?" he said, cracking a smile.

"If anyone did, then the scholar would simply strike them with the book, ending the argument."

"You did mention it was pretty thick."

"Thank you for reminding me," she said, sniffing self-importantly. "It was a crucial detail."

Picket couldn't keep from smiling wide now, and Weezie laughed hard. How had she made him laugh in this dark, forsaken place? She was, he thought, very special. They sat in silence a little while, their laughter subsiding and the heaviness returning.

"Who runs this underground now?" Picket asked.

"Good question," Weezie said. "Seems a perfect place for Daggler's Black Band to operate out of. Like I told you, Picket. They drag away suspects and insurrectionists, and no one ever sees them again. It's happened a thousand times. They warned Mother that they were watching her and, if anything happened, her only surviving daughter would be gone."

Picket winced at this, as a stab of guilt pierced him. "So when we came," he said, "the explosions were blamed on the resistance. They took the younglings and promised worse. Then Master Helmer and I showed up at your house, and now they've taken you."

"Daggler is our Prince Winslow's right-hand assassin," she explained, "and the terror of the resistance. They would have been on high alert after the explosions. So..."

Picket didn't need her to go on.

"They'll kill me," she said. "But you—Picket, they'll want answers from you."

Picket nodded.

The bolt on the door shifted with a clang, and the door swung open. Three guards entered. Picket launched at them, lashing out with desperate kicks. They subdued him quickly.

"Don't hurt him!" Weezie cried. "He was just visiting our farm. It's me you want to punish! Leave him alone, will you?"

"Quiet now," one of the band said, softly and with surprising kindness. But Weezie went on as they dragged Picket to his feet.

"Let him go. It's me you swore to murder. I'll tell Daggler anything he needs to hear. This rabbit isn't in the resistance."

"Quiet now," the rabbit said again. "You can speak in a few minutes."

The Black Band marched them down a dim hallway, past several similar cells, which all seemed to be empty. Then they passed into another part of the warren. There was more light here and less of the dank disused coldness of the cells. Picket looked at Weezie. She wore a determined, defiant expression. Her blood was still hot with her efforts to save him. *Brave Weezie.*

Picket was lost in dark thoughts, trying to find the courage to sustain him through the harrowing ordeal ahead. Then, softly at first, he thought he heard music. He shook his head. But it persisted and grew louder, so that his mind, which had initially dismissed it as impossible, now had to recognize that, in fact, music was being played nearby. The lieutenant governor, this Daggler, must like a lively tune to drown out the screams of his victims.

But the music was so happy, so infectiously wonderful, that he couldn't see how it could fit in the den of a torturer. Picket glanced at Weezie. She wore the same look of confusion. They exchanged looks, smiled warily at one another, hunching their shoulders.

They came to large double doors and pushed through.

Inside, there was a large public house like you might see at any of the free citadels. It was full of happy rabbits, some dancing, some singing around a set of energetic musicians. Others sat and watched, but all seemed to be smiling.

Their bonds were cut loose. A tall rabbit clad in green came forward and, with arms open wide and a bright smile, said, "Welcome, to the Citadel of Dreams!"

Chapter Thirty-Eight

The Citadel of Dreams

Picket was confused. He'd been preparing for suffering, but these rabbits were welcoming them with open arms. He glanced at Weezie and saw she was caught between a frown and a smile, puzzling out this odd turn.

"Come have a drink," the green-clad leader said, leading them to a table already set with glasses. "Sit down and relax! You're among friends here."

"I don't understand," Weezie said, standing behind the offered chair.

"You will soon," the leader answered, motioning for them to sit. Picket did, though he remained on guard against a sudden attack. Weezie followed, slowly lowering into her chair. Maybe this was how Daggler prepared his victims.

"Isn't the Citadel of Dreams something Fay wrote of in her book?" Picket asked.

"Aye," said the leader. "It's in the Lost Book."

"And why do you, whom I assume are Lieutenant Governor Daggler, take this name?" When Picket said

Daggler, everyone at the table spat, and the leader's face twisted in revulsion.

"You are welcome here, son," he said, suddenly serious. The music had stopped. "And you can be forgiven, since I haven't given you my name yet. But never call me that again. Any rabbit here would trade his life to end that villain. For my part, I am under a vow to destroy him for the crimes he has committed against our kind, and against my own family."

"I understand," Picket said, "and I beg your pardon. I only assumed it, since we've been captured and kept in prison."

"All necessary precautions, my lad!" he said, his smile returning. "We must be careful how we bring our guests into this oasis."

"If you aren't…him, then what should we call you?" Weezie asked.

"Call me Captain Moonlight," he answered, grinning wide. He was a tall ruddy rabbit, strong and jolly. His eyes glittered in the lamplight.

"And what is this place, Captain?" Picket asked. "What is the Citadel of Dreams?"

"It is a haven," Moonlight answered, "a resting place for those who oppose the tyrants."

Picket glanced around. There were fewer than fifty rabbits within. "Is this all the resistance there is?"

A little of the spark left Captain Moonlight's eyes. He looked down, sipped his drink, then looked up again. "We have taken heavy losses. We are far fewer now than we were when we started. It's been a long, hard war. But we're always happy to add two more."

"I'm in," Weezie said eagerly.

"Wait," Picket said, holding up a hand. "Wait, Weezie. We know nothing of these rabbits. Begging your pardon, *Captain Moonlight*," he said, pronouncing their host's name with some skepticism, "but this could be nothing but the waiting room to Daggler's dungeon." They all spit again, and Weezie joined in. "I'm as eager as any to overthrow these tyrants, all the way up to Morbin Blackhawk himself. But I've been fighting this war for some time, and our side can't afford to trust just anyone."

"We don't have much reason to trust either of you, either," Moonlight said. "You've been fighting this war, you say? Where? I know every resistance fighter from the dam to the far gate. I've never seen you till today. Weezie, we know about. We knew of her sister and father, bless them. We know her mother, though we've left her alone, as she asked. But who are you?"

Picket smirked. *They'll love to hear I'm a Longtreader, I'm sure. Or rather they'll love to hear that I'm Picket Packslayer himself.* "I'm General Sunshine," he said, smirking.

"There's no reason to mistrust them," Weezie said. "If they worked for Morbin's puppets, then they'd have no reason for this." She pointed all around the friendly inn.

"Sorry, Weezie," Picket said, "they have every reason to lull us into letting our guard down. They want information on what happened with the disruptions yesterday. They want to root out the offenders and crush the resistance. They've been watching your family for a long time. We...I mean, *I*—suddenly show up, and now they want to get answers. So they put on this play of being friendly so they can lure us into giving away secrets."

Weezie looked from Picket to Captain Moonlight, her eyes narrowing. "Good point."

Captain Moonlight laughed; then his expression grew serious. "It's sad that the world is so deformed that we, on the same side, can't trust one another. I'm grieved at your lack of faith."

"Hey, we didn't attack and capture you," Picket said.

"Good point," the captain answered. "How can I prove my sincerity to you? How can we prove that we are really your allies and friends—that is, if you truly are opposed to Morbin?"

"You can start by letting Weezie see her mother," Picket said. "If you know her situation, as you claim, then you'll know what her disappearance will do to her mother."

"That's true," Captain Moonlight said. "We had planned to grab her mother and the other one as well, but they never came into the open."

"You can go in the house, can't you?" Weezie asked, increasingly distressed. "Or are you under a vow not to enter a house and put bags over grieving widows' heads?"

"They watch the house," Captain Moonlight said, frowning. "That's why we took you on your walk. It was a way to rescue you from being snagged by Daggler." They all spit.

"So they're in danger?" Picket asked.

"Of course they are, " the captain responded. "We all are."

"Then why are we here?" Picket asked. "Why bring us here?"

"This is what we do, stranger!" he answered, slamming his hand on the table. He pointed all around the room. "We snatch rabbits from their ordinary lives of grim submission and bring them here. We take them back in time!"

"Back in time?" Weezie asked.

"Shall I tell you my story?" he asked.

"Please," Weezie said.

Captain Moonlight bowed, then began. "Before the old king fell, my father had an inn near the square. We had happy families in there every evening, and the public house was a center of our common life. Of course, it was a happy place in a happy time. There was peace, and the Great Wood was open to travelers from Nick Hollow all the way to Kingston. We had rabbits from all over stay at our inn, and our common room was a hub for music, art, storytelling, and games. We had regulars who supped with us each night, and my family ran it. My old father..." He looked away and wiped at his eyes. "My parents ran it, and I worked there growing up. Then I left to join the army, and, I'm very sorry to say, was away when the end came. By the time I had returned, the war was over. Garten Longtreader's scheme was so perfect that we never even had a chance to fight. We had to retreat. The secret citadels were formed, and I came here in the early days when it was possible to come and go.

"I was a soldier, and I helped organize the resistance here. In time, they closed all the gates. And Winslow's bucks blew up much of the old First Warren, the deep down-belows. But I knew my way around here. I found a section that had partially survived. I reclaimed a portion and rebuilt it. We tried for years to tunnel out, but that enterprise failed. Eventually, after heavy losses, we had to abandon it. We carried on clandestine raids and ran anti-propaganda broadsheets for years. But we found that, more and more, it was hard to convince others to join the cause. In time, many didn't remember, or even want to remember, how free we had once been. They simply adjusted to the new order."

"So you hatched a plan to remind them?" Picket asked.

"I did. We shifted our focus. I remembered, with deep fondness, how it felt to be in our old place in its day. The laughter, the music, and the families all together. Regulars mixed in with travelers, from younglings to the oldest around. It was humming with life. So, to help recapture the imagination of the community, and to honor my own family legacy, I created the Citadel of Dreams. We snatch rabbits, yes. We take them from their lives of bleak indignities, and we bring them to an inn of life and light. We bring them here to remind them of what we had, and what we might have again."

"You help them know why it's a good thing to resist," Weezie said.

"That's our aim, friends." Captain Moonlight smiled at them again and had opened his mouth to carry on when the door opened. The black-masked rabbit, the one who had spoken kindly to Picket earlier, hurried in. He nodded to them, then whispered in the captain's ear.

Captain Moonlight's eyes widened, and he stood up. "The enemy is moving on the farm," he said. "Daggler's on his way."

Picket shot up. "We have to help them. It's vital that my friend isn't taken."

"We'll send a team," Captain Moonlight said, "but we have a way of operating. We can't add anyone to our—"

Picket didn't let him finish. "Listen, you have more to worry about than Daggler." He spit, along with the others. "My friend is in that house, and he won't be as easy to take as we were."

"You weren't exactly easy, lad," the black-masked guard said, rubbing his shoulder.

"Handling me is like dealing with a ladybug compared to him," Picket said. "Listen, Captain," he went on, looking into his host's eyes. "That rabbit with Airen, he's her brother. Helmer's his name."

"Captain Helmer?" Moonlight asked, surprise in his eyes. "The old hero?"

"Yes. He's a leader in the resistance outside First Warren. That's where we're from. The explosions were a distraction to get us in. We're sick over the reprisals, but we needed to get in because we have a mission here. We need to get him and bring him here."

"And my mother," Weezie said.

"Yes. And Airen, too," Picket added.

Captain Moonlight looked at Picket long and hard, as if measuring him. After a long moment, he nodded. "We'll send our best squad."

Picket frowned.

"Okay, I'll lead the team myself," Moonlight said.

"Get me my sword," Picket barked at a nearby buck. "I'm going with you."

The buck glanced at his captain, who nodded, frowning. "You ever been in a real fight?" Captain Moonlight asked.

"One or two," Picket answered.

"What's your name, lad?" Moonlight asked.

"Picket Longtreader."

Captain Moonlight just stared, then shook his head. "Of course it is."

"I'm coming too," Weezie said. "Bring my bow and a fresh quiver, if you've got one handy."

Captain Moonlight shrugged. "Anyone else want to come?" he called to the room. He pointed to a one-legged fiddler in the band. "Want to come, Stompy? How about we bring Blind Watson too?" he asked. Another of the band members, an old grey rabbit with milky eyes, raised his head.

"I'll lead the way, Cap," he said. The band, and everyone around, laughed.

"Give us a jig, bucks," Captain Moonlight said, still shaking his head. "We're going snatching!"

Picket received his sword belt and buckled it on.

Chapter Thirty-Nine

Left and Lost

After a winding jog through the shadowy passages of the warren, the band emerged into sunlight. Picket felt the stiff wind hit his face and turned to see the cleverly concealed opening covered again with a tangled gate of thorns and limbs.

"Whit," Captain Moonlight called, speaking to the white rabbit whose black mask was now matched by all the others, "take the north trail and bring your team to the ridge. Wait for my signal." They were all armed with black bows and quivers slung at their sides. Most also wore swords.

"Aye," Whit said, and, nodding to his team, he scampered off. They followed him, and so the group was split. Picket followed Moonlight into a thicket, picking his way through a dense tract of trees and brush. Weezie stuck close by Picket, twisting as she went to preserve her bow and the full quiver she had been given. Three more bucks came behind her.

In a few minutes they emerged from the thicket and darted along a well-worn path. Picket flashed a questioning glance at Weezie. She understood that he was asking, *Is this the right way?* She nodded.

"Captain," Picket whispered, hurrying up beside the leader. "What's our plan?"

"We do this only a few ways. So our team knows the protocols. If you stick close to me, you won't be in the way."

"We want to help."

"Is she any good with that bow?" he asked, nodding back at Weezie.

"Hold on," Picket replied, then slowed and moved beside Weezie. "Hey, when you shot at Helmer and me and the arrow went right between us, what were you aiming at?"

"Your head," she said. He nodded and jogged back up. The leader raised his eyebrows with curiosity.

"She's not that great," Picket said. Then to himself he muttered, "Thankfully."

"Stay close," Moonlight said. "We'll approach the house from the south, and hopefully we can extricate them before Daggler arrives. We can deal with his advance team, but when he comes, it'll be too late."

"Have you ever faced him?" Picket asked.

"Just once," the leader said, a grimace twisting his face. "He drove me back, and I was lucky to escape alive. He's the best fighter I've ever seen. More than a match for me. And he's the cleverest tactician, too. Always two steps ahead of me."

"Maybe you'll pip him this time," Picket said, then froze when they heard a rustling ahead. Wordlessly, the team dispersed into the thicket on either side of the path. Picket dived in beside Weezie, who recovered quickly to nock an arrow and peer into the trail. She relaxed.

"It's Whit," she said. The white-furred rabbit, his face still covered in the black mask, hurried toward them.

Captain Moonlight emerged as well, brushing his clothes. "What is it, Whit?"

"The advance team has already taken them," he said, "though they took heavy losses from the look of the house." Captain Moonlight glanced at Picket, who nodded.

"Where are they now?" Picket asked.

"My team is tracking them," Whit said, his voice hard to understand beneath the mask. "They're meeting Daggler at the river."

"Let's go!" Captain Moonlight said. "We've got to get there first, or it's over for them."

They ran at full speed now, tearing through the trees in a rush. Weezie hurried past Picket, who didn't know the area, and ran alongside Moonlight. They came to a thin path and sped down it for a few minutes before breaking into the brush again. Weezie surged ahead, redirecting the course through a brittle patch of dying trees. Their feet snapped through dry sticks as they passed through the patch and onto another path. Moonlight smiled at Weezie, and they hurried on. Picket worked hard to keep up, tracking the shifting course with keen concentration.

Finally, they slowed and then stopped at the edge of an orchard. "They have to come this way," Moonlight whispered, breathing heavy. He motioned for them all to surround the path and get well-hidden. The band acted fast, and Picket crouched inside a thorny tangle of brush. In seconds, they heard footsteps and a labored scraping sound. Picket bent back a thin limb to glimpse the bending curve of the path.

They were coming.

He laid an eager hand on the hilt of his sword and watched. They came, fifteen soldiers, alert and well-armed. Two held Airen by her arms, and two dragged a body in a long black sack. Picket's heart sank, and his eyes went wide. Then an anger started inside him that swelled like an unstoppable wildfire till it was all he could do to wait for Captain Moonlight's signal to attack. It came soon enough.

They leapt at his word, flashing out with death-dealing strokes. Picket's sword found the first soldier, who was exposed badly as he blocked an overhead strike from Captain Moonlight. They moved on quickly, this time picking different targets and bringing their opponents down with agile force. In a moment, Airen was free, and Whit was pulling her into the forest. Weezie followed them, sending her speeding arrows into the thick of the enemy as she covered her mother's escape. After a few well-aimed shots, she hurried back to help with her mother. Picket saw them go with great relief.

Then he saw he was in trouble. He twisted to meet the savage swipe of an opponent with his blocking stroke. He brought his blade around quickly to finish the frenzied attacker just ahead of the rabbit's certain death stroke.

Picket's heart was racing. He lunged for the bag and tore it open. Helmer lay motionless on the ground. While Captain Moonlight and another of his band fought back the last soldiers, the rest of Whit's company crashed in, sending their enemies running for the woods. Captain Moonlight, now free to assess the situation, ran ahead and gazed down the path.

"We have to go," he said calmly as he trotted back. "Daggler's band of fifty is nearly here." They all spat.

"He needs help," Picket said, checking Helmer over. "He's been hit in the head again and again."

"If his skull's as thick as they say," Captain Moonlight said, signaling for another buck to come and help, "then he'll recover." The three of them hoisted Helmer together and hurried back the way they had come.

They were going too slow. They heard the sound of Daggler's band finding the site of the rescue. They heard his furious cry and urgent orders. Picket glanced at Moonlight, who shook his head. They both knew they couldn't get away while carrying Helmer. Captain Moonlight glanced at Picket, then Helmer, and then at his few fellows. He frowned.

Hearing the pursuit, he dropped Helmer and hurried ahead.

Picket's eyes went wide as he was left alone with Helmer, unable to drag him with any haste.

"Hold!" someone shouted from behind. He spun to see the massive form of Daggler himself. He leapt into view, followed by a cadre of lethal warriors. "If you move, you and your friend die."

Chapter Forty

Old Enmities

Picket glanced around. No escape. His master was coming to. Helmer felt his head and squinted up through a badly swollen eye.

"Steady," Picket said as Helmer swiveled up on his elbows.

"Who are you?" Daggler asked, stepping forward with an inquisitive expression.

"I'm General Sunshine, and this is Private Misgivings," Picket said, smirking.

"I know you," Daggler said, ignoring Picket's remark. "You're *Helmer*. We were in the same unit in training."

"Dag?" Helmer asked, getting slowly to his feet.

"The same," Daggler said, smiling proudly. "My, how you've aged, Helmer. Where have you been hiding all these years?"

Helmer felt around his head, wincing as he probed for the sources of his various pains. Picket held his arm to steady him. "You're leading a unit?" Helmer asked.

"I'm leading the entire army," Daggler said, tilting his chin upward. "I've come a long way since the days we knew one another. I have risen, like a bird in flight."

"I thought you couldn't get any lower than being discharged for torturing a fresh recruit," Helmer said, shaking off Picket's assistance. Picket saw that Helmer was steadily resuming his usual vigor. "But I see you've descended lower still. You have a part in this treachery? I'm not surprised."

Daggler's face bent in a disgusted frown, though his eyes still held their haughty aspect. He nodded to the two massive guards standing nearest Picket and Helmer. The two grinned and stepped forward. Picket lifted his hands, "Wait," he said, but he was shoved aside and pinned by three more of Daggler's rabbits. He watched as the two glanced back at their chief, then turned on Helmer. Helmer stood still, his feet shoulder width apart, his arms loose at his side. The first attacker lurched forward.

It was a feint, and Helmer didn't react but blocked the thundering punch from the second attacker, turning it aside and rising to kick him in the face. The burly rabbit twisted and fell, shaking his head and trying to regain his footing. Picket saw Daggler roll his eyes. The first attacker came on now, angry to see this smaller, far-older rabbit best his fellow so quickly. He came straight forward, extending his arms out wide to seize Helmer by his middle. But Helmer rose again and sent a straight, hard kick to his stomach. As the stunned rabbit bent, gasping from the blow, Helmer brought his elbow down hard on his head. The rabbit attacker crumpled as Helmer resumed his calm stance, glancing around for who was next. Picket smiled.

There were far too many in Daggler's company to be bested by Helmer, but it still made Picket's heart swell to see his master answer this initial assault with such a decisive reply.

"I see you haven't changed much," Daggler said, disappointment dripping from his words. "But I believe I can change your proud look." Picket saw that Helmer's bearing showed only the confidence of a warrior ready to act, and not one of pride. Daggler, however, wore the disdainful expression of an entitled brat whose plans for humiliating another child had been spoiled. Daggler drew his sword and advanced.

"You coward!" Picket called, trying unsuccessfully to shake loose. "You come at an unarmed foe with a blade? Is there no honor in this army?" he asked, appealing to the surrounding crowd. The grip on him loosened a moment, then quickly grew harder as the rabbits who pinned him bore down with their weight, driving knees into his back and head.

"Your young colleague is a mouthy brat, to be sure," Daggler said. "I don't think I shall attack you, Helmer, but this young buck." He turned toward Picket and stepped forward.

"No, Dag," Helmer said, raising his hands. "Take me, please. I'm done showing off," he said, falling to his knees and folding his hands behind his neck. "Please."

Daggler stopped and swung on Helmer. He extended his sword point to touch his neck. He smiled, and his eyes widened with excitement. "This is an unexpected pleasure. To kill you, who at one time seemed to surpass me, will give me no small delight. But first I will kill your student," he said, glancing over at Picket. "It will be good to report to the Preylords that I have found out and shut down the source of these disturbances. And when we gather on Victory Day and they swoop in to slay all the younglings, you will be blamed. And the futile resistance will be blamed. The wretches will turn on each other, and Captain Moonlight, their imbecilic icon, will be handed over to me."

"Are you truly happy to know our enemies will kill all the younglings?" Helmer asked, rage barely contained beneath his thin facade of calm.

"I'm not troubled by their deaths. I have executed so many myself," Daggler said, "including your young niece, Layra." He laughed at the expression of anger that played over Helmer's face. Picket felt sickened to see the glee on Daggler's face, and he understood why free rabbits spit when they heard his name.

"Your kingdom will fail," Helmer growled. "And whether or not I'm there to see it, you will be crushed in the rubble of its fantastic fall."

Daggler laughed. "Been reading poetry, Helmer? You need better bedtime stories. You have lost, and you will lose. And everyone you love will die."

Helmer nodded and said, "I give you permission to kill me, soldier." He closed his eyes and opened his arms wide.

"You don't have to give me permission!" Daggler barked, his face twisting in sudden anger. "I'm in charge here!" He stepped forward, lunging at Helmer's chest with his sword.

Picket cried out. Helmer's heart was inches from the steel point of Daggler's blade.

At the last possible moment, Helmer's eyes flashed open, and he twisted quickly. Daggler's jab sent him spilling forward, where Helmer took him in a constricting grip. Helmer's legs were pinning Daggler's, and his one hand held Daggler's blade to the cruel chief's throat. The other hand pinned both of Daggler's wrists behind. Picket's cries of protest had been barely uttered when Helmer reversed the situation entirely.

"Let him go, or this fiend dies," Helmer said, motioning toward the three rabbits who bore down on Picket. They looked at one another and complied, backing up slowly. One made as if to grab at Picket, and Helmer brought the pommel of Daggler's blade down on their chief's throat, sending him into throes of breathless gagging agonies. They stepped back.

Picket drew his sword and stepped to Helmer's side. There were still close to fifty of them, and some of them were subtly moving to surround Helmer. "You there," Helmer said, arresting the creeping progress of some. "Move one more step, and I cut him down."

"To the river," Picket said, motioning with his sword.

Helmer nodded. "When you get to the other side of the river," he said, "we'll let this creature go."

The soldiers were unsure of what to do. It was clear they were divided. "You'll just kill him and run away," an officer, trying to take charge, said. He stepped forward.

"Listen," Helmer said. "We were as good as dead a minute ago. This soulless wretch just informed me that he murdered my niece. He, a full-grown buck, killed a doe child. I have nothing to lose. I will kill him."

"That's what I mean," the officer said. "We can't trust you."

"I understand," Helmer said. "Let this buck go, and you can have me." He motioned to Picket.

Picket scowled. "Master, I won't leave you," he began. "I won't—"

"You are bound to obey me by our vows, Picket," Helmer said, pushing Daggler to the ground. The chief was recovering his breath, so Helmer drove him down and pinned him to the earth, bringing the blade point down on his back. "Please go, and fulfill our mission. Do it not only for duty but for love. Take care of my family. They're your family now. I would do it for you," he finished.

Picket's mind raced and his heart beat faster. Helmer was right. He would want his master to do the same if the situation were reversed. He nodded.

"So the young buck goes free, and we keep you?" the officer asked. He glanced back at some of the other officers, then back at his prone chief and the wild-eyed rabbit ready to drive a sword through him. "I agree," he said. The soldiers began to slowly move back toward the river.

"Go, son," Helmer said. "Now."

Picket looked at Helmer for a moment, and his expression said all he wasn't able to with words. Helmer nodded.

Picket sprinted away, heading for the thickest part of the forest. Just before he leapt into a dense thicket, he looked back to see an arrow from a keen archer loosed. Picket's backward glance of a moment was stuck in slow motion. The arrow arcing toward his master. Helmer looking up as the arrow caught him, spinning him down with an agonized cry.

Picket fled.

Helmer had fallen.

Chapter Forty-One

Run-In

Picket's heart felt pierced by arrows unseen by any eye. He had seen Helmer fall, seen the angry band surge ahead and Daggler begin to rise. It was too awful to contemplate, but he could see little else. As he sped ahead, his eyes spilled blinding tears that he wiped away to clear his view. But in his mind's eye, he saw Helmer fall again and again.

Picket inhaled and tried to focus on the task at hand. He had to honor his master's last wishes, had to be sure that Airen and Weezie were okay. He tried to blot out every other emotion, all thoughts that distracted him from his desperate flight.

A barrage of strangled curses and breathless barked orders filled the air behind him. Daggler was after him. A hail of arrows followed, most landing just behind him and filling the surrounding woods. One arrow zipped by his ear and sank into a tree just ahead as he dodged past.

He considered scaling a tree and trying to hide aloft, but he felt he was better off on the move, using his gifts for calculation to his advantage. He ran on, desperate now, with the sound of soldiers crashing into the forest behind him. Ducking under low limbs and dodging through thickets, he hurried back in the direction from which they had come. His mind was mapping a route he believed best to evade his hunters but would also twist back toward the secret entrance to the warrens below.

Despair soon threatened to overwhelm him. Failure, fierce and sudden, loomed everywhere he looked. Backward glances and careful listening told him his plan couldn't work. He determined that they were gaining on him and flanking his position as they came. These were no fools. They were an elite band of killers in familiar territory, and he was incapable of eluding them.

But he had to press on. He ran more directly back toward the disguised entrance they had emerged from not long ago, though he doubted he could make it in time.

Through trees and brush, he saw the telltale black uniforms everywhere he looked now except dead ahead. They closed in on him from every side. Picket was trapped, and there was no way out. He swerved back and forth, trying to throw them off the trail. But on they came, closing him in with the deadly expertise of trained hunters. From behind, he heard Daggler's choking calls, raggedly bellowing his angry orders. Picket realized with some satisfaction that Helmer must have really damaged the twisted chief's throat. Too bad Helmer hadn't ended him when he could have.

Increasingly sure he would never get away alive, Picket's intent narrowed to a somber certainty. He couldn't escape, but he might do one good deed before he died. He slowed a moment, listening for the urgent calls behind. Hearing Daggler's hoarse curses, he turned and hurried toward the source of the sound.

One final blow to land. One final gift to the cause.

Picket gripped the handle of his sword, clenched his teeth, and ran. Beyond the knot of trees ahead, he knew he'd find his foe. Flashing through painful memories of the past, he blinked away an image of Helmer spinning to the ground and imagined the thrust he must send through Daggler's heart.

Picket reached the knot of trees and prepared to dart around them, reaching for his sword, when he was astonished to see the tree before him open up. An unseen door flew open, and he was pulled inside. He nearly killed the grasping blur of a rabbit, but he let himself be hauled within. Then, in the dimness of the hollowed-out tree, he saw a single finger poised over the mouth of his rescuer. Captain Moonlight mouthed, "Quiet," and both rabbits stood still, cramped inside the hollow tree.

Picket tried to control his breathing and calm his heart from its awful intent of moments before. He closed his eyes and focused on taking deep, slow, quiet breaths. In a few moments, he was more relaxed. They heard urgent footfalls and wary voices, angry orders followed by consternation.

"Where is he?" Daggler choked out, coughing as they heard him stomp around.

"Disappeared, sir," a soldier answered.

"Kill him," Daggler said, still unable to speak clearly. "Kill the daft rabbit who thinks our target merely disappeared." An awful sound followed as his evil orders were carried out. "Now," Daggler added, gasping. "Find him. And burn it down if you have to. Burn the whole forest down, but find him!"

It took the soldiers only a few minutes to set about the task of setting the thicket ablaze. Picket, whose eyes had now adjusted to the dim light inside the hollow tree, made his questioning face clear to his companion. Captain Moonlight smirked but held up a hand for patience. He pointed to his long left ear. They waited, the smoke starting to reach them.

"Back up, you fools," Daggler rasped. "And stand ready with your bows."

Captain Moonlight smiled, then pointed at his throat, making mocking faces at Daggler's ragged threats. Picket smiled, though he quickly remembered Helmer. He mouthed his master's name, and Captain Moonlight frowned. "Tried," he mouthed, and Picket understood that they had tried to rescue him. "Failed?" Picket asked, mouthing the word in a silent question. Captain Moonlight shrugged his shoulders. He did not know.

The smoke was growing thicker, and the heat was reaching them now. They heard the cracking pops of brittle limbs burning. Captain Moonlight put his hand up and motioned to Picket. He placed a finger over his mouth again and then crossed his flattened hands in a gesture Picket understood as a demand for silence.

Picket, eyes wide, made open-handed gestures to say, *Of course I'll be quiet,* then pointed out toward the devouring flames, *until I start catching on fire.*

Captain Moonlight nodded, then placed his hand on a jutting lever that was fixed just over his head. Then he held up three fingers. Dropping one, he now held up two fingers. Then another dropped, and only one was left. When the last finger fell, he pulled hard on the lever. Picket heard the swishing sound as a mechanism within released.

The floor was gone.

Chapter Forty-Two

Descent into Songs

Picket was in the hollowed-out tree one moment, and the next he was not. When Captain Moonlight pulled the release, the bottom dropped out of the hideaway. Picket fell through a narrow hole that funneled into a long slick surface of rock and slid down with exhilarating speed. He heard Moonlight behind him and realized the captain must have held on a moment in the tree while he fell first. The slick wet surface of the rock was smooth and sent Picket speeding down in a wild spiral of rapid descent. It reminded him of the terrifying ride he'd had back in Nick Hollow at Seven Mounds, escaping in the darkness with Heather and Smalls. He was going so fast! Alarmed and thrilled at once, he slid down into the dark, twisting deeps. Sometimes he slipped through something like a narrow tube and other times a massive cavern with eerie echoes of his sloshing fall. He was still picking up speed.

The stone slide banked hard, and Picket felt he was coming off and tried to steady himself against slipping too far. He heard the hollow wash of swishing water in the vast cavern below, then shot into a narrow cave. All was pitch black. Then he issued through an opening into a lighted dirt-walled room where two rabbits sat laughing. They stood up at once as Picket slid onto the floor before them. His entrance was less than spectacular. Picket hit the ground and rolled over several times, ending in a breathless heap, arms out wide, mouth open, and eyes starting like two moons.

The surprised guards reached for the pikes that had been resting against the wall and leveled them at Picket, who did not move. Then he heard the swishing sound of another entry and watched as Captain Moonlight glided into the receiving room, standing as he came in and lightly leaping to the ground. He loomed over Picket, smiling wide, as the two guards stepped back, saluting their chief.

"Pretty fun, isn't it?" Moonlight asked. Picket nodded. Moonlight reached for Picket's hand and helped him up. "Come on. Let's find out how our friends fared."

Picket hurried after the captain, dripping as he went. They ran through corridor after corridor, then into another torchlit room, where Captain Moonlight leapt onto a sliding smooth-rock path that wound around into a twisting tunnel, plunging to a deeper level of the warren. Picket followed fast behind, and this time, imitating Captain Moonlight's motions, rode the wild turns far more nimbly.

Again they issued into a torchlit room with two guards waiting, these more alert than the last. Picket tried to slide in with the same grace that Captain Moonlight displayed, but he again toppled onto the floor with a tumbling spill.

Captain Moonlight pulled him up, and they raced into the passageway ahead, taking several more turns before finally ending into a place Picket recognized.

The Citadel of Dreams.

Weezie was there, and, seeing him, she rushed over and smothered him with a hug. "You're all right?" she asked. He nodded.

"Your mother?"

"She's fine," Weezie said, pointing aloft to a stairway that led to several of the inn's rooms. "Resting comfortably."

Picket smiled.

"Did Dekko's team find Helmer?" Captain Moonlight asked, walking to where Whit stood talking with several others.

Whit nodded, and Picket, hand in hand with Weezie, hurried to join them. "Is he—?" Picket began.

"He took an arrow in the shoulder before Dekko was able to get to him," Whit said, speaking from under his black mask. "He's with the doctor now." Picket's heart swelled to hear that Helmer had neither been killed nor taken prisoner.

"Where?" Picket asked, eager to be with his wounded master.

"Just there," Whit said, "in room four. But it's best to let the doctor work. Helmer's in no great danger. Doc's given him something to help him sleep while he sees to the wound. He'll be fit for company again in a few hours."

Weezie squeezed Picket's hand. "There's nothing you can do for him now," she said. "He would want you to rest."

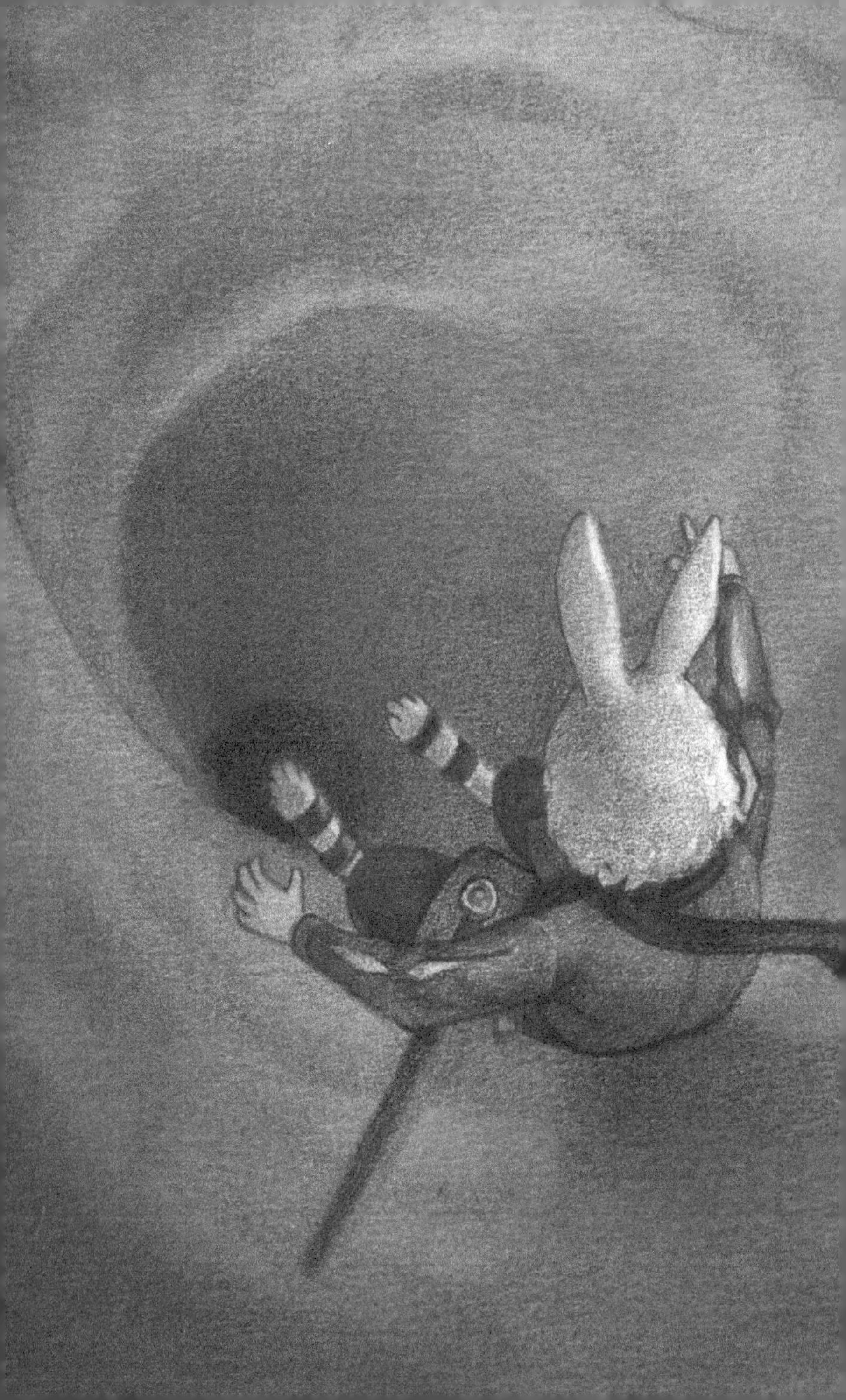

"And celebrate!" Captain Moonlight said, raising his glass and helping to pass out drinks to everyone around. "There's mud in Daggler's eye!" he said, spitting along with the rest.

"Confusion to Morbin and all his hosts!" Whit cried, raising his glass.

"Confusion to Morbin!" they all cried, and they drank. Picket winced at the sour taste of their brew but said nothing as the smiling band laughed and clapped each other's backs.

"Stompy!" Captain Moonlight called. "Get up a jig this instant! We have to celebrate a snatching that was the completest thing!"

"Aye, Cap," Stompy called, motioning for the band to reassemble. They did, each in turn adding to the spritely tune dashed out by Stompy's fiddle. As the music rose and the bandleader's wooden stump struck the floor in time with the clapping and drumming, the Citadel of Dreams filled with more and more celebrants. It was true that they were a small band, that the resistance had suffered tremendous losses and couldn't hold out much longer. But maybe they wouldn't have to. Maybe the end was near.

Picket let himself be carried away on the tide of joy. He joined in the common dances, making everyone laugh with his spectacularly bad form. But he tried again with every dance and laughed loudest of all as he failed and failed again to get it right. He danced with Weezie, laughing as he hadn't laughed for what felt like ages. The free and faithful rabbits of First Warren sang their raucous songs, few of which Picket knew but all of which he loved. They sang, full-throated and damp-eyed, of the love they had for their home and their enduring hope for the Mended Wood. Picket wept along with them, one arm around Weezie and the other around Captain Moonlight, as the band played and the crowd sang on and on.

And the night stretched on into a long happy fancy that felt to Picket like something unreal in its flood of delight. He remembered his duty, remembered the hard days behind and grim work ahead. But he was completely and happily present, alive and awake here, in the Citadel of Dreams.

As the night wore on, he learned their songs. And he sang along when they sang.

"Come all you travelers, wounded and worn,
Come over your mountains and streams.
Though bruised and abused, come be introduced
To the Citadel of Dreams.

The road has been hard, you're harried and hurt,
And the wide world's unkind as it seems.
You're soak'n and broken, but kind words are spoken
At the Citadel of Dreams!

Come, come, and rest, forget your pains,
Or remember them among friends.
At the Citadel of Dreams you'll find
A welcome that never ends.

Come, come and find your friends inside,
Come while the kind light beams.
Lend your voice and your ear, we'll sing and we'll cheer
In the Citadel of Dreams.

We have a hope, but for now it's buried,
It's a seed stuffed with stories and schemes.
For now it's the winter, but we can't be bitter
At the Citadel of Dreams!

Come, come, and rest, forget your pains,
Or remember them among friends.
At the Citadel of Dreams you'll find
A welcome that never ends.

The time will come, when the dark becomes dawn,
And the ember bursts into a flame
That lights up the sky, showing the world is my
Own Citadel of Dreams!"

Chapter Forty-Three

Victory Eve

Picket woke up smiling and saw Whit standing over him, shaking him awake. The rabbit's eyes were friendly, and Picket could tell that beneath the mask there must be a smile to match his own.

"My, but you're hard to waken. Get up, lad," Whit said. "We have work to do today. It's Victory Eve."

"Of course," Picket answered, stretching. "Tomorrow is the so-called Victory Day."

"Hurry up," Whit said.

Picket nodded, standing up. He had slept hard in the inn section of the Citadel of Dreams. Late the night before he had crashed into bed after checking on Helmer, following the enchanting evening of song and dance. He felt happy and hopeful. "I didn't dream, Whit," he said, stretching. "I feel like I didn't get what I was promised."

"That's disappointing," Whit answered. "Maybe we shall have to change the name to the Citadel of a Good Night's Rest."

"Why do you wear the mask, Whit?" Picket asked. "I understand why you wear it on missions, but aren't we all friends down here now?"

"We are friends," Whit said, looking down. "But I have many scars." He moved toward the door, then turned his head and removed his mask. He was white, with some splashes of black fur. But he had not exaggerated. Whit was cruelly scarred, with a missing ear and marks of hardship all over his face.

"You remind me of the prince," Picket said, wrapping the black scarf around his own neck. "Prince Smalls, my very dear friend." It had been nearly a week since Smalls had fallen, though so much had happened since. Still, the wound in his heart felt very fresh.

Whit nodded. "He was my little brother, though I never really knew him."

"You're one of King Jupiter's sons?" Picket asked, astonished. "I thought they were all loyal to Winslow."

"I am a son," Whit said, frowning, "and I was unfaithful for a long time, going along with Winslow's betrayals. I mended my ways and turned back to my father's cause a few years ago. I have paid for the change," he said, looking down. "I was once considered quite handsome."

"You have a great heart, Whit," Picket said, "as your brother had. And your scars are marks of valor to me. I would wish you to never cover even one but to bare them all with honor."

"Thank you, Picket," Whit said, then nodded to the door. "Cap calls a council. Come to the common room when you're ready."

"Yes, Your Highness," Picket said, bowing.

"Here I am only Whit, and Cap alone knows my secret."

"Then when we are with the others, I will help guard your secret," Picket said. "But in my heart, I will keep the old ways and honor your birth and blood. More than that, I will honor your scars."

Whit bowed quickly, then turned and quit the room.

In a few minutes, Picket left his room and crossed the hallway, quietly opened Helmer's door, and crept in. The bed was empty. He left the room puzzled and walked the length of the hallway, then descended the stairs overlooking the common room where so much joy had been shared the previous night. As he left the final step, he saw that Helmer sat with Captain Moonlight, eating and talking quietly, as many other rabbits ate around the large table that had been brought in. Picket's heart swelled to see Helmer. He had no doubt that the old rabbit ought to have been in bed still, but to see him there sent a thrill through him. He loved Helmer, and he was happy to see him alive. But mixed in with the selfless devotion was a deep relief that his master had not left him to contend with this impossible errand alone.

"Picket Packslayer!" Captain Moonlight said, laughing and motioning him over. "Come and eat at my table, now that I finally know your name."

Picket walked up to the table and nodded to Captain Moonlight. Then he looked at Helmer with plain tenderness. His master returned his look, and the two rabbits regarded one another with unabashed understanding, though no words were spoken. Picket was grateful to see his master alive, and Helmer plainly felt the same. But there was more. Much more.

Picket sat and took the vegetable pie extended to him by a kind-eyed doe. It was good, and the water offered to wash it down was even more gratefully received. He was parched.

In a few minutes, Weezie appeared at the bottom of the stairs, walking beside her mother. "Airen!" Helmer said, standing so suddenly that he knocked over his chair. He limped to his sister and folded her in his arms. "My dear," he said softly, holding her tight. She returned his embrace, and Picket saw the tears from her eyes drip onto Helmer's back. But her face was happy, and she looked closer to what she must have been at one time. Weezie beamed at Picket, and he smiled back. She looked fresh and happy. The fire that he understood to have marked their family's history seemed to be rekindled in some small way. He loved seeing it spark to life.

Making room for them near where he sat, he pulled back a chair for Weezie while Helmer did the same for his beloved sister.

"Thank you, Picket," Weezie said. "Did you sleep well?"

"Like the dead," he said, and Weezie frowned. "But with more snoring," he added.

"You should have heard Mother," Weezie said, whispering. "She sounded like a battle horn plunged underwater all night."

Picket laughed. "So you didn't sleep well?" he asked.

"It was fine. Woke up a few times to enjoy the, um, music," she said, nodding at Airen, "but I feel great."

"Good," he said.

"Good," she agreed. "So what happens now?"

"You eat some of this delicious vegetable pie," he said, making a plate for her and one for her mother.

"I don't usually like to eat..." she began, "only one piece."

Picket laughed and piled three more of the round pies on her plate. "Happy now?" he asked. Weezie nodded, cutting into the first golden pie.

"How are you, Uncle?" she asked, speaking through a mouthful.

"I am well, Weezie, my dear," Helmer answered. "I see you have the family appetite."

"I'm still growing, I think," she said.

"So is your uncle," Airen said, patting her brother's tummy.

Picket was amazed to hear her speak so casually. So were the others.

Helmer looked surprised a moment. Then he smiled, and his eyes filled with tears. Weezie froze, forgetting to chew. Picket was the first to recover, and he laughed. "Thank you, Airen, for supporting my position," he said. "He's always training me to make myself a more difficult target to hit, but he's not being a very good example."

They all laughed, and Helmer put his arm around Airen.

"You see I am not all the way gone, yet," she said quietly. It was true.

"Clearly, neither is Uncle Helmer," Weezie said. Picket laughed along with the others, and Helmer held up his hands.

"Enough," he said playfully. "I'm down, I'm down. There's no use kicking me."

"Funny," Picket said, "but that's exactly the training method he used on me. Kicking me while I was down."

"Did it work?" Weezie asked.

"It was best when he kicked dirt in my eyes first."

"Well, that does help," Weezie said.

"I see he's using his past sibling experiences in his military training now," Airen said softly. Everyone laughed again, and Helmer smirked at his sister.

They ate and smiled and laughed some more, returning again and again to needle Helmer where Airen had begun. Picket could see that, though Helmer weakly played at being offended, nothing had brought him this much happiness in many years. He could not keep from smiling.

After a short time, Moonlight stood and motioned to some active rabbits at the bar. "Bring everyone in," he said. They nodded and hurried from the room and, in a few minutes, brought back scores of rabbits. They lined the walls and filled the stairs, perched on landings and crowded into corners. When the Citadel of Dreams was packed, Captain Moonlight leapt onto the bar and raised his hands for quiet. A hush fell, and every eye and ear inclined to the energetic chief.

"Friends, today is Victory Eve," he began, and a grumbling rumble began in the room. "You know, as I know, the history of the day. Tomorrow is the anniversary of the fall of King Jupiter the Great. We know the ruin that came to us in the aftermath of that murder. And they rub it in our faces every year. They make us celebrate the death of our king and the end of our liberty. They mark us as prey with red at our necks, make a show of our weakness, and steal our young."

The crowd murmured angrily, and several rabbits called, "No more!"

"No more, indeed!" Captain Moonlight shouted loudly, and the crowd quieted again. "Tomorrow they aim to take every youngling in First Warren. Every single one. These, the most vulnerable members of our kind, will be carried off into slavery in Akolan. Or worse. We hear the vilest rumors of dark rites and ceremonial meals. You have heard them too. They murder the great, prey on the small, and hold us all in their thrall. No more!" he cried.

"No more!" they echoed, fists in the air.

"Today is a day to prepare," Moonlight said. "We have heroes among us, friends. Captain Helmer was a hero of the last wars and is a hero of this one too. And Picket Longtreader, of whom some of the stories are true, is here with us. We are not alone, and there are thousands of rabbits rallying to the cause all across Natalia. I have been speaking with Captain Helmer for some time this morning, and it's plain we have a shared objective. We must prepare like we never have before. It will take all our resources and all our courage. Many of us will fall, like our own king fell. Many of us will die, as King Jupiter's son and heir died fighting for the Mended Wood. But we must press on! There's an heir who lives: Princess Emma. And she is the bearer of our hopes. Tomorrow, we rise. We rise for the cause of the Mended Wood, the story we have believed and worked for over these many years of darkness. We wait for the mending. We hope for the healing." He clenched his fist and thrust it in the air. "Tomorrow, we fight for the rising!"

Chapter Forty-Four

Cell of Sorrow

Heather was dragged from her home, into the street, and past the lifeless body of Stretch. She turned away, horrified at the sight and bewildered by the dwindling chances for her hopes—for all the free rabbits' hopes—to be realized. They shoved her toward the District Six gate. She staggered, less from exhaustion and more from the weight of the terrible series of events leading up to her and Mother's arrest.

She had been asked to treat and help keep alive the Tunneler for a short time more. His almost-certain successor was against any action that would launch the project the faithful Akolan rabbits had worked toward in secret for over a century. Their bold escape.

But she had failed.

The Tunneler was dead.

The plan to kill all the younglings on Victory Day—tomorrow—would proceed. She was captured, along with Mother. Father was missing. Jacks was being held at the administration headquarters, where he had gone to inform on his own family. Young Jacks didn't know it, deceived as he was about the authorities he had been trained to trust, but he was destined to become part of a ritual meal for Morbin Blackhawk's table.

And there was nothing Heather could do. She put one foot in front of the other as they shoved her forward, her hands bound. Primly swatting flakes of ash, Captain Vitton came to walk beside her, his languid gait sickeningly smooth. "Tomorrow is Victory Day, Heather Longtreader. A very special day, and we have so much planned. Don't worry about young Jacks Longtreader," he said, cackling. "We'll see he stays safely in good hands until his…last meal."

"You vile pet of the predators!" she cried. "You're no buck. You're a coward."

Vitton laughed his smug laugh, then crossed to where Mother was walking along, gazing at Heather with terrible concern. Vitton drew out a knife and, looking at Heather, sliced at Mother's leg.

"No!" Heather screamed as Mother buckled to the ground.

"What do you say now, Heather Longtreader?" Captain Vitton asked in a sickly prim retort. "Nothing? I thought so."

Heather gasped, twisting to try to free herself. "Let me help her, please!"

"Perhaps I will," Vitton said, "once you're both in my cells."

"Yes," Heather said quickly. "Whatever you say."

As they walked, Vitton mused about the city, as casually as if on a stroll with friends. "The Fourth District is the filthiest of all, I find. Being so close to the lepers has infected them. But all the outer districts are grotesque." His guards nodded. Heather saw they would not speak unless directly spoken to. "The Commandant should, at last, let me go forward with my plan to eliminate the lepers and torch their horrible district," he said, motioning vaguely toward the L.D. "And while we're at it, we should do the same in the Fourth. That would dispense with much of the pathetic outwaller resistance."

They soon reached Longtreader headquarters, several guards dragging Mother roughly while Heather bit her tongue. A lieutenant reported to Vitton as he arrived, saluting silently.

"Go and find Whittle Longtreader," Vitton commanded. "I want him caught by Victory Day dawn. He ought to be at the outer aqueducts. If he resists, kill him." The lieutenant saluted and set off, signaling several guards to follow him.

Elude them, Father. You're the only one safe.

They descended a series of stairways and found themselves at the beginning of a long passage with dim cells on either side. They were shoved into the tenth one on the left. Heather went first, followed by her mother. She caught Mother as she fell into the cell and laid her down gently on the one cot.

"I've got you, Mother," Heather said, fighting back tears. "Just rest easy. I have my satchel, and I'll treat the wound."

"Thank you, Heather," Mother said weakly.

Heather couldn't see well, but still she found her tools and, after cleaning the wound as well as she could without water, applied an ointment and bandaged it. Heather rose from her work to look at Mother's face and saw a sad smile. She kissed Mother and stood up.

"Thank you, Heather. Did it stop bleeding?" Mother asked.

"I think so. It's not the worst wound I've ever seen. Still, I do wish that you could rest easy for a week and not move."

"I will have to bear it, my dear. I'm sorry to say that we may have worse to face from that monster."

"I fear we will."

"Perhaps your father has gotten away. And Picket," she said, trying so hard to keep a brave face, "I believe he is somewhere safe right now, working like a good'n for the mending."

"I'm sure he is, Mother," Heather said. "Why don't you rest now?"

"I will if you will, dear. We'll both need our strength for the ordeal ahead."

"There's so much to be done!" Heather said, pacing the length of the dim cell. "We were so close to having a chance."

"Others will take up the work," Mother said, squinting against the pain. "It doesn't all depend on you."

"I know, Mother," Heather said, worried eyes moving from her mother's face to the wound. "I wanted to save

Jacks, at least. I wanted to see the younglings safely into the Seventh District. I wanted—"

"You wanted to save the world," Mother said, smiling. "I know you."

"This is a nightmare!" Heather shouted, crossing to kick the bars of the cell that held them in. She gripped the bars and shook them with all her might, but they didn't budge. She sank to the ground, weeping.

"Come here, my dear," Mother said. Heather rose and slowly crossed to her mother's side. Mother winced and moved over, making room for Heather to lie beside her.

"But, Mother," Heather began.

"You will help me rest," Mother said, arms open. Heather slid in beside her mother, receiving the wrapping arms around her neck. She lay there, in that familiar embrace, while Mother sang softly.

"I dreamed I saw a valley,
When I woke, it was a mountain,
I climbed to the peak and fell asleep
And rolled down in the fountain.

In the morning when you're shaken
It might be you were mistaken,
The things that seemed, were only dreamed,
So sleep and dream and waken.
I woke to windy weather
And had dreamed the sky was clear,

So I said, I'll go back to bed,
And that's just when the rainbow appeared.

In the morning when you're shaken
It might be you were mistaken,
The things that seemed, were only dreamed,
So sleep and dream and waken.

Oh, sleep and dream and waken."

Heather finally fell asleep, calmed somewhat by this familiar remedy to her nighttime fears. But her last thoughts were worried ones. Of Mother's weakening voice. Of Jacks and Father. Of Picket far away. Of rabbitkind's dwindling hopes. But she slept at last.

And dreamed.

Chapter Forty-Five

The Edge of Death

When Heather woke, shaking off the dim disturbing dream, she felt Mother's limp arms around her. She rolled off the cot, heart racing, and spun to check her mother's condition. She was breathing, though with some difficulty. And the wound had bled more, but not so much as Heather had feared.

Heather crept to the edge of their cell and leaned into the bars to try to see down the passage. Nothing yet. Maybe they had been forgotten? Somehow she didn't think so. Vitton enjoyed his cruelty too much to abandon them as projects of his sick fancy. It was not enough that they were suffering. He would want to see it. To cause it. To revel in it.

Heather spat. "Vitton the Skinner," she whispered.

As if she had summoned him by her cursing, Heather heard a door open and footsteps approaching. The villain himself appeared outside her cell, sneering at her by torchlight. He was accompanied by ten stout guards, all dressed in their wing-shouldered Longtreader uniforms, neat red bands around their necks.

"Happy Victory Day, Heather Longtreader," Vitton said. "The city center is filling with the filth of the outer districts, all bringing their delicious little outwaller younglings along. What a day this will be!"

Heather seethed beneath a calm expression. "What will you do with us?" she asked, jaws clenched. "Mother needs medical care."

"Oh, she'll receive the attention she deserves," Vitton said, nodding to his guards. "Bring them."

The cell was unlocked, and guards shoved Heather out, while others stomped inside, roughly woke Mother, and dragged her out into the passage.

"Be careful with her, you monsters!" Heather yelled. Vitton nodded to a guard, who struck Heather hard in the stomach with the end of his pike. She doubled over, sagging in the grip of her captors. She felt sick and coughed, going to her knees.

"Now," Vitton said. "I take you to the roof, where you can see the ceremony. I do not permit you to speak unless I invite you." He drew out a knife and stepped toward Mother, whose tired eyes showed a grim determination.

"I understand!" Heather gasped, staggering to her feet. "You're in charge, Captain Vitton. We'll do as you say."

Vitton paused, pursing his lips in a show of disappointment. "Our fun will have to wait," he said, resuming the march down the passage, through tunnels and up stairways. They emerged onto the roof, just as Heather had her first morning in Akolan.

When her eyes had adjusted to the morning light, she saw an incredible scene in the city center below. There were rabbits all over, filing in from every corner of Akolan. The center was decorated with bright banners, and music was playing from a balcony opposite their own position. Two enormous banners were draped down the sides of the two tallest buildings. One bore the Akolan administration's anthem:

We are here and alive,
Let us make a life for ourselves,
Among our own kind,
And end our rebellion,
Against destiny.
Peace and prosperity forever!

The other banner bore the startling silhouette of a vast black hawk with a sickle in his grip and a crown on his head. At his feet were piled rabbit skulls. Heather winced at seeing again this cruel emblem, now mounted on this massive scale at a gathering—a celebration—attended by multitudes of red-throated rabbits. Her face contorted in a disgusted sneer.

"You do not approve, Miss Longtreader?" Vitton asked, smiling proudly.

"I find it troubling that rabbits must celebrate an image with rabbit skulls piled at the feet of their oppressor, who is a murderer and tyrant."

He crossed to strike her, lashing out with a deft punch. But Heather ducked the blow and sent a driving kick into his middle. Vitton buckled to the ground, breathless and grimacing. Two guards grabbed Heather and held her up while Vitton swiveled up and staggered to his feet.

"Oh, I love this!" he said, eyes wild. "I love this!" He nodded at a guard. "Retrieve my claw," he said, and the guard, saluting, retreated back through the door. "I needed that, Heather Longtreader. That was a fine gift. Now, watch!"

The guards spun Heather to where she was forced to see the city center and all the bustle of Victory Day. She watched, heartbroken, as the preparations neared completion. She gazed as sad-faced rabbits glanced at the massive banner featuring Morbin. Heather saw the divided stands where the District Six elites were kept from having to interact with their outwaller guests. The smug looks of the Sixes, mixed with their genuine pleasure at the festivities, marked them over and against their kindred from the outer districts. The visitors to the city center were uneasy, uncertain where to go. Most kept their heads down, hiding unhappy faces. For some in the galleries, it was a kind of sport to point and laugh at the poorer rabbits. Heather's eyes filled with tears.

We have become our own worst enemies. What could we have accomplished all over Natalia if we had only worked together?

Heather watched on while the city center filled, watched with a sinking heart as an open space was roped off in the midst of the gathered rabbits and the younglings were gathered there. They were so small, and their oversized scarves and neckerchiefs marked them for what they really were. *Prey.* She watched frenzied parents and terrified friends be pressed back, often with brutal force, from the abandoned younglings. There were guilty glances everywhere as disgusted bucks and horrified does watched helplessly. Most did not know what was coming, but their dread steadily increased as the number of younglings multiplied.

The clamorous music wasn't loud enough to drown out the screams.

Heather's weeping eyes grew wider, and her heavy heart sank ever lower. A sickening helplessness overwhelmed her. She had forgotten where she was. Her heart was with the mothers and all the other helpless rabbits who watched their children be exposed to the baleful horrors that would surely come. She longed to see Flint and Fay, impossibly large, leaping from standing stone to standing stone, coming to rescue them all. Fay with light in her eyes and Flint bearing his stone sword. Rescuers. Justice. But they were not coming. No one was coming.

There are no heroes here.

"You do not enjoy our Victory Day festivities, I find," Vitton said sickly. Heather turned slowly to find him kneeling before a small forge that had been brought up while she watched below. Orange coals, stoked by a broad rabbit pumping large bellows, heated several instruments. Smoke puffed out in twisting wisps, and mingled with the falling flakes of ash. Vitton smiled, seeing her alarm. "Are you crying, Heather Longtreader?" He cackled with glee. "You're perfect! You still care so much. I find so often my victims have given up. But you still care, and you still believe in your hopeless cause." He laughed louder still. "I love it!"

Heather hung her head. He was right. She did care. And she did, somehow, still believe. She looked up as Vitton was fitted with a thick metal-rimmed glove. The stout blacksmith took tongs and secured a five-bladed claw, which he then settled onto the glove, clicking it in place. Now Vitton's eyes were lit with a fell frenzy as he rose, brandishing this orange-hot claw. His other hand was fitted with a thick glove, and he drew from the forge a heated sword, its end glowing white. Heather saw the air ripple above the claw hand and the sword. She saw Vitton's twisted glee as he stepped forward.

"Now," he said, his voice high and frantic, "you will feel the burning. There will be no mending, only an ending—to you, your family, and your cause!"

Chapter Forty-Six

A New Betrayal

Captain Vitton advanced, rabid in his glee. The door opened behind him, and Heather's heart rose. Then she saw the Commandant walk out onto the roof, and her hopes died.

"Commandant," Vitton said, his eyes still bright and his sharp teeth showing a bright, wild smile, "you're just in time for the burning."

"Very good, Captain Vitton," the Commandant said. "I have brought you more players for your sport. After you've finished with this girl and her mother, then enjoy exercising your particular skills on these." The Commandant motioned, and five rabbits were led out onto the roof, canvas bags covering their heads. Uniformed guards shoved them forward, and they stood behind the Commandant, whose half-scarred face and callous expression made Heather shudder. *These are the leaders of Akolan. A cold, heartless bureaucrat and a twisted fanatic.*

"Are they rebels?" Vitton asked, waving his hot-metal talon back and forth.

"They tried to keep back their younglings from the gathering," the Commandant said. Heather's heart lurched. "They are traitors and deserve whatever fate you may…enjoy to give them."

Vitton motioned them over, and the guards dragged them toward the maniacal captain. "I will get to you, bagheads, after her!" He twisted toward Heather, his eyes wide with dark delight and his bright blades bearing down on her.

The door opened again, and a frantic guard ran through, saluting.

"You may speak, Lieutenant Anders," the Commandant said, his face betraying a mild concern.

"Sir," the breathless Anders said, "I've been interrogating all morning and have just found out the most incredible intelligence."

"How did you obtain this intelligence, Lieutenant?" the Commandant asked.

"The outwaller volunteered it, sir," Anders replied. "He wanted to trade the information for the life of his twin younglings. I agreed, knowing we could always do what we wanted anyway once the intel was secured."

"You did very well. Go on," the Commandant said, while Captain Vitton turned to listen.

"Sir," Lieutenant Anders continued, "the rebels… they have built a tunnel into the mountain behind the Lepers' District."

"What?" Captain Vitton said, eyes still wide with frenzy. Heather's heart sank, and she barely stifled a scream. It wasn't only that she and mother, Jacks, and all the younglings were going to be killed but that the whole project of escape was in jeopardy.

"Silence, you!" Mother cried at Anders. The Commandant spun, and Vitton nodded to her nearest guard. She was herself silenced with a crunching blow. Heather screamed as Mother fell back, unmoving.

"No!" Heather cried, and she strained at her captors. They held her tight as Vitton swung his hot blade around, pointing it at her and motioning for her to be silent.

"Say on, Lieutenant," Vitton said, a savage hunger in his eyes.

"Yes, Captain," Anders answered. "They have a council, a kind of government, and a leader. And they have a vast cavern back in there, and they call it District Seven. They have ships—massive ships—intended to take most of the city away in escape! They have trained soldiers called battlebucks and a whole scheme that's been worked on for over a hundred years!"

The guards and officers atop the roof gasped and looked at one another. Vitton whistled, then cackled and bobbed his head. The Commandant frowned.

"Stay here a moment, Anders," the Commandant said. "I have heard similar rumors today. When Captain Vitton is finished, we will go and question this buck together. Then we will uncover all."

Vitton smiled grotesquely, nodding thanks to the Commandant, who stood behind the five prisoners by the door. Then Vitton turned again on Heather, walking forward and raising his incandescent claw. His crazed eyes were wide as he stepped forward. "And now, the painful end to your pitiful story!"

Heather closed her eyes as the claw swept toward her. She braced for the horrifying end.

But she felt nothing.

All she heard was a clanging ring. Her eyes flashed open. She saw the claw, orange-hot, on the stone rooftop beside her. She looked up to see Vitton's face overcome with confusion.

"What is this?" he demanded, turning around. Heather saw what he saw—five bags on the deck and the former prisoners rushing toward Vitton and his guards. She couldn't take it all in at once, but she saw one of the prisoners had a bow. He had shot a guard and was nocking another arrow. Another of the freed prisoners, a familiar form, charged hard at the wicked captain. She had to look twice to be certain.

Her heart leapt. *Father!* He rushed at Vitton, who brought around his white-hot sword with tremendous speed and drove it down hard on Father. Father brought up his weapon, an ordinary pickaxe that looked ancient, and blocked Vitton's stroke. Vitton stumbled back toward Heather, his maniac glee giving way to hysteria.

"Who are you?" he screamed.

"I am her father, and father to more," he said, "and now I am a father to all."

"What do you mean?" Vitton shrieked, rising with a last effort to face this envoy of death.

Father raised the ancient pickaxe and said, "I am the Tunneler and the Truth." He struck then such a devastating blow that Vitton had no chance to deflect it. The white-hot blade snapped in half, and the ancient tool sped down, finding, and finishing, that dreaded captain of a thousand cruelties. Heather looked away.

Then Father was with her. "Are you all right, Heather?"

"Yes," she said, hugging him. "But Mother. We need to get her somewhere safe."

"There's only one safe place now," Father said, looking down at the city center. It was full now, and the ceremony was beginning. "And it's nowhere near here." He ran to his wife and handed the pickaxe to another of the former prisoners. Heather recognized Dote. Father took Mother in his arms and dodged through the chaos of the ongoing battle with what was left of Vitton's band.

"The Commandant!" Heather cried, recalling his presence with a jolt of terror.

Dote pointed, and she tracked the path of his outstretched finger. She saw that the Commandant's drawn sword was pointed at the neck of Anders, the young lieutenant who had revealed the secret of District Seven. "He's with us," Father said, smiling. "The Commandant has always been with us. He's betraying the betrayers."

She was astounded. "But all the evil he's done! He knocked me off this roof!" she said.

"I know," Father answered, "right onto a series of awnings that were meant to bring you to the ground

unharmed. But we'll speak of it later. Right now, we have work to do!"

"Yes, Father," she said, leaping to action. "Where's Jacks?"

Father swiveled toward the Commandant. "Will Jacks still be in the holding area?" he called.

"No, Father Tunneler," he answered. "They'll be moving them to the city center now. They will call the birds at the first alarm, so we have very little time."

"Okay," Father said, turning to the archer, who Heather noticed was Stitcher. "Do it!"

Stitcher nodded and then called for his fellow archers to step to the edge. They lit the soaked bundles on the ends of their arrows in the forge that held Vitton's twisted weapons. They raised their arrows and aimed. "Fire!" Stitcher shouted.

The flaming arrows sped through the sky, arcing over the anxious crowd below. Heather watched as they found the massive banners and burst into flame. Heather shouted a defiant cry along with the others on the roof as the image of Morbin began to peel away in the flames.

At that signal, the gate filled with a horde of rabbits rushing into the city center. None wore the red preymarks at their necks. They were lepers, Heather saw with amazement, and they ran in with a tremendous shout, scattering the galleries of the shocked residents of Sixth District.

"Lepers!" the inwallers cried, knocking one another down in their efforts to avoid the diseased horde. "They'll infect us all!"

Heather saw, with a mounting shock and wild joy, that Harmony was at the head of the leper insurrection. Harmony, her fur mottled and with apparent sores scattered through rips in her tattered rags, was leading the lepers into the city center. Soon there were gaps in the crowd, and the lepers sped in, surrounding the terrified younglings. Harmony shouted instructions, and the leper host went to work. Heather watched with rising hope as the lepers encircled and began to pick up the younglings and carry them off. Many rabbits screamed and fought off the rescue, but scores more joined in, rushing away with younglings in tow.

"The trick of a century!" Stitcher cried out in joy.

And what a deception it had been. Heather finally understood that the so-called lepers were not truly sick at all but were part of an old ploy to keep curious foes away from the ongoing project inside the mountain—in District Seven. They had sacrificed to provide cover for the great project of the ages. Heather knew they were heroes. And how heroically they acted now!

Heather smiled as she saw the burning banners fall and, though it seemed impossible to her, two new banners were revealed beneath. One bore the red and green double-diamond emblem and the other the old oath:

My place beside you,
My blood for yours.
Till the Green Ember rises,
Or the end of the world!

Stitcher stepped up beside Heather, smiling wide with tears in his eyes as others patted his back.

"Good work, Mr. Weaver!' Dote said. "I don't know how you did it."

"Thank you, son," the old rabbit said. "It's an old trick, but I've never tried it on that scale before."

"Mr. Weaver?" she asked, mouth gaping open. "Mr. Edward Weaver? Maggie Weaver's husband?"

"Yes, Heather. You have seen my wife?" he asked, his brimming eyes eager.

"Oh, dear Mr. Weaver!" she cried, plunging into his arms. "Your wife is the dearest, most wonderful rabbit! She was very well the last I saw her. Very well, indeed. She's the wisest counselor the heirs have had and the heart of our cause. She has looked for you, Mr. Weaver, every day from her porch at Cloud Mountain. She has never forgotten you."

They embraced for a long moment, and Mr. Weaver wept. "My dear Maggie! Oh, my Maggie," he said.

They broke apart and stood staring, first at one another, then up at the magnificent banners Mr. Weaver had fashioned for this incredible occasion. "How?" she asked, pointing at them. "The top layer burned, but these don't. How?"

"The bottom banners are sealed with flame-retardant ointment," he answered, his arm around her as if she were his own granddaughter, "and the tops were highly flammable. It's not too complicated, just daring."

She gazed with wonder at the banners. She thought of Emma and of her beloved Smalls and then looked down at the scene unfolding below.

It was chaotic still but beginning to turn toward order as the lepers' gamble paid off. Most of the younglings were on their way to District Seven while the inwallers fled in a panic. The Longtreader guards couldn't manage the bedlam, and they regrouped on the edge of their headquarters. Heather reveled in their retreat.

Then she spotted Jacks. He was running against the retreating tide of lepers carrying younglings. He fought off any attempt to carry him away, even sidestepping Harmony and ducking under an upturned booth. Harmony lost sight of him and was pressed by other, urgent, dangers. But Heather tracked his movements. She saw his face plainly, and it showed a panicked confusion. He looked as if he believed his world were coming apart.

"Jacks!" she cried, though he was far too far away to hear her.

"Where?" Father asked, rushing up to the edge of the roof.

"There!" She pointed, then spun to take in the scene on the roof. The Commandant, who Heather could hardly believe was really their ally, had subdued the remainder of Vitton's force and now held the rooftop. Mother was lying still, and Heather longed to help her, but she saw how delicate Jacks' situation stood.

"The Lords of Prey will be coming soon, Master Tunneler," the Commandant called. "I'm late to setting the cover fires."

"Will they believe that the younglings, and many more," Father asked, "were maddened by the rush of the lepers and are now infected?"

"I hope so," the Commandant said. "I have my script prepared. It only remains to be seen if your brother will believe it or acknowledge the fiction."

"Our hopes rest on that!" Father said. "Now, go!"

The Commandant hurried through the door along with Dote, Mr. Weaver, and their other remaining allies. Vitton's band was tied up and gagged, with the bags over *their* heads now.

"Heather," Father asked, "can you carry your mother to District Seven? I have to get to Jacks!"

They both knew the answer to that question. Heather wasn't strong enough to carry Mother that far.

"Take her, Father," she said. "And lead these rabbits to freedom."

"But, Heather," Father began, tears starting in his eyes. "I can't lose you again."

"You'll always have me, Father," she said, crossing to kiss him. "You're strong enough to carry Mother and to set the grand project in motion."

"And you?"

"I'm strong enough to carry Jacks," she said, and she leapt from the rooftop.

Chapter Forty-Seven

Heather's Departure

Heather struck the canvas awning, careful to keep her balance as best as she could, rolled again to the next level, and so on before spilling onto the ground. But this time, knowing what to expect, she kept her feet and landed firmly on the ground. Then she dug into a sprint.

All around her, chaos reigned. The inwallers were fleeing in every direction, running inside whatever buildings would let them in. The last of the lepers were hurrying their comrades off in the direction of the Fifth District—the Lepers' District—and then into the Seventh.

Heather sped on, dodging through the raucous rabbits. She kept her eyes on where Jacks had been and ran there with all the speed she could manage. She was still fast, and still, even in this mad moment, she felt a thrill at the speed she could achieve when she didn't hold back.

She saw him! Jacks was climbing up an upturned cart and leapt from it to a stage to escape the trampling tumult on the ground.

She saw Harmony nearby, patiently coordinating the rescue of several elderly rabbits. She had a team of large strong rabbits, and they began to carry the elders off. Heather almost stopped a moment, thinking she saw the large form of Master Mills, the rabbit she had seen fade toward death before her very eyes. Perhaps he had a twin? She saw him drape an elder over his shoulder and follow Harmony's route of escape.

Heather sped past the elder evacuation and toward the stage where Jacks knelt, terrified.

As she approached the bottom of the stage, she looked down to dodge through a wreck of scattered debris. Looking up toward Jacks again, she saw him, and then the sky above her brother filled with birds.

She swallowed a scream and sped on, skipping up the upturned cart and then leaping onto the stage. Jacks looked at her with a bewildered expression. He reached back, feeling desperately among the tools and broken boards scattered across the stage. Laying hold of a small hammer, he knelt atop a hinged door on the floor of the center of the stage and made to defend himself.

"I've come for you, Jacks!" she shouted above the screams and tumult on the ground and the terrifying shrieks of the approaching birds.

"You're a traitor!" he said, tears in his eyes, while waving the hammer. "You're on the wrong side."

"No, Jacks!" she cried. "I am for rabbitkind and for the cause of the Mended Wood! And I'm on your side!"

"Stay away!" he shouted as she rushed at him. He swung the hammer, but she blocked his strike at the wrist, and the hammer clattered to the platform deck. She wrapped him in an embrace.

"Jacks," she said in his ear. "You are far from home now, but I remember you. I know who you are."

His resistance diminished, and he allowed her to hold him tight in a hug. She lifted him off the ground, then turned to survey the mad scene.

The Lords of Prey were descending into their midst.

Fifty raptors dropped into the city center, striking out at the scampering rabbits with razor-sharp talons and snapping beaks. It was a horrific scene. Heather noticed birds circling high above the Lepers' District, hesitating. But they dived and destroyed with vicious energy in the midst of the city center.

Heather looked to the left and right, searching for an escape from this stage and then the town. Her gaze rested on the Longtreader headquarters roof from which she had just come. She saw a large eagle, ridden by a grey rabbit, alight. The rabbit dismounted and came to the edge.

She knew who he was.

Garten Longtreader, her betraying uncle, was on the scene of what might be his great failure. She felt a surge of pride, seeing how this spectacle must vex him. Then he appeared to see her.

He pointed at her.

"We have to go, Jacks," she said, as calmly as possible, as her uncle hurried to remount his eagle. Jacks would say nothing. He was a lightly clinging burden for her as she mapped out an escape. Her uncle's eagle leapt from the rooftop.

Just then, much closer, a brown hawk banked on the edge of the now-sagging banners and beat his wings in an aggressive approach toward them.

She stepped back and tripped over the lip of the trapdoor, hinged on one side and bolted shut on the other. She tugged at the door but without any success. The hawk shrieked and dived at them. Heather and Jacks lay on the door, unable to get it open.

Then Heather saw the hammer Jacks had tried to use to fend her off. She grabbed it and swung furiously, not at the lock but at the hinges. They held a moment, then bent, finally breaking at her last roaring blow. When the hinge was broken, she leapt up as the hawk's beak extended to rip her apart, and then she landed with a shattering kick, breaking the trapdoor open. She and Jacks disappeared below as the hawk's beak closed on air.

They were falling down stairs, rolling over and over, until they spilled on the dark bottom of the under-stage. Heather leapt up, took Jacks' hand, and rushed through the slatted passage beneath the long stage. When they were only moments gone from the stairway bottom, the stage above was shredded by slicing talons. They sped away, barely keeping ahead of the frenzied attack.

Heather ran out from the bottom of the stage and into an alley adjoining the city center, pulling Jacks along and darted into a connecting street and so on toward the edge of District Six. They ran through neighborhoods filled with fleeing inwallers, and they dodged through scattered wreckage of the ruined Victory Day preparations. At last they came to the wall at the edge of the district and were speeding along under the aqueduct that provided water to the district and to potato fields just outside.

Heather and Jacks came to the base of the water tower. She pulled Jacks onto her back and began to ascend the scaffold, climbing as fast as she could.

The gate was no doubt clogged with horrible carnage, so she had to find another way out of District Six. Halfway up the scaffold, she saw the hawk that had so closely pursued them and, just behind him, an eagle bearing an angry grey rabbit.

She hurried to the top and thrust Jacks over the aqueduct lip as the hawk swept in. She heard Jacks' startled cry as he slid away, and she vaulted in behind him as the hawk's shriek echoed in her ear. She hit the bottom of the aqueduct and was amazed at the force of the water surging down from the high water tower. It took her in a sudden spurt, just before the hawk could crush her.

Heather was speeding down the aqueduct at an alarming pace. She saw Jacks disappear around a bend ahead, dropping in a wide curve that soon took her, spinning and slipping down the wild plunging slide.

The bend sped her into a section where the pipe was covered all around and the water was thick. She took a deep breath before plunging in, and she shot through the section with shocking speed.

Just when she thought she couldn't hold her breath any longer, she broke into the open and slid down a long open-top section of the aqueduct that was outside the wall. She spurted free of the slide and rolled into the potato fields. She saw Jacks sputtering nearby and was with him in a moment. She wasted no time but grabbed Jacks and hurried toward the Lepers' District and the salvation that lay just beyond in District Seven.

The hawk seemed to have disappeared, for her panicked backward glances showed no sign of him. She smiled and sped on, reaching a point where the birds simply circled high above and dared not drop in and infect themselves in the vile-smelling lepers' community.

The ruse was holding.

She had never greeted that malodorous stench with such gratitude. They were nearly there! She patted Jacks as she sped on, ecstatic to have been able to save her baby brother. Picket would be so pleased.

Heather saw the ragged tents and smelled the disgusting brew concocted to keep away all inquisitive advances. A force of lepers came out to greet her, arms open to take Jacks to safety. They had been receiving and rescuing younglings in great numbers and were eager to do still more before the chance was lost.

Harmony herself ran out at their head, waving Heather in with desperate urgency. Many of the others looked up, behind and above Heather, skidded to a halt, and hurried back for what cover they could find. Their eyes told Heather of the terror they felt. She ran on.

A massive shadow engulfed them, and Heather saw at its edges the fringed feather tips she dreaded. She turned her head to see, blocking out the sun, a massive eagle and his rabbit rider.

Uncle Garten had found them.

Harmony bravely came on, despite the fierce cry of the eagle, his talons extended and his brutal beak open.

Just as Harmony came near enough for Heather to heave Jacks into her arms, Heather felt the talons close around her. Squeezed breathless, she was rising up, banking above the smoking chaos of Akolan. She saw the city center, its banners torn and several buildings burning. The smoke twisted into the sky, and they flew through it, ascending above and into the white clouds that hovered over the palaces of the Lords of Prey.

But they did not fly that way.

They banked again and headed southwest. Heather was exhausted by her attempted escape, overwhelmed by the sudden failure, and half choked by the pincer grip of the eagle's talons. She fainted.

* * *

Heather awoke from time to time, seeing below her mountains she did not know and a river she did not recognize. Every time she awoke she tried to identify her surroundings, but she saw nothing familiar except for that river flowing out of the mountains.

Where was Uncle Garten taking her? Was he rescuing her? Would she reunite with her brother and Emma? Had he turned back to their side?

It couldn't be. The look she had seen in his eye back in Akolan was not one of friendship. He was furious. Akolan's Longtreader administration had been his invention. It had been his achievement, and she had, after being there only a few days, inspired the community to its most decisive act of defiance ever. She hoped they would survive this phase and be able to carry out the rest of their audacious plan.

The clouds faded to black.

When she woke the last time, the eagle was descending over a long lake that she assumed the river had led to. There were several islands. Near a large dam, a high-peaked central island was flanked on either side by three smaller islands. In the distance she saw a wall—a dam wall on the lakeside—and a city within. It was larger than Akolan and surrounded by a wide black ring wherever the water wasn't present. Peering more intently, she saw that the black section was merely burned-back wood and grass, beyond which grew a thick forest.

The city itself seemed to hum with activity. She saw a large square and a crowd gathered there. She longed to see it closer because she knew what it was.

It was First Warren, the seat of rabbitkind's rule for over a century. This was Whitson Mariner's home, and that of all his noble descendants. It was the place that Emma ought to rule from. It would have been where Smalls' kingdom started. He would have been crowned there, were they to win the war. He would have been married there, had he survived. She wept then, for all she had lost.

Though she wept, still a part of her was glad she had been able to save Jacks and to use her gifts to help the cause in Akolan. She had done what she could.

Heather wondered why Uncle Garten was taking her to First Warren. She knew that Smalls' and Emma's brother, Winslow, ruled the city as a puppet governor for Morbin, and she wondered what fresh torments awaited her there. They were descending lower and lower, just above the water. Heather prepared herself to see First Warren, trying not to think of what might have been had things turned out differently. She gazed ahead at the dam wall and braced for what was there.

But the eagle banked before they reached the dam and circled around to the large high-peaked island. Swirling ever closer, he dropped toward the crown of the deserted rocky peak. The eagle released Heather, and she fell, rolling over and over on a small plateau atop the island. The eagle landed, and Garten leapt off, walking toward Heather with an angry expression.

"I leave you here, you troublesome girl."

"Why not turn back, Uncle?" she asked, getting to her knees as the wind whipped on the island top. "There's still time for you."

"You think this will turn your way?" he asked, incredulous. "I assure you, it won't."

"Shall I open the gate?" the eagle asked from behind Heather.

"Yes!" Garten shouted, and his cry echoed around the lake.

"What gate? Uncle, what are you doing to me? Will you leave me for dead, chained on top of this desolate island?"

"The rebellion cannot succeed, Heather," he said, looking at her with intense exasperation. "You have been undoing the work of years!"

"I am glad to undo the work of traitors. May many more do so after I'm gone."

He ripped free his sword and pointed it at Heather. "You don't understand, because you are only a child. But we live in a world with certain realities."

"Realities, like Morbin eating our young at his feasts?" she asked, defiant. Garten's face changed from cold anger to hot rage. She went on. "Realities, like we are betrayed by our own flesh and blood?"

"Yes!" he said, lunging forward.

He plunged his blade into Heather's middle.

The pain was intense, but the shock was greater still. She couldn't believe he had done it. She stood and staggered back, hands pressed to a wound she knew was mortal. She gasped, eyes wide, and lurched farther back still. Uncle Garten advanced, his face set in a simmering glower. She tried to speak but coughed painfully instead. Her vision blurred, and she struggled to stay upright. Garten stepped closer still, glancing behind her before returning his angry gaze to her terrified face.

"I was building a world where rabbits could survive," he said, his voice cracking and his face taking on an almost tender expression. "I was making order. I was making a way. All we had to do was bow our heads and bend our knees. That was the price of peace, the price of survival. But you! You and your agitators rose up and raised your heads." He took a deep breath and looked out over the dam to First Warren and sighed. He turned back to Heather, his eyes wet and his voice hoarse. "And so Morbin will come. He will take our raised heads and pile a stack of skulls so high it will blot out the sun. You don't understand, little doe, what you've done. But all these deaths are on your head."

Then Garten Longtreader kicked Heather hard, so that she stumbled back and fell into a deep black pit.

Chapter Forty-Eight

The Challenge

It was Victory Day morning in First Warren, and Picket was walking to the governor's palace in broad daylight. He shook his head, glancing across at Helmer, who limped along on the other side of Whit, the tall white rabbit whose face was so horribly scarred.

"We're taking a terrible risk," Picket said, and Whit nodded in agreement.

Helmer shrugged. "You have to jump in order to land," he said.

"But you don't have to jump on a spike," Picket replied. "This is madness."

They had gained the gate with a word from Whit, to whom the guards bowed as they passed.

"Moonlight was certain Whit could get us in," Helmer said, "and we have a job to do."

Picket frowned but walked on in step with his fellows. At the governor's door, a nervous servant with a splendid red neckerchief stepped forward ahead of the fifty guards who surrounded the door, holding up his hands.

"I'm so sorry, but Prince Winslow is very busy with the Victory Day ceremony set to begin soon. He may not be disturbed today."

"Out of the way," Whit growled. Stepping past the servant and through the unsettled soldiers, he pushed the door open. Picket breathed out relief as they passed the soldiers, and he and Helmer followed Whit in. Inside, they saw a spectacular entrance with a double stairway leading up to the higher floors. They took the steps in threes and, reaching the top of the stairs on the fifth floor, walked into a large room that opened onto a wide balcony overlooking the square.

Whit walked ahead, flanked by Helmer and Picket. They were all three dressed sharply, with military precision and detail. Helmer wore all black with a cape draped over his strong shoulders. Picket looked a complete officer in his neat uniform set off by his black scarf. Whit was dressed like a prince. None wore a trace of red.

They walked onto the wide balcony and found Prince Winslow there, surrounded by several officers and councilors, including Captain Daggler. Daggler, who had been sitting and speaking, stopped and rose quickly. He moved his hand to the sword hilt at his side.

Winslow dropped his cup, spilling wine down the white gown he wore. Picket noticed how old Winslow looked up close, how fragile he had become.

"Whitbie?" Prince Winslow asked. "What…what is the meaning of this?"

"Greetings, brother," Whit said. "Do I still have the honor of protection here?"

"Do you still swear allegiance to Morbin?" Daggler asked sharply, stepping forward.

"I'm speaking to another member of the royal family, Daggler," Whit answered calmly, spitting after saying the name, as did Picket and Helmer. "I'll address you when I'm ready—if I wish to."

Daggler growled and nodded at the guards, who stood ready. Picket felt an insistent urge to draw his sword, to strike out at Daggler, but he maintained a steady expression.

"You come back *this* day?" Prince Winslow asked, and Picket saw from the balcony heights overlooking the square that Victory Day preparations were nearly complete. The crowd was already gathering for the imposed festivities. "Of all days, you choose this one?"

"Do I still have your safe conduct?" Whit asked. "And that of my companions? As per the terms, I brought only two."

"Yes," Winslow said, agitated. "Daggler, please sit down." The captain backed away, sneering at Winslow as he did. He didn't sit but stood apart, whispering to his nearest lieutenant.

"Thank you, brother, Lord Governor of Morbin's Second City of Slaves," Whit said, bowing briefly with a smirk. Helmer and Picket stayed stiffly upright, neither betraying a hint of fear.

"So you come here," Winslow said, "a disgraced failure, accompanied by almost a child and an old cripple, by the looks of it. Though the cripple looks familiar," he said, peering at Helmer. Then he turned back to his brother. "What does it mean, Whitbie? Do you turn yourself in and beg for my mercy? You're right to. The resistance is so pathetically small now, and its reach grows shorter every day. What can you mean by coming here?"

"I am the second son of Jupiter the Great, killed this day, years ago, by your master, Morbin Slaver. Our youngest brother and the first rightful heir, young Smalden, died fighting for Father's cause. Did you know this?"

"And so the rebellion outside is dashed to pieces and that little upstart is silenced forever," Winslow said bitterly. "I call that good. *I* am the oldest!"

"Our father was not the oldest, brother," Whit said. "You had a chance to be better than Uncle Bleston and accept the decision Father made. But you were only too eager to assume a hollow throne and accept a false crown."

"The bearer of the Green Ember is dead," Winslow answered, "and so I am right to rule, by all accounts. It is settled. No more troubles. Rabbitkind can unite behind my outlook, first envisioned by Ambassador Longtreader, for a new world based on peace and prosperity for all. But why are you here?"

"You are wrong," Whit said. "There is an heir. Peace with Morbin is slavery and degradation for rabbits."

"My patience is at an end, my sad little brother," Winslow said. "I say again, and for the last time, why are you here?"

"I will trouble you no further. We will share our message," Whit said, "and I invite the Lord Captain of Her

Royal Highness's Army to bring it." He bowed to Helmer, who stepped forward. Winslow's face showed recognition now, and then a spreading alarm. Helmer, a dismissive frown on his face, reached inside his cloak. At this action, the guards, along with Daggler, grabbed at their swords, and Winslow staggered backward with a fragile gasp, his wine-stained shirt looking like a wound. Helmer drew out a scroll, still frowning, and began to unroll it as the tension eased a little.

"So says Princess Emma, heir of all Natalia and rightful bearer of the Green Ember," Helmer began. "To the usurper's marionette, Winslow the Coward, greetings. You were once my elder brother, but I disown you. I disinherit you and will soon turn you out of the palace you have stolen." Helmer read this first part of the letter looking at the paper, but soon enough his eyes rose to meet those of Winslow, and he spoke the message straight to the wide-eyed rabbit's face. He had it by heart. "Your time for pretended rule is at an end. Your savage policies are overturned. When the sun sets tonight, I will have made an end of your intrigues with our enemies, and rule shall be returned to its rightful place in rabbitkind. You are warned, therefore. Fly before my wrath, Winslow Coward. Or stay and face it, I beg. But know this. The reckoning that has long haunted your steps will this day overtake you and strike the pretended crown from your head." Helmer paused. "So says my princess, and my message is ended." He made a curt bow, then retreated to stand beside Whit again. Picket kept his steady eyes on Daggler, whose fierce anger was stoked beneath a mask of haughty reproof.

"What can you be at?" Prince Winslow asked, his face showing a mix of confusion and fear. "Is this a jest, Whitbie?"

Whit glanced over at Picket, who shook his head coldly. "I assure you, it is not," Picket said.

"This part is not in the letter," Helmer said, cold and ruthless. He pointed at Daggler. "You and I will meet this day, and you will never see another sunrise."

"I will hang you by the feet and beat the life from you—" Daggler began, ripping free his sword and stepping forward. Helmer did not move.

"Stop, Daggler," Winslow said. "My brother has safe conduct here for himself and his guests. But I ask you now," he went on, turning to Whit, "to leave my house this instant."

Whit nodded, then turned and walked back toward the stairs. Picket and Helmer followed him at his right and left, and they walked down the steps with no great haste. They quit the steps and marched out the door, their faces grave and contemptuous.

"Will they come?" Picket whispered after they passed the gathered soldiers at the gate and were back on the path toward the woods.

"I hope so," Whit answered.

"Even if they don't," Helmer said, smiling, "that felt good."

Chapter Forty-Nine

The Rattling

Picket never turned around, but he could feel they were being followed. They moved as fast as they could with Helmer's bad leg. Rounding a bend, they dived for the cover of a hollow in a thicket, while three rabbits dressed just as they were appeared and continued along the path. Picket peeked out a thin opening in the hollow and watched as Captain Daggler's band walked past not long after.

"They bought it," Whit said.

"I suppose," Helmer replied, peeking out at the creeping band. "Though that fake Helmer's limping a little too much."

"Hopefully he won't crack a smile," Picket said.

"Let's go," Whit said.

In a few minutes they were at a safe house near the square, and they followed Whit down stone stairs into a dim basement.

"You made it!" Weezie said, rushing up to them. "We were so worried." Airen nodded and hugged her brother.

"Did you stoke a fire, friend Whit?" Captain Moonlight asked, smiling eagerly.

Whit glanced around the room and nodded. "I think it was more like blastpowder than a simple stoking. Captain Helmer's message wounded and alarmed my—um, well—Winslow. But Daggler is certain to be coming for us now."

"Good. Then we proceed," Moonlight said. Whit nodded, and Moonlight turned to Helmer. "I think you speak for the princess here, Captain. There is no turning back for us now. There will be no place to hide after this. If we fail, we fail forever."

"For the princess, I say let the end come," Helmer answered. "Let us shake this place and, after all the rattling clamor, see who is still standing."

"For the Mended Wood," Picket said, and every head nodded in steady resolution.

"To your places!" Captain Moonlight roared. The room emptied as rabbits hurried to their assigned tasks.

Picket accepted his heavy pack from Weezie, and they hugged quickly. "I'll *see* you," Weezie said. Picket nodded as Weezie hurried up the stairs.

Picket and Helmer followed Whit through a door on the far side of the basement. This led into a dark tunnel, around a cleared section of a collapsed passage, and then through another long tunnel. After descending a spiral ladder and crossing several more dank passages, Whit turned and placed a finger over his mouth. It was time to be silent. They climbed up again, coming finally to the lip of a disused cistern. What water was left there was brackish and foul-smelling. Picket's pack was heavy, and he shifted its weight to ease his cramping back. Whit turned again and whispered. "This used to supply the palace, but it hasn't been used in ages. Almost everyone's attention will be on the palace front, the side facing the square, and the crowd gathered there. If we break through just above here, we'll be northeast of the palace, with a short sprint to the trellis. There will be guards, so stay sharp."

"I'll be sharp again when we're aboveground," Helmer said, grimacing, "and away from this sewer."

"Oh, this isn't the sewer," Whit said. "But I considered that route."

"Be grateful, Master," Picket said, patting Helmer's back and smiling. "You always say, 'Things will get worse.' But they didn't this time."

"The day is young," Helmer said, smirking, "and so are you."

They hurried on and reached the ladder's last rung, which brought them to a long iron platform. Whit opened a small door, and they climbed through the narrow opening and into blackness. Picket crawled on, just behind Whit, through a low-roofed tunnel. He had to drag his pack, as the space wasn't high enough for him to crawl through with it on his back. He heard Whit stop ahead and a sound of scraping metal.

"Picket," Whit whispered, and Picket crawled ahead. In the darkness, Whit found Picket's hands and pressed them up against a rotting door. "Push!" Whit said in a soft but urgent tone.

Picket pushed. He strained against the heavy door, and he could tell that Whit was doing the same. There was no room for Helmer in the tight space beneath the old door, but he and Whit shoved with an intense final effort, and Picket heard a crack. Soon they were pushing through thick clods and grass, emerging at last into sunlight in an overgrown field. Whit surfaced first, and Picket followed, imitating the prince by lying low in the tall grass. Picket at once thought of the high grass fields of their Nick Hollow home, where he and Heather had spent so many happy hours playing Starseek. Beyond the grass to the north, a field, and some barracks, there rose the high wall. Atop the wall, which Picket knew at this part was a dam against the large lake beyond, sat a large fort. Picket remembered that this fort was where a large company of wolves was housed. He and Whit were trying to get the cold clods off their fur and clothes when Helmer emerged and began peering around. He frowned at them and whispered harshly, "We're not going to a fancy dress party, bucks."

Picket rolled his eyes, but he stopped knocking the dirt free. Whit smiled and whispered, "Maybe it will hide some of my scars."

"And some of his ugly," Helmer added, nodding at Picket. Picket smiled, and the three intruders crawled forward. Picket saw only two guards at the back of the palace. They were scouting the perimeter, and they seemed to have just passed the prowlers on their route. Both walked on with their backs to the three.

Helmer nodded at Picket. Picket leapt from their cover and rushed across the gap. When he reached the wall of the palace, he froze, his back to the lattice-covered wall. He was prepared for the guards to turn, but they never did. They continued their course on down the row of old stone buildings while Helmer hobbled forward, with Whit at his side.

"Up the lattice," Whit whispered, and Picket launched into the effort. He made quick work of it, nimbly climbing high without much fear of falling. What a difference there was between the old fearful Picket and the one who thought nothing of scaling a flimsy trellis on the side of a many-storied building. *Everything doesn't get worse.*

Picket glanced down and found Whit right behind him, though Helmer was laboring up the side at a much slower pace. They had walked too much, put too much strain on Helmer's bad leg for one day. But the stubborn old buck hadn't allowed any discussion about whether he would be the one to deliver the princess's message. And he climbed on despite the agony in his shoulder, his teeth clenched tight and a fierce determination on his face.

Picket reached the rooftop at last and slid over the lip of the dizzying edge. A guard was keeping careless watch near the ledge, and he observed Picket coming over the top with a stunned, uncomprehending look. Picket had him to the ground, knocked out, before his friends reached him on the roof. He hadn't had time to give the alarm. Whit bounded over the edge, and Helmer slid over, gasping as he came. Five soldiers were guarding the far side of the rooftop, all gazing out over the crowd in the square on the other side, not noticing Picket or his companions.

Whit led them, creeping along, to a shed halfway to the front edge. They crouched behind it, and Picket went to his pack. They could hear the noise of the crowd in the square below, the unsettled hum of thousands of voices merging into a common rumble. Then a trumpet, and a strange sudden silence.

"Greetings, on this glorious day!" Prince Winslow's voice, though more brittle than it should have been at his age, was strong enough to be heard over the silent square. "Today we celebrate the victory of our king, Morbin Everstrong, and the new order of progress and peace he has brought to us." A slow, unsettled applause began, then intensified. Picket worked on, imagining the soldiers inciting the crowd to clap. He scowled as Winslow went on, praising the vile creature who murdered his own father. "Our savior gave us this city and the gift to live in the light of his kindness. Morbin Invincible is our lord forever! Rabbitkind's alliance with our king, forged through the brave and noble efforts of Ambassador Longtreader, is celebrated today. Ambassador Longtreader joined us last year but this year will be at our sister city, Akolan, for their celebrations. He sends his regards through me." More tepid applause, followed by increasingly vigorous cheers.

"We don't have much time," Helmer whispered, glancing first at the guards, then up at the sun's location. "Are you ready, Ladybug?"

"I am," Picket answered, fastening the last buckle.

"Remember," Helmer said, "that symbols matter, more than you might imagine."

Picket nodded, then peeked around the edge of the shed. He couldn't see the balcony from which Winslow spoke but remembered it clearly from the morning's challenge. No doubt the prince was dressed in splendor, flanked by guards. He hoped Daggler wasn't there. Picket gazed at the crowd below, extending to the edge of the square and beyond. So many rabbits. For so long they had been slaves and had been told, year after year, that their slaver was their savior. The center of the square was split by the sacred standing stones, now desecrated by the raptor statues set atop them. Garten Longtreader kneeling was the first statue, of course, and the lone rabbit exception. Then the six Lords of Prey, with Morbin on the last step and the First Warren's particular tormentor, Falcowit, on the second. And more than merely his stone representation, the snow-white falcon himself was perched atop his memorial. He glowered over the crowd with a brooding woe that Picket felt in his bones.

"Now it's time to gather all the younglings. We will, uh…bring the young together to…to recite together our vows of honor," Winslow said with a sham tenderness. A worried whispering began in the crowd, and Picket could sense the hesitation parents had to bring their children forward. "Bring them, now!" Winslow cried. When the murmuring crowd wavered a moment more, Falcowit screeched a piercing command. It was so loud and terrifying that Picket himself, atop the palace and hidden almost entirely from view behind the shed, felt a jolt of paralyzing fear pass though him at that sound. He ducked again behind the shed and saw that his companions both felt the terrifying shiver as well.

"How can we oppose that?" Picket asked, gasping.

"They say the Six have calls that can almost kill," Whit said, breathing deep to restore his calm. "Part of Morbin's power is this power to command. It works on their own kind to compel, on rabbitkind to undo."

"It is a woeful sound," Helmer said, swallowing hard and nervously examining his weapons.

Picket peeked around the edge again and saw that the red-throated younglings were being brought forward. He ground his teeth together, and the fire inside him, which had gone cold at the white falcon's call, began to blaze again. He saw that the other sentinels, massive raptors all, were circling overhead.

"As the younglings gather, I am happy to announce that we have at last located the base of operations for the rebels." Prince Winslow went on, and Picket scowled at the scene as he resumed his post peering around the edge of the shed. Parents were leading their children to the center of the square, beneath the standing stone and statue atop which loomed Lord Falcowit. "Just this last hour, Captain Daggler has sent his best forces to infiltrate and destroy the last desperate scraps of the defeated resistance. Their location, beneath the forest in the remnants of the old warren, has been found out at last." Picket could hear the relish in his words. These were the confident pronouncements of a rabbit who had outmaneuvered a bitter enemy. "Captain Daggler's forces are inside now and are no doubt killing off the last of these traitors. Their disruptions are forever ended. Morbin rules here, and everywhere. He is the king of all Natalia!"

Chapter Fifty

The Battle for First Warren

It's time," Helmer said, and Picket stood. Helmer and Whit had fastened ropes to the foundation of the shed and held the other side of the long coiled rope in hand. "Are you sure this is the right length?" Helmer asked Whit.

"Reasonably sure," Whit answered. Then, "You can always go with Picket."

"No thanks," Helmer said, pulling on the rope to test its strength.

Prince Winslow talked on and on. "The resistance, which troubled us so much recently," he called out from below, his voice triumphant, "has been dealt with. The rebellion against Lord Morbin is over!"

At that moment, a large blast was heard—and felt. Picket looked out past the square as the earth shifted, knocking many in the crowd off balance, and the forest collapsed in several places. Picket pumped his fist, and it seemed that in the square below they understood what had happened. The old warrens beneath the forest had been blown up and collapsed in on whatever—and whoever—was down there.

Picket watched as the guards atop the roof scrambled to the middle stairway, awaiting orders from their senior commanders. He hoped that they would leave, but they stayed. In fact, they were reinforced by a team of ten archers.

"Great," Helmer said. "It's worse."

"It doesn't change anything," Picket said.

The crowd was nervous, uncertain of what to do. Some began to flee the square while guards struggled to pen them in. Picket scowled down at the brutality of the officers against their own kind, against does and the elderly. He bristled, then tried to calm down by breathing deeply. *I have to stay focused on my task. I can't own it all.*

The crowd surged, moving dangerously near to a panicked rush that might crush hundreds. Then the blast of several trumpets and a piercing shriek from Lord Falcowit brought them under control, and something like order resumed.

"Lord Falcowit will see what has happened," Winslow shouted. "Stay calm! All is well. No doubt Captain Daggler's forces have destroyed the rebels below." Picket could hear in his voice that Winslow didn't believe what he was saying. The prince was worried and unsettled. Almost panicked.

They watched Lord Falcowit and the raptor sentinels fly toward the forest, no doubt to ascertain the damage.

Falcowit banked hard and screeched again, then cried out to the crowded square, "If one redthroat moves from this place, I shall release the wolves!"

"Everyone, stay where you are!" Winslow called. "We have not had the wolves set on us here since the afterterrors. None of us wants to see that again!"

"They're going," Whit said, watching the raptors approach the collapse and disappear into the ruin.

"Now, Picket!" Helmer whispered.

Picket nodded. He tore around the side of the shed, heading for the now heavily guarded edge of the palace. He ran past the first startled guards, who called out, alerting the remaining guards on the edge. These turned to see a rabbit with a loose black cape draped around his back and a strange series of buckles and belts around his body. Picket wore a sword at his side, but he did not draw it as he sped toward the guards, who gathered to block his approach and raised their own weapons.

Just before Picket reached the outstretched points of their blades, he leapt, flipping over them and ending on the other side. The astonished guards looked on because there was nothing where he had been.

Nothing but air.

Picket dipped a moment, dropping near the edge of the balcony, where Winslow cried out for calm. Then, jutting out his arms, he felt his taut glider catch the air, and he rose in an elegant arc.

The gathered rabbits gasped and pointed as Picket flew over the younglings herded in the square's center. Then he swept up and landed on the seventh standing stone. He stood there, poised beneath the iron-wrought feet of Morbin's massive statue. The crowd buzzed with an uneasy awe while Picket looked down to see Weezie. She smiled up at him.

"Ready?" she asked.

He nodded. Weezie was lifted up so she stood on the shoulders of two stout bucks. She ripped the red preymark free of her neck and tossed it toward the balcony. Then her confederates produced several small barrels from their packs and carefully handed them up to Weezie, who tossed them high to Picket. Picket caught them cautiously one by one and set them all around the iron talons at the base of the monstrous statue. Finally, Weezie tossed up a torch.

Picket caught it and immediately raised it high, thinking of his sister. "The seed of the new world smolders," he cried. "But a fire comes first. Bear the flame!"

He set the first barrel's fuse alight, then leapt from the top of the standing stone.

"Get back!" Weezie called, joined by others from the resistance, who forced back the part of the crowd surrounding the ground beneath the statue. As Picket swept once more over the exposed younglings, the small blastpowder kegs ignited in a quick succession of explosive bursts. Orange flames spit amid plumes of acrid black smoke as the massive statue blasted free from its desecrated pedestal.

The watching crowd gasped as Morbin's statue rose amid the explosion, then turned, slowly twisting through the smoke, and began to fall. It sped down, knocking against the seventh standing stone, sending a spiderweb of cracks along the outside of the sacred pillar. Then it struck the ground, half-sinking in a smoking wreck at the stone's base.

Picket swept around the square, and every eye followed his flight. Winslow, from his balcony, had one hand over his heart and the other covering his speechless mouth. Aides were helping him stand. Picket swept back and landed atop the seventh standing stone, his feet feeling the heat of the blast. He raised his hands for quiet, and, for a few moments, he had it.

"Now, rabbits of First Warren, join your fellows in the fight. Free the younglings! Fight the enemy! For the Green Ember and the Mended Wood!"

A shout rose up, and many things happened at once.

Arrows aimed at Picket just missed as he leapt from the seventh standing stone, now free of the tyrant's statue, and swept over the crowd in a graceful glide. He saw Captain Moonlight, followed by a hundred bucks, rush on the greatest concentration of guards, overwhelming them at that spot.

He banked back and saw parents of the exposed younglings surge toward their children, many finding them at once. Others joined in, helping to free and connect the families. Weezie was among them, helping guide the fleeing families toward the safest havens in the city.

A screech in the distance chilled the hearts and arrested the flight of the rabbits. But Weezie and the other resistance rabbits who had infiltrated the crowd worked all the harder to focus the escape.

Picket swept up, seeing with alarm that the raptor sentinels, led by Lord Falcowit, were speeding back toward the square. He glanced up and saw that the fortress on the dam wall was opened, and wolves were pouring out by the hundreds, leaping down the long stone steps toward the short road to the square. They would be there in a very short time.

Arrows whizzed past him, shocking him back to focus on the present danger. He dipped and swerved, then banked to fly over the heads of the largest concentration of Daggler's soldiers in the square. Many missing arrows found marks among these soldiers, and the barrage slowed while Picket swept up once again, aiming for the balcony where Winslow staggered and Daggler shouted angry orders.

Nearly to the balcony, he looked up to see several enemy soldiers knocked from the roof above and two rabbits leaping far out over the edge. Helmer and Whit held ropes that uncoiled in the air and then went taut. The two rabbits then jerked and swung in a tight line toward the balcony, just ahead of Picket. They swung in, Helmer quitting his grip so he sailed into a huddle of officers, whom he bowled down in a tackling tangle. Whit held on longer and landed gracefully, drew his sword, and set the point to Winslow's neck.

Helmer stood, ripping free his own sword with a blood-curdling shout. He brought it down on the nearest officer's blade, snapping the startled soldier's sword in half. The officer shrank back, but two more were there. Helmer had disarmed one and was near to ending the other when Daggler darted behind him. He drove his sword toward Helmer's back, a coward's move that would kill Helmer for certain, but Picket swept in at the last moment, tackling Daggler with a vicious cry. Daggler's sword fell to the ground behind Helmer as the old captain kept up his alarming assault on his foes, who far outnumbered him.

Picket rose from the jarring impact and saw Daggler scamper away down the stairway. He started to go after him, then turned to see Helmer fighting off eight officers, who were slowly regaining their nerve. Picket leapt into the clash, ripping free his sword and sending it into action at once. Whit had secured his brother in a chair, and now he joined in the battle as the three, led by an irrepressible Helmer, beat back the eight.

When this desperate battle was done and the eight enemies were stretched on the ground, Picket turned back, gasping, and hurried to the edge of the balcony to look out over the square.

Picket's eyes widened, and his heart seemed to stop. He saw wolves pour into the square just as the raptors arrived back, talons flashing in the sun.

Chapter Fifty-One

Breech and Banner

Picket forced himself to look away from the horrific scene beginning to unfold in the square below. He turned his gaze to the west wall. That part of the wall was past the dam and the lake, and on the other side of it lay the Black Gap, with the Great Wood beyond.

He gazed at the wall, willing it to fall. But it stood, and so at last he tore his gaze away and looked again at the scene below. Most of the younglings had been led out of the square, but they hadn't gone far. After the wolves and raptors made quick work of the small band of resistance fighters, they would be set loose on the rest. Picket had hoped more rabbits of First Warren would have joined the fight, and some had. Most had fled. He couldn't blame them. They had been trained to cower for so long.

But Picket had been trained to fight.

He looked up at the white falcon and saw him call out commands to the attacking raptors and the horde of murderous wolves.

Picket sprang onto the banister of the balcony and sheathed his sword. He nodded to Helmer, then bent to leap.

Before he could launch, an ear-splitting explosion ripped through the west wall, shaking the palace and the square. Several more blasts followed, and Picket's heart leapt as he turned and saw the wall splitting apart and the stone crumbling down in a series of terrific billowing blasts.

"Yes!" Picket shouted. And he heard the resistance fighters echo his shout for joy. The wolves were put off a moment, then resumed their craven assault, while the raptors arced toward the smoking gap in the west wall.

And it was a gap.

In moments, the gap was filled.

Rabbits, in great numbers, charged through the smoldering ruin of the west wall and poured into First Warren. Picket felt hope flooding every fiber of his body, and he gave another shout, then hopped down off the banister and clasped Helmer in an embrace.

"It's not over yet, son," Helmer said. "We have work." Picket nodded.

"I'll keep watch over this one," Whit said hoarsely, standing over his brother, Prince Winslow. Whit's eyes were filled with tears as he gazed out at the army of rabbits entering the city under the double-diamond banner.

"What should I do, Master?" Picket asked.

Helmer's intelligent eyes took in the scene, and in a moment, he nodded. "The unbroken section of the wall. The enemy has a huge advantage by air with the raptors' return, but they have left the wall top unguarded. Lord Hewson will know it. We must win those positions."

"Understood!" Picket said.

Picket saw the wolves turning, at Falcowit's command, to charge the vanguard of the rabbit attack. The resistance fighters were pressed back hard, but Captain Moonlight shouted for them to fight on. Picket watched until Falcowit's attention was turned away from his direction. Then he sprang onto the banister and leapt off the balcony, sending his arms out to engage the glider. He swept over the thin ranks of the resistance, calling out encouragement. Then he rose in a banking turn and glided up, losing his momentum just as he crested the top of the west wall. He landed on the stone top, about as wide as two carts, and hurried to look out over the waist-high wall on the outside edge. Just as he reached the edge, a large iron claw swung over the top and nearly took him apart. He dodged away just in time as the grappling hook found its grip, setting a firm hold in the wall. He rose and cautiously looked over and saw that Helmer was right. The army was sending large numbers all along the wall with grappling hooks and rope ladders, aiming to take the heights. He saw stacks of arrows in bundles being lugged up rope ladders behind archers with bows fixed over their shoulders as they scampered up the high wall.

"Come on!" Picket shouted, and he swept his arm toward the city. An answering cry echoed off the wall and into the Black Gap, which was now teeming with soldiers who poured in from the woods. Picket saw a set of stout rabbits pulling an empty cart, ahead of others who bore one of those large crossbow launchers he had seen at Harbone. He thought he might even recognize Heyward among those running alongside in support of the weapon. Despite their strength and haste, it would be a while before they could get the weapon in place. Perhaps too long. His gaze swept over the approaching army.

They must get into the city. If they were blocked out, the vanguard, along with the small resistance, would be routed by the wolves and raptors. Picket gave another defiant cry, then helped set several ladders, easing the approach of the archers nearest him. He ran along doing all he could on his section of the wall, until he came to the part that had been blasted apart. He stopped on the crumbling edge, almost losing his footing, then turned back to the city, to the scene unfolding below.

Surging ahead, the rabbit vanguard met the menacing wolves on the threshold of the square. Picket saw Cole and Captain Frye at the head of the army. Beside Cole, a stout rabbit bore the banner of the heirs of Whitson. The flag flew high, a white field with a double-diamond sign, red, then green. A fierce clash ensued, and Picket struggled to find his friends again in the kicked-up dust and ferocious fighting.

These wolves were nothing like the ones they had encountered outside Harbone. Instead, they were more disciplined and deft than any he had yet seen. They kept together and attacked in well-led packs, then regrouped at barked orders. They were still savage and merciless, but they matched this ferocity with organization.

Picket saw the banner, so close to the front line, and knew that Cole must be near it still. He watched as the banner dipped, then fell, as the massive staff split in two in the midst of a violent clash. It came down, rippling as it descended like a blanket over the fray.

Picket didn't hesitate. He leapt over the edge and swept down on the battle.

He was flying too fast, and he adjusted his approach. He aimed for the heart of the conflict and prepared his mind for the fight. Where was Cole, and Captain Frye? How could he help them? He knew he could help them most by shifting the battle in any small way. He glanced up at the seven standing stones, now with one fewer threatening statues. Then he remembered Helmer's words. *Symbols matter, more than you might imagine.*

Picket's heart was pumping fast, and he wanted badly to join in the battle. But he banked and swept over the center of the skirmish. He dipped low and, skimming the tops of the tangled warriors, snagged the edge of the now-tattered flag and gripped it tight as he rose again in a curving ascent. He concentrated now, holding firm and adjusting the drag on his flight, and just made the top of the third standing stone. He stood atop the grim stone image of Falcowit and gripped the broken pole as the flag, tattered though it was, streamed out beside him in the wind. He waved the torn banner back and forth.

“For the Mended Wood!” he cried. He heard an answering shout over the din of war and felt inside the fire of the good fight. He knew that all around, from the desperate fighters in the square to the hundreds rushing into First Warren through the west wall breach, the sight of this renowned warrior waving the true king’s banner atop this desecration of a statue was one to set the faintest heart on fire.

Chapter Fifty-Two

A Banner in Your Heart

Picket stood atop the statue of Lord Falcowit, waving the double-diamond banner like it was a beacon in the darkness and the survival of many souls depended on its light. He relished the moment. Then came a screech that rippled through his spine like ice. He turned to see Lord Falcowit himself high above, ordering an attack that was fast descending on him.

One of the black raptor sentinels sped toward him, talons flashing as he let out a terrifying shriek of his own, causing Picket to almost miss his footing. The raptor was flying so fast that Picket had no chance to sidestep the strike, not if he wanted to keep hold of the flag. And with every eye in the square on him, he dared not let go of this banner.

The shriek repeated, and he saw the hungry look in the eyes of the giant bird. There was no time. He was on him. The raptor raised his talons, poised to slice Picket to bits. At the last moment, Picket desperately swept back the banner and its broken pole, in line with the striking attacker.

The collision came with the bird's thunderous strike. Picket was knocked off the statue with tremendous force. He barely had wits enough to send out his arms to engage the glider briefly so his tumbling momentum was arrested enough that his landing was rough but not mortal. Still, he rolled over and over on the ground, finally coming to a stop.

Shaking his head free, he tried to stand, stumbling as he did, until strong hands gripped his arm. "Steady there," he heard. He looked over to see Coleden Blackstar.

"Cole!" They embraced, Picket still trying to shake off his confusion.

"What happened?" he asked.

"You just sent our flag through a raptor sentinel, for one," Cole said, looking carefully at Picket and breathing heavily. "That was very creative, by the way. And there are a few other things happening."

Picket's wits were coming back, and he surveyed the scene from where they stood in the square. "Where's Emma?"

"She's coming," Cole answered. "The vanguard's been joined by the next waves, and we have the wolves pinned back there, and there," he said, pointing. It seemed that the battle was twisting in their favor. "Jo's up there with the archers," Cole went on, pointing to the west wall, "and they are giving us some cover from your raptor friends. Emma is with the rear guard, with Lord Morgan and Vandalia's elite soldiers. Father is there as well, acting as field commander. She's fine."

"Lord Hewson isn't leading the attack?"

"No, Pick. Lord Hewson fell," Cole said. "After you… they didn't make it back."

Picket nodded gravely. Lord Hewson—and how many others?—had died getting him and Helmer into the city.

Cole pulled Picket behind an upturned cart and the wreckage of several battered stalls. "Listen, Pick. One reason we took the wall up there—at such a great risk and with horrible losses—was to try to be sure that none of the raptors escaped. We can't let word get to Morbin this quickly. If we can take the city back, we need time to fortify before Morbin organizes a massive assault."

"True," Picket said, frowning. "Our best hope is that Lord Falcowit is proud."

"What do you mean?"

"I mean he's kept this city for a long time," Picket said, "and he won't like the idea of going back to Morbin with the news that it's fallen. He might stay to the end and fight like mad to keep it."

"I'm not sure that's good news," Cole said, rising to look out over the top of the upturned cart. "Okay, Captain Longtreader. Where to now?"

Picket scanned the field. He saw the rabbit army encircling the wolf army, pushing them back into the square. The sentinels dealt with an increasing hail of arrows as they set in to wreak havoc on the rabbit forces in turns.

"Back into it!" Picket said, and he rose to rush into the fray. But as he turned one last time, he saw a skirmish playing out beneath the balcony of the prince's palace.

Daggler's rabbits were clashing with Captain Moonlight and a few of his remaining band.

Picket grabbed Cole, who had begun to tear off toward the main battle. Picket pointed. "That's the rabbit who murdered Helmer's niece, his brother-in-law, and a hundred other rabbits over the years."

"Let's go!" Cole said, and the two friends darted toward the fight.

Daggler's band outnumbered Moonlight's, and they were pressing their advantage, pushing the weary resistance fighters farther and farther back. Captain Moonlight had battled bravely on, though covered with gashes. He was on the ground now, and Daggler stood over him, sword poised and cackling haughtily. Picket was enraged and pushed his tired legs to go faster. Daggler rained down a hail of scything slices, each deflected desperately by the valiant rabbit, with less and less effect. Daggler laughed and took a deep breath. He dragged back his blade and brought it around in a windmill stroke. Picket cried out as Daggler's blade met Moonlight's feeble effort to deflect it. The blade broke in two, and the resistance leader was struck down.

Moonlight lay stretched on the ground, and Daggler loomed over him with a craven leer. He raised his sword to finish the job. Moonlight was wounded badly and lay motionless on the stone.

Picket and Cole finally reached the edge of the clash, and Picket leapt in, head over feet, sailing over several soldiers to land a crushing kick on Daggler just as he was about to drive home his blade. Picket fell hard as Daggler was sent clattering to the ground.

Picket sprang up. He had been prepared for the impact, while Daggler slowly dragged himself to his feet, shaking his head. Meanwhile, Picket was pressed by Daggler's guards, and he had to roll back and rip free his sword to block an assault by two soldiers.

His side was still outnumbered, though Cole was making a swathing circle, driving back and cutting down many enemies. Still, Daggler's band regained the ascendency, and Daggler himself, though jarred and likely injured, swept back into the battle with renewed rage.

Picket was pressed back, fighting for his life, and unable to do anything to help his fellows. He had just gotten his footing again with the two rabbits who were on him when a third joined his enemies, and he was driven back. He knew he couldn't hold out much longer. He glanced at the center of the battle, where Cole was facing Daggler, and he longed to help his friend. Cole was one of the best fighters he knew, but Daggler was dominating the encounter, and Cole was already bleeding from several wounds.

Picket's heart went out to his friend, and he rushed forward, taking a brutal wound to his hip but surprising his enemies. He sidestepped another mortal strike, then kicked down one opponent and struck another so that he would never rise again. Cole was on his back, desperately defending against Daggler's relentless assault. Picket didn't wait to deal with the third opponent but sprang away, painfully, to try to reach Cole. He lunged ahead, desperate to get to his friend in time. But he felt a blow and searing pain in his knee as he was knocked hard to the ground and rolled over and over.

The third of his opponents hadn't let him escape but had struck out as he tried to spring away. Now this enemy rabbit, a massive white-furred monster, rushed to finish Picket off, bringing his blade down in a powerful strike that Picket only just dodged, rolling over in agony. Grimacing, Picket tried to stand, but he crumpled immediately, his injured leg giving way. He forced himself up, balancing his weight on his good leg. Then another thundering strike fell, and he just caught it on his blade. But the blow sent a numb shivering up Picket's wrists that made his hands cold and almost useless for a moment, while his enemy rounded back with a kick to his face. This sent Picket spilling backward, and he rolled over again, barely holding on to his sword. He recovered just in time to bring his blade up to block the next killing stroke meant to end him, and he risked a glance over to Cole.

Cole was on his knees, swordless and wounded badly, while Daggler poised his blade over the defenseless rabbit.

Picket could do nothing to help.

Chapter Fifty-Three

A Traitor's Fate

Picket couldn't even cry out, so desperate was his own situation. On his back, he watched as the blade came round on Cole. Then an amazing collision, and Daggler was struck hard by the falling form of a black rabbit.

Helmer!

Helmer had leapt from the balcony and smashed into Daggler, and now both lay sprawled on the ground. Cole sagged and fell, and Picket's massive opponent, arrested by the same sight that had so distracted Picket's attention, rushed toward his own captain. Picket himself rose, putting his weight almost all on his good leg, and limped as quickly as he could, stumbling several times, toward Helmer and Cole. But the big white rabbit reached the scene first, and all Picket could do was call out a warning.

Helmer, hearing Picket's call, looked up at once and just ducked a strong slice meant to take off his head. Helmer sprang up then, an angry scowl displacing his shocked expression, and he rounded on the attacker. Picket hobbled on, reaching Cole just as Helmer sent the big white rabbit to his end. Picket knelt by his friend, checked his wounds, and stood guard over him. "I'm with you, Cole. I've got you. They'll have to get through me to get to you."

Helmer, fresh from overcoming the last opponent, turned toward Daggler. Daggler was on his feet and staring across at Helmer with intense hatred. Helmer was wounded, limping, and tired, but there was a fire in his eyes.

"Even if you take this city today," Daggler said, beginning to circle like the raptors he served, "it will only be for a moment. Morbin will bring such an avalanche down on you from the High Bleaks that you'll wish you had stayed in your cave." Helmer said nothing, only slowly stepped in the rhythm of the circling standoff, bearing his blade before him and moving carefully. "But you won't be around to see it—to see these weak fools finished off by Morbin himself and his hosts. I'm going to cut you down, gimp," Daggler went on, smiling wildly, "just like I did your niece. With this very sword."

Helmer's form didn't change, but Picket saw his eyes narrow into thinner slits. He waited and seemed calmer and calmer, while Daggler's eyes grew wilder still. Finally, Daggler screamed and charged.

Helmer met his charge, deflecting the series of strokes in the aggressive complicated attack. Daggler was half-mad but masterful. He wasted no stroke and fought with intensity and intelligence. Helmer concentrated on defense, blocking and gaining a better position with each new offensive from Daggler. Picket kept watch on Cole, but the clash all around seemed to stop while all gazed at Helmer and Daggler battling in their midst.

Daggler came at Helmer again. Helmer deflected stroke after stroke, sending only a few counterstrokes back at Daggler. Daggler grew more and more angry, and his thrusts came harder and faster. He was gasping for breath while Helmer breathed easier.

Finally, after a series of glancing blows, Daggler lunged for Helmer's middle. Helmer sidestepped and tripped Daggler, causing him to stumble. Daggler twisted back, off-balance, to deflect Helmer's slicing strike. Daggler overcompensated from the stumble and came too close to Helmer, who then struck up with his pommel, catching Daggler's chin and snapping his head back in a crunching blow. Having dazed his foe, Helmer wasted no time. He spun on his enemy and brought his cleaving blade around with fury.

Daggler fell dead with two thuds.

Picket's heart leapt, and he stumbled to his feet, waiting for the next enemy to come. But seeing their captain fall so decisively, Daggler's band fled. Picket saluted his master, and Helmer nodded back grimly. They met near Cole, who was sitting up drinking water offered by a medic. *Wait. A medic?*

Picket looked around the city for the first time in a while. He had been so engaged in this skirmish with Daggler's band that he had been unaware of what was happening elsewhere. But the scene was remarkable.

The wolf army was all but beaten, and several raptors lay dead on the ground.

Princess Emma rushed in, flanked by Vandalia Citadel's recently-elevated Lord Morgan, Lord Blackstar, several other lords and captains, and an exhausted Captain Frye. "Picket!" she shouted, and they embraced. Heyna Blackstar, who had been right beside Emma, ran to her brother. Then, seeing he was wounded, Emma hurried toward Cole.

"Your Highness," Lord Morgan called, "the medics will see to him. We must get you to the balcony to rally the city. We almost have them!"

"He's right, Your Highness," Lord Blackstar said, checking his son over. "Cole will be fine. I'll stay with him till he's safe. Heyna, go with the princess."

Emma nodded, "You're right. Let's go," she called, hurrying toward the palace.

Heyna squeezed her brother's hand, then followed Emma and the entourage as they left the square. Picket hobbled along for a little while beside Helmer, who was also limping, though not as badly. Then Picket collapsed, unable to put weight on his leg anymore. Emma saw and went to his side.

"Your leg," Emma said, examining his wounds. "It's bad, Picket. You need attention, now."

"Go, Emma," Picket said, gritting his teeth. "Get to the balcony."

Emma glanced back and forth from the palace to Picket, frowning. "Bring him!" she called. "Lord Morgan, Captain Parn," she commanded, "carry him up with us."

They obeyed, grabbing Picket between them and rushing on. As he was carried along, Picket saw, through a gap in the fighting, a clear view of the west wall and its blasted gap. The last of the reinforcements were charging through, and strong rabbits were pulling a cart into the city. His view was blocked again as Emma reached the palace and they hurried inside behind her. Picket saw in bobbing glimpses the changes to the palace from that morning. It had been a settled, orderly, fortified stronghold. Now it was as open as an abandoned shack.

The great room was empty, and Picket winced as they made for the stairs. Emma was in front, flanked by a Harbone soldier and Heyna.

One of the royal guards appeared from a secret door behind a wall and rushed at Emma with frantic eyes and a drawn sword. The attacker cut down the Harbone soldier before he was seen and lunged at Emma with his blade.

Heyna struck out with a deft kick to the attacker's wrist, sending his sword clattering to the ground. She balanced quickly, then spun and kicked the guard hard in the face. He fell back, dazed a moment, and by the time he was able to try again, he was subdued by strong rabbits in Emma's retinue.

Emma, eyes wide and scowling, hurried ahead. She ran, hand in hand with Heyna, to the stairs.

They rushed up the stairs, then raced through to the balcony. They stopped, seeing Prince Winslow sitting on a chair in the corner of the balcony, watching the battle play out with tears in his eyes. Whit stood beside him. Whit turned, saw Emma, and smiled, reaching for the mask he almost always wore. But it wasn't there.

"Your Highness," Helmer said, wheezing, "this is your brother, Whit. A noble rabbit without whom we...would not have had a chance in this battle."

Whit bowed to his sister, and then kissed her hand. "My sister, and my future queen, welcome to your home."

Emma kissed his forehead. "Thank you, brother," she said, squeezing his hands. "I'm so glad to see a brother who has kept faith. I hope we'll have time to speak soon. For now, we must finish the job here."

"Of course," Whit said, and he led the way to the edge of the balcony. "Your forces have routed the wolf division below, and there are two raptors left." Lord Morgan and Captain Parn sat Picket in a chair on the edge of the balcony, where he could see well.

"I see Falcowit," Emma said, pointing to the white falcon flying high above the city, "but where's the other?"

"There!" Whit said, pointing to the west wall, where a lone archer stood atop the wall, firing arrows as a massive raptor swept down on him like lightning.

Picket's eyes widened.

"Jo!"

Chapter Fifty-Four

The Last Shots

Picket's heart sank as he watched Jo's heroic stand. Jo Shanks was Picket's loyal friend from Halfwind Citadel, a comrade who had fought by his side through dark days. Jo had left his elite archer unit, the Bracers, in order to follow Picket and join Helmer's Fowlers.

Whit explained that the archers had been battling with the raptors since ascending the wall, and all the rest had apparently fallen in the fight. Picket could see the broken tops of the wall where raptor attacks had devastated the brave archers.

Now Jo would be next. Jo would be last.

Picket winced against the pain in his leg, but he wasn't worried about that now. Jo was firing over the lip of the wall, ducking back under to nock another arrow, then emerging to fire again. The attacking raptor dodged as he came, but still Picket saw shafts bristling from his body where Jo's arrows had hit.

The raptor was done dodging now. Beating his wings, he bore down on the lip of the wall, preparing to shatter all with his massive talons. Picket groaned as the raptor rushed ahead.

A murderous glare. An awful screech. A frantic beating of wings, and the massive bird was there.

Picket cried out in anguish. "No!"

At the last moment, Jo leapt onto the rim of the wall, and then, as the talons swiped and the crushing attack came, he sprang high into the air. The raptor tore through the wall's edge, shattering stone and sending a spray of mortar all around. Jo seemed to hang in the air a moment as the terrific collision hit. The raptor's momentum took him through the lip of the inner wall, and then, bursting stone once more, he smashed through the outer rim of the wall, sliding out of the city and into the air beyond, disappearing from Picket's sight.

Jo landed on the rubble left behind and lost his footing. He slid down the outer lip remnants and nearly plunged from the heights. He snagged a brittle tangle of bricks, still somehow attached atop the ruined wall.

The rabbits on the palace balcony were in agony, but Picket saw that Emma was calling out orders, listening to suggestions from her advisors, and working hard to rally the various forces into a unit. Captain Frye was busy trying to get archers from the field to the west wall and had quit the balcony to help the effort himself. Lord Morgan of Vandalia and Captain Parn of Harbone were overseeing the tactical assets on the ground, desperately trying to get weapons in place to help. Helmer stood by Emma, with Whit on her other side, keeping a side-eye on Winslow. The brittle rabbit was a wreck and posed no apparent threat.

Picket's attention was all on Jo. His dear friend was clinging to a shabby section of a crumbling wall. Picket felt helpless.

He glanced down at his leg. It was bleeding badly, and he could put no weight on it now. He hated being out of commission at this crucial point in the battle. Then a thought struck him hard.

You don't need legs to fly.

He hobbled up to the edge and looked over at Helmer. Helmer saw the determination in his eyes and hurried to Picket's side. He lifted Picket to the balcony rail and steadied him as he, balancing on his good leg, bent and launched into the air.

Picket sent out his arms to engage the glider, caught the quickening wind, and rode it up in an arc toward the west wall. He was aiming for Jo, who struggled to get a grip on the debris crumbling on the edge of the west wall heights. Picket began to believe he would reach his friend in time.

Then, beyond the battered wall, the raptor rose into view.

The Preylord was banking back for another attack. Picket willed himself ahead, but he could see he would not make it in time. He would only be closer—close enough to see the end clearly. And powerless to stop it.

The bird bore down, building momentum again and setting his talons to tear Jo to pieces.

Jo heard the shrieking screech and made a last effort to climb the crumbling rubble. Though the bricks gave way in alarming near misses, Jo managed to scramble up the side and regain the height again. He staggered around, searching for something. Then he reached down and raised his bow. He unlocked his quiver and drew out his last arrow.

Massive beating wings and a gaping beak. Talons, razor sharp and slicing through the air. The raptor came.

Jo sagged. Then, taking a deep breath, he raised himself to his full height and nocked his arrow. Stretching back his bowstring, he calmly waited for the racing raptor to raise his head again.

And he did. So close that Picket cried out in desperate fear for his friend, the raptor raised his head and bellowed as he readied his awful talons for the strike. But Jo, aiming carefully, let fly his arrow. It sped away, and for Picket the time seemed to slow. The arrow was true, and it found the raptor's throat. It pierced the bird, silencing his ominous screech, and the life left his angry eyes. He sped on, dead weight hurtling toward the lonely archer's high perch of rubble.

Jo had no time to leap over his attacker. He didn't even have time to lower his bow. Picket was close enough to see the dead bird's wrecking fall. Losing little of his attacking speed, the raptor collided with the wall just below where Jo was perched precariously, shattering the peak of the wall entirely. Jo fell, among a hundred bricks, spinning down into a chaotic plunge.

Picket saw the bursting bricks, the rain of ruined stone, and the spray of mortar. The death-dealing debris fell,

and his aching body called out for him to bank away and save his own life.

Then he saw Jo.

Picket flew into the shower of stone, diving into the murderous chaos of the crumbling wall. Jo was there, falling just beyond what was left of the west wall. Picket swept in, dodged a series of shattered stones, and reached Jo just as he was halfway down.

Picket tried to plan for what came next, but there was no way to do this well. He disengaged the glider, grabbed Jo, and tried to secure him on his back as he reengaged. But the glider plunged, unable to bear the added weight, just as a hail of stone fell all around them. Desperate, he somehow wrestled the glider into softening their landing as they rolled and rolled along the outskirts of the crashing debris. Stone rained down around them, sending up a cloud of dust amid a terrific rattling din. On the ground, Picket tried to leap to cover Jo, but his leg gave way, and they merged together in a heap. Picket covered his head and Jo's as best as he could.

As the dust cleared, Picket saw that Jo wasn't moving. He called for help, trying to find a medic. Picket's own pains were beyond what he could process. His ears rang. His vision blurred. He saw the battle, but it made no sense.

At last help arrived, and Picket stumbled out of the ruins of the wrecked wall. Medics went to work on Jo, and several soldiers came along and helped them get clear. They headed back toward the square, Picket's leg giving way so badly that the soldiers finally carried him to the edge of the square. There he met up with Heyward, who was with Emerson and a team settling the bowstriker in place. Picket came awake as they pointed at Falcowit, who was streaking away overhead.

That roused him up from his stupor, and he pointed at the bolting bird. "There! We can't let him escape!"

"We know, Picket," Emerson said as the team of rabbits worked to secure the base of the weapon. "Forget securing it!" Emerson shouted. "We have to fire!"

Picket remembered that Emerson's father, Emery, had been killed by Falcowit while he was trying to enter the city for the cause.

"Stand clear!" Heyward shouted. Stout rabbits held the bowstriker onto the cart, and Emerson trained the blastarrow at the escaping form of Falcowit.

Picket watched with intense anxiety. *He'll only get one shot.*

Emerson aimed, carefully tracing the pattern of the white falcon's flight, then fired. The blastarrow leapt from the launcher. Unsecured, the machine recoiled violently and came apart on the cart. Its wreck sent rabbits sprawling all around, including the brave strong ones who had held it to the cart with their own hands.

Picket watched the shot sail into the sunlit sky. It sped ahead, a slender shaft in a vast canvas of blue.

By the time Lord Falcowit saw it, it was too late.

The blast came. A loud cracking explosion, and the raptor lord came apart in a terrific unmaking eruption that sent white feathers scattering across the sky. Picket watched, disbelieving, as the bowstriker crew recovered enough to cry out with joy as the huge white feathers fell in aimless arcing dips all around them.

That blast was the last emphatic note in the song of the retaking. The city belonged to the free rabbits of Natalia. The First Warren was liberated.

Chapter Fifty-Five

The Return of Shuffler

Picket woke a few hours later and heard cheerful singing in the distance. There were large numbers of singers, of that he was sure. An attendant told him he had passed out in the aftermath of the battle, amid the cheers and hustle of the post-battle work. When the attendant saw him awake, she left quickly. In a few minutes, Doctor Zeiger came in, clearly tired but smiling wide at Picket.

"How's is mine friend, Picket?" he asked. "Big knuckles-head hero all the time flying and fighting like some kind of mad rabbits from story-tales! Them medics says Picket captain's fighting wars like Zeiger-doctor speaking. Crazybuck!"

"It's good to see you, Doc," Picket said. "Is the city secure?"

"Mine work to fix soldier body, sick body, every kind of rabbit-bodies," Doctor Zeiger answered. "But I haven't hearing no bomb-booms in long time. No hurrah-shouts nor yikes-oh-me shouts for long times."

"Is Emma okay?"

"Doctor Princess doing work now. She talk to city in just little bit of time."

"What about Jo, and Cole?"

"These friendbucks hurt, but Cole come back fine. He's stout and has big will inside his soul-heart. Jo hurt worse, and sleeping. Hope for good, but he still have a bit of dangerbad."

"When can I see them?"

"Soon, mine think. Need healing for your leggy."

"Will I ever walk again?" Picket asked, deeply fearful of the response. He was afraid he had given his last contribution to the cause, and, even on this day of tremendous victory, it filled him with gloom.

"Can walk now, treaderbuck," he said. "But some help-self need for times. Hip cut-wound yes, knocked socket twist, but I'm setting this correcter. Knee got nasty knock, but will heal okay."

Picket was relieved, and he hoped he understood Doctor Zeiger correctly. One was never quite certain. "Thank you, Doc. I think the knock on my knee was lucky. He caught me with the flat of his blade, I think."

"That's being a close miss," Doctor Zeiger said, laying his hand on Picket's wrapped-up knee. "But Picket One-Leggy make great name for sister story when this war finish. I see you again, soon." Doctor Zeiger left.

Picket thought of Heather, wondering if she was well and where she was. He wished she could be close, to hear the sounds of victory in First Warren. He believed he was in the palace, and the singing must be coming from outside in the square.

Then Emma came in, her hands behind her back, walking with her attendants behind her. This included a few doctors, Heyna Blackstar, and Mrs. Weaver.

"Mrs. Weaver!" Picket cried, and the old rabbit moved to Picket's bedside and bent down to kiss his head.

"My dear Picket," she said. "You're getting into some very bad habits of getting yourself hurt." Then she bent over his head and whispered, "I'm so proud of you."

He smiled, tears starting in his eyes. He coughed and then tried to get out of bed. He wanted to sit up and pay the proper respects to Emma, but he was struggling inelegantly. He found that his injured leg was wrapped straight and couldn't be bent.

"Your Highness," he said, bowing his head as best he could.

"Captain Longtreader," she said, smiling down on him with a hint of mischief. "Or, should I say, Shuffler? Yes," she said, looking at his leg. "I believe that is appropriate once again."

He laughed. "Doctor Zeiger said I was nearly Picket One-Leggy, so Shuffler doesn't sound too bad by comparison."

"I brought something for you." Emma smiled wide, then brought out a crutch from behind her back. It wasn't as ornately made as the one she had given him long ago at Cloud Mountain, but it looked like it would do the job.

"Thank you, Emma. I mean, Your Highness."

"You're welcome, Picket. I mean, Shuffler." She handed him the crutch and bent to embrace him. Both shed tears, and both felt joy breaking stubbornly through a strong barricade of pain.

Emma helped him out of bed and onto his feet. He found it awkward at first, but soon was hobbling around the spacious room on the crutch. Weezie came in then, and she ran to Picket and wrapped him in a hug. Helmer and Airen followed her in, and the reunion was sweet. Helmer asked the princess if he could introduce his sister and niece, and Picket watched happily while Airen and Weezie pledged their faithfulness to the heir and future queen.

Lord Morgan and Lord Blackstar came in after, nodding to Picket, then bowing to Emma. "Your Highness," Lord Blackstar said, "all is ready."

She nodded, and they left the room, followed by the lords and captains. Picket followed behind, hobbling along with help from Weezie.

"Can you believe it's done, Picket?" Weezie asked, a wide smile on her face. "I saw what you did! I saw you soar in and blow up the statue."

"With your help," Picket said, wincing through a smile.

"And when you saved your friend Jo," she said. "I saw it all. I didn't know, until hearing from the leaders of the other citadels, what a hero you've been. That the Picket Packslayer song was almost true. But I didn't need to hear it from them, really. I saw it myself."

Picket hobbled on, pain playing up and down his leg but his heart glowing with joy. He was, he found, getting over the thrill of being a hero to rabbitkind. But he liked being one to Weezie. "And you," he said, "sent up those blastpowder keglets and then helped lead the younglings to safety. Without you, they would have been destroyed."

"Well, not everyone made it out," she said, bowing her head. "But we did save so many. And I did make a difference."

They walked on in silence until they reached the stairs. Picket found that he had been put in a room on the bottom floor, and now Emma was beginning up the stairway, surrounded by her wartime court. Then she stopped, turning back to where Picket stood with Weezie.

"Picket," Emma said, "will you come with me to the balcony? I'm going to address the city."

He looked up at Emma, glanced over at Weezie, then back to Emma. "Is it all right, Your Highness, if I watch from the square?"

Emma's eyes seemed to shine a moment, and she blinked, then smiled. "Of course, Picket."

"I know you will do an amazing job, Your Highness," he said, and he bowed low, using the crutch to support himself. When he looked up, she was hurrying up the stairs.

Chapter Fifty-Six

Victory Day

Picket, helped by Weezie, walked slowly out into the square. He couldn't help but smile at what he saw and felt. He saw so much to swell his soul, but it *felt* so different here. He couldn't quite put it into words, but his leg hurt less, and Weezie squeezed his arm as they walked into the busy square. He saw that now all of the seven standing stones had been restored to their former order, with the vile statues blasted off and hauled away. *Symbols are important.* Weezie was leading him into the crowd, which gave way before him as many bowed when he passed. They whispered his name, and a circle of murmuring awe surrounded him.

He wanted to get away.

Picket turned then, gently pulling Weezie back, and they moved to the base of the first standing stone. The entrance was being watched over by several blue-robed votaries, including one who looked as old as Helmer.

"Picket," Weezie said, pulling him back, "I don't think we're allowed—"

But the older brother in blue, who knew Picket from Halfwind, had seen how the wounded warrior was pressed by the crowd and nodded for them to come up. Picket nodded, touching, with his free hand, his eyes, ears, and mouth. The old votary bowed and motioned for them to pass. Very slowly, Picket hobbled up the countless stairs leading up the first standing stone. There was no railing, so he leaned on Weezie and looked out over the square as he made his ascent, marveling at all he saw.

Even though the scars of war were plain and the square itself and the west wall nearby were wrecked in many ways, the city was teeming with joy. He saw the same children who, only a short time before, were meant to be slaughtered by the raptor sentinels or taken away for the feast of the Six, now happily playing games near their joystruck parents. Near the forest where he and Helmer had first seen the horrors of Winslow's treachery, the long-oppressed residents of First Warren mingled with soldiers from every free citadel. Picket glanced from face to face, and he marveled at what he saw. The same warriors who had, only a few hours before, been hard at the brutal work of battle now showed tenderness toward the residents. Picket saw many soldiers listening intently to the natives' stories. Picket's heart swelled to see these

heroes, so fierce on the field, show such kindness. Soldiers from Halfwind, some of them votaries, taught a small knot of children the game of bouncer. He laughed as the ball bounced off the stone and the little ones all collided in the middle just under its rebounding arc. It rolled along and merged with a game of hoopvolley, which was being explained to an overly energetic youth by an exasperated soldier from Harbone. The two games collided and became a new game—an old and simple game—where the players all rushed wildly and tackled whoever had the ball.

The steps went on and on, and Picket was beginning to wonder if this decision had been wise. But he felt such energy from the happiness all around and inside him that he pressed on, sweating as he made his uneasy way up. Finally, as they neared the top, Weezie whispered to Picket as she gazed out over the square. "I'm proud of you, Picket."

"Thank you, Weezie," he answered, squeezing her hand as they finally arrived on the top of the standing stone. Five votaries were working to break away the last remnants of the statue that had stood so long there.

The kneeling form of Garten Longtreader.

Picket felt a stab of anger, mingled with worry, as he thought of his treacherous uncle and how he had, among his many crimes, taken Heather away. What had happened to her? Would he ever see her again?

A stout brother chiseled away the last scrap of the statue's base. The top was smooth again, and, after a brief cleanup, the brothers took their tools, gathered the statue scraps, and headed for the steps. Weezie and Picket were alone.

They sat then, Picket stretching his well-wrapped leg while Weezie settled down beside him. There was no higher point in the city than these stones. And Picket could see the tops of the buildings, the wall, and the lake beyond First Warren. There, out among the blue water, stood seven islands. The middle island was taller than the others, and it looked to Picket like a desolate rock. *Forbidden Island.* The island Helmer and Sno swam to in their reckless younger days. He felt a strange pain inside when he saw that island, another stab of worry.

"What is it, Picket?" Weezie asked.

"I miss my sister," he said, a tear starting in his eye. He wiped his eyes with his black scarf.

"Me too," she said, and they stared off into the distance for a little while. Picket turned back toward the forest and frowned. Part of it had fallen away when Captain Moonlight blew up the Citadel of Dreams and the deep belows collapsed on Daggler's wicked band. Now there was only a gaping pit, a maw of death that fed on the destroyed wolves and raptors that had fallen in the fight.

"It's the Brute's Gorge," Weezie said, "though some call it the Chasm of Death. Whatever it's called, after the bodies are dumped, the rabbits stay far away. It's a cursed place now."

"It's not close to the farm, is it?"

"No," Weezie said, smiling. "It's far away."

"Good."

A hush fell over the crowd, and Picket turned to watch Emma walk out onto the balcony. His heart rose once more to see her there, in the place of her fathers, in the place where King Jupiter the Great had once addressed First Warren. She needed no gesture for quiet, for the gathered rabbits fell into reverent awe when they saw her. She looked out over them for a long moment, and Picket was happy to see her so confident and bold. Even though she had never desired the task and they had all wished for her beloved brother to have this honor, she was becoming the queen they needed.

"Friends," she began, and her voice echoed over the square, "we are home again. Rabbits truly rule, once more, in First Warren, the heart of the Great Wood. This is a great triumph, and we do well to celebrate this day!" Cheers erupted through the square and beyond, where thousands stood and cried out with joy. Picket believed he could almost feel the rising tide of joy lift him on his perch above the square. When the crowd had quieted, Emma went on. "I look out on you, and I see many different kinds of rabbits. I see the long-suffering citizens of this city, whose painful wait for liberation is over at last. I see soldiers and support forces from every secret citadel. And our citadels are no longer secret, for here we are, out in the open, defying Morbin and his dark legions." Some in the crowd murmured when they heard Morbin named, and a ripple of disapproval rattled some in the square. "I know, for many, that name has filled you with fear. I know that many of you are wounded by even whispering these words. But we will not allow words to destroy us; we will not make sacred our cursed foe's name. Morbin Blackhawk is the vile tyrant who slaughtered my father on this very day years ago. I will not bow to his rule nor honor his name. I say his name is cursed and his rule is ended. I will never hesitate to say it, though the name is like bile in my mouth." She paused a moment, looking down to gather her thoughts, then went on. "He will come, we know. He will bring his army down on us, and we will not have long to prepare. But prepare we will. Already, our military council is at work to make the best defense of this, our home, reclaimed after long resistance and never to be lost again!" A slow cheer began, but Emma shouted over it. "I have been advised by some to leave the city, to seek protection to ensure against the loss of the bloodline of my father. I was also advised not to come on this day. But I tell you, my friends, that I will not quit this city until Morbin is defeated. He shall know where to find me," she cried, thrusting her fist into the air, then pointing down at the square, "for I will be here!" A thunderous cheer met this defiant cry, and the city once more rose with one voice to clap and loudly shout their approval.

Emma raised her hands for quiet, and once more the crowd settled in to listen. "Today we came together and fought together. We, who are many, became one fighting force. An unstoppable force. The innovation of Harbone met the devotion of Halfwind. The resolve of Vandalia met the valor of Blackstone. The heart of Cloud Mountain met the soul of First Warren's resistance!

"We have been divided by treachery and betrayals, divided by distance and distrust. We have been divided and carved up like a ritual meal for their perverse feasts. We have been torn apart. But not today. Today, we joined. Today, we fought for a cause bigger than any single citadel. We fought for the cause for which the citadels were formed. We fought with passion, and we fought *together*!"

Again, they cheered loud and long. The good feeling spread all over the square as thousands shouted and raised their hands.

Princess Emma stood there, nodding at the glad cheers, bending her arm before her with a clenched fist, and scanning the crowd with a bold and determined expression.

Then Emma stepped to the left side of the balcony while Helmer led out Prince Winslow to the right. The crowd was unsettled by seeing him alive, and an angry current spread quickly, ending in jeers and angry cries. Picket frowned and sat up straighter.

Emma let it go on awhile. She let the crowd, still mostly made up of citizens of First Warren, have their say. Then she raised her hand again.

Helmer bowed low to Emma, then spoke loud enough for all to hear. "Your Royal Highness, here is the traitor Winslow, sometime pretended ruler of this city. His crimes are many but include submission to Morbin, capitulation to our greatest enemy's evil plans, and tyranny in his name over this place. Prince Winslow has allowed the kinslayer Daggler to perform unthinkable acts, including the murder of many innocents. He had not, perhaps, direct knowledge of these atrocities. But he still bears responsibility for Daggler's years of evil work, for they were done in Winslow's name and by his authority. Finally, Prince Winslow has usurped your place as rightful heir to your father's throne. So then, Your Highness," Helmer went on, bowing again in crisp military precision, "I await your orders as to the punishment of this wretched rabbit who has betrayed his blood and all of rabbitkind." With that, Helmer shoved Winslow roughly so that he staggered forward.

Winslow kept his feet and came to the center of that balcony from which he had spoken so often as the tool of Morbin and the bane of his own kind. The crowd, which had, in angry silence, heard Helmer's account of all his evil, now erupted once again in a torrent of angry cries. The citizens of First Warren shouted and shook their fists at him. Winslow winced as he looked out over the crowd, then over at Emma, and then down. He sank to his knees and hung his head. Picket thought he could see tears in Winslow's eyes.

Emma stepped toward her eldest brother, the symbol in this city of those rabbits who had bowed to Morbin and worked his villainous will. Winslow took the crown from his head, a crown that had been the gift of Morbin, and handed it reverently to Emma. She held it in her hands a moment there in the center of the balcony. Then she cast it down with such force that it shattered into pieces, sending the jewels it contained spraying over the balcony's edge. None in the square below would dare drop to recover them. Emma resumed her poised posture, though a high fury imbued her expression. She looked at Helmer and held out her hand. He bowed again, then unsheathed his sword, placing the hilt in her hand. She lifted the sword while the crowd, which had so loudly jeered, fell slowly silent as they watched in awe as she stood before her brother and raised the heavy sword.

"Have you anything to say for yourself, Winslow Joveson?" she asked.

Winslow coughed and, still hoarse, said, "I am guilty of all I am accused of, and more besides. I deserve the death you so justly deal. But I *am* sorry," he began; then, choking on these words, he continued softly, "for the evil I have done, and allowed to be done, in my name."

Emma raised the sword. Winslow never moved. He held his head high, offering his neck for the end he knew he deserved. The square below fell silent but for a thousand breaths catching in a thousand throats. Picket's eyes widened, and he stumbled up as Weezie helped him to his feet.

Emma brought the sword around, and Winslow closed his eyes.

She touched it gently to his shoulder.

"By my right as heir and rightful bearer of the Green Ember, I pardon you, Winslow, son of Jupiter, for all your crimes." There was an audible sigh from the crowd, and Picket too breathed out in relief. "You will be watched, brother Winslow, and your influence will be limited during this war, but you will be spared the grim ending you deserve."

Helmer received back his sword, sheathed it, and bowed to Emma once more. Then he helped Winslow to his feet and led the awestruck buck back from the balcony's edge and into the palace.

Emma turned back to the square. "I have come home today. I am, at last, in my father's house. It's good to be home. So let me proclaim it now, a blanket pardon for all who are willing to come home to our cause, to come home to their own. To pledge to fight the enemies of rabbitkind together."

The space beneath the balcony was cleared, and the crowd stepped back almost in the same way they had made a space for the younglings who were that day to be slaughtered. Out of the palace, with Winslow at their head, came a large band of soldiers who had worked at the palace or formed the guard that had carried out the traitorous mission of Winslow's governorship. They came, heads hung low, and filled the space available. But Winslow looked around, eyes wet, his expression one of startled gratitude. Many in the crowd came forward. From the edges of the square and from the edge of the woods, they came. They knelt at the base of the balcony, and Emma pronounced pardon on them all. She charged the others to welcome them back and work together for the good of the cause and the battle to come. "Many disputes will be settled when the war is over, but for now let us all work hand in hand, turning our swords on the true enemy.

Morbin is coming, and we must meet him when he does. But we must never forget that beyond that clash comes the Mended Wood!"

The crowd cheered again, and the relieved rabbits around Winslow joined in. Music struck up, and Picket saw several places where bands were positioned around the city. And they sang a song of the resistance. Picket and Weezie joined in from atop the first standing stone, and the song echoed over the square and filled the city. The song echoed over the lake.

"I'm right here in the story,
I don't know the ending.
But I know one thing,
I'm meant for the Mending.

And we're meant to be allies,
Sisters and brothers
To fight against evil,
And fight for each other.

My place beside you,
My blood for yours,
Till the Green Ember rises,
Or the end of the world!

I'm a part of this story,
Though I'm not the great king,

But what I do matters,
So I fight and I laugh and I sing!

My place beside you,
My blood for yours,
Till the Green Ember rises,
Or the end of the world!"

Chapter Fifty-Seven

Heart of Hope

Heather thought she heard singing. Faint, and far away. But it made her come suddenly, and painfully, awake. She remembered falling. She felt in her belly the brutal wound from her uncle's blade. She was weak, sore, and sad. She knew, even before she opened her eyes, that she was in a dark place. The dank smell was familiar. She recognized it from a hundred nightmares. Heather knew what she would see before ever she opened her eyes. But she opened them still.

Heather was in a deep cavern, dark except for a single shaft of light high above. That was the gate through which she had been kicked. Her head and back ached. She was lying on thick wet moss. It had cushioned her landing. All around the top of the cavern she saw dangling patches of dripping green. She had believed she could convince her uncle; she had believed in the power of her persuasive words. But she was wrong. He stabbed her, then kicked her down into a pit where she would, in agony, die alone.

But in her dreams she had not been alone. There had always been the scaly hand, the slippery voice, and that memory filled her with terror. Maybe she wasn't alone down here. She closed her eyes again, breathing hard. But that wasn't all her dreams had shown. She forced herself to roll over to her right and open her eyes.

He was there.

The unmoving body of a white rabbit.

She had been, as Morbin once warned her she might be, buried with Smalls. She swallowed hard and crawled slowly toward his body. Her physical pain was intense, but it was nothing compared to the emotional agony she felt. She reached his side and bravely gazed at his face. Heather saw by the dim light that it was set forever in a sad expression. She felt overwhelmed with woe. It seemed like a long time, but it had been only a few days since he fell in a fight to free slaves.

Part of her was almost grateful to be with him at the end of her life and glad that they would be sealed together in this vast tomb, forever.

She could almost make herself believe that the cause would succeed, that Emma would ascend the throne she had never really wanted, and that her family would all survive. Hadn't Jacks made it to District Seven? All would be well, and she would rest forever beside the one she loved most in all the world. She would die lying beside Smalls.

Heather took off her satchel and set it aside, then looked into his face once more. A well of grief came flooding up again, and she sobbed as she never had before, rocking back and forth as the weight of all her pains came rushing over her heart. When the worst was over, she bent and laid her head on his chest, resting there a moment over his heart.

In a few seconds, her expression changed. She gasped. Her eyes grew wide with wonder.

The End

About The Author

S. D. Smith is the author of The Green Ember Series, a children's adventure saga. When he's not spending time writing tales in his writing shed, dubbed The Forge, S. D. Smith loves to speak to audiences about storytelling, creation, and seeing yourself as a character in The Story.

www.SDSmith.com